# Unusual Oregon

WILD LIFE

Edited by
**Mark
Christensen**

&

Designed by
**James Kiehle**

**SASQUATCH BOOKS**
SEATTLE

ACKNOWLEDGMENTS:
"Laser" excerpted from *Night Dogs*, by Kent Anderson. Copyright 1997 by
Kent Anderson. Reprinted by permission of Bantam Doubleday Dell.
"Flaming Dad" excerpted from *Patio Daddy-O*, by Gideon Bosker. Copyright
1996 by Gideon Bosker. Used by permission of Chronicle Books.
"Best Inner Turmoil: Crisis One [through] Ten" excerpted from *Goat Brothers*,
by Larry Colton. Copyright 1993 by Larry Colton. Used by
permission of Doubleday, a division of DoubledayDell Publishing.
"Best Memoir: JD" excerpted from *Shot in the Heart*, by Mikal Gilmore.
Copyright 1995 by Mikal Gilmore. Used by permission of Doubleday,
a division of DoubledayDell Publishing.
"Best Prelude to Suburban Apocalypse" excerpted from *The Deus Machine*, by
Pierre Ouellette. Copyright 1993 by Pierre Ouellette.
Used by permission of Villard Publishing.
"Small Town Girl Makes Loud" excerpted from *Queen of Noise*, by Melissa
Rossi. Copyright 1996 by Melissa Rossi. Reprinted by
permission of Pocketbooks, a division of Simon & Schuster.

Library of Congress Cataloging in Publication Data
Wild life : unusual Oregon / [edited by] Mark Christensen.
p. cm.
ISBN 1-57061-050-9
1. Oregon—Guidebooks. 2. Oregon—Miscellanea. I. Christensen, Mark.
F874.3W55 1997
917.9504'43—dc21                                        97-9948

SASQUATCH BOOKS
615 Second Avenue
Seattle, Washington 98104
(206) 467-4300
books@sasquatchbooks.com
http://www.sasquatchbooks.com

Sasquatch Books publishes high-quality adult nonfiction and
children's books related to the Northwest (Alaska to San Francisco).
For more information about our titles, contact us at the address above,
or view our site on the World Wide Web.

# Contents

# Introduction

This is an anthology.

Oregon has produced writers of great renown: John Reed, Ken Kesey, Katherine Dunn, John Shirley, Ursula K. LeGuin and Raymond Carver. Sadly, with the exception of Katherine Dunn and John Shirley, you won't be hearing them in WILD LIFE. Either they were dead, too expensive, or didn't return our phone calls.

You will, however, be hearing from a generation of Oregon writers who began publishing between the late 1960s and two weeks ago, and whose visions have contributed mightily (okay, significantly [all right, *credibly*]) to contemporary American literature.

WILD LIFE is a no nonsense, hit-and-miss guide to breaking the back of boredom in the Beaver State. We bring you the best of Oregon—and the best of the worst, delivered in the form of either factoids or literature. Just the stuff that makes Oregon life worth living: restaurants, bars, poetry, loud music, beer, guns, progressive politics, post-modernism, mindless violence, smack, salvation, the woods, and golf.

–MARK CHRISTENSEN

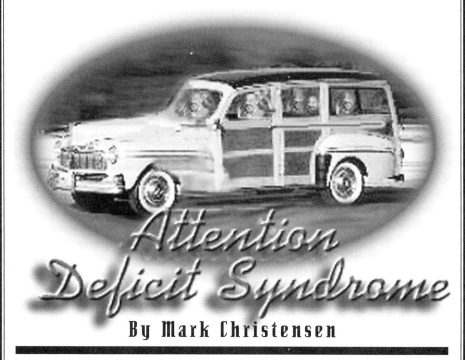

# Attention Deficit Syndrome

## By Mark Christensen

# OREGON MINI-VACATION HARD POINTS

Read this and forget the rest of the book. Sorry you already paid for the thing, but here is your Oregon vacation in a nutshell. In this scenario, you're in your car, heading north on I-5 from California with 2.3 children and a husband or a wife and $2,000 in cash, plastic, and traveler's checks— enough for one fast week in paradise. Here are the ADS hard points—great places to hit on your drive through the state.

**WILD LIFE's guide to the best of Oregon's beaches— an intimate grain-by-grain tour of 326 miles of sand.**

## ASHLAND

Ashland is the first great thing you hit after you cross the California border on Interstate 5. Located along the foothills of the Cascade and Siskiyou Mountains, Ashland used to be a sleepy little logging burg where the action was playing Pong in a local tavern while listening to choker-setters chortle about blowing up I-5 North at Medford and Yreka to seal off their woodsy little paradise from the rest of the irradiated world when nuclear apocalypse comes.

But Ashland has evolved into the bed and breakfast capital of the world, the only tourist trap in the United States run almost entirely by English professors.

Try the Royal Carter House, an immaculate 1909 two-story Crafts-man home. Intricate breakfasts and wonderful touches: 40-year-old copies of *American Girl* magazine in the dramatically decorated-to-period bedrooms.

Downtown, dine at the rurally urbane Plaza Cafe, delight at the "extinct robotic beasts"—the saber-toothed cat and giant ground sloth—at the Pacific Northwest Museum of Natural History, and check out Ashland's hippies, who seem to have been preserved exactly from 1967. Delight at the Orange County prices tacked up in the win-dows of the local real estate offices: Fabulous Craftsman classic has five bedrooms, four and a half baths, a housekeeper's apartment, two offices, five fireplaces, and a barn. All for just $1,300,000.

## COOS BAY

Oregon is the best place ever to kill and shop. Before you get ready to hunt black-tailed deer, black bear, beaver, nutria, and muskrat, or to visit the brand-new monster factory outlet stores in Lincoln City (or perhaps "America's first mall," Lloyd Center in Portland), stock up on guns and ammo in Coos Bay, a town that used to have some real economic muscle before the forests ran out of trees and the ocean ran out of fish. Thank God they haven't run out of tourists.

## REEDSPORT

Ah, so nice. A place on the Oregon coast where people—commercial fishermen and loggers, mostly—still actually *do* something besides pull designer beer and hawk geegaws.

Once a marshland, Reedsport was constructed on pilings and, until 1926, travel between buildings was by boat. Every three centuries or so, the Reedsport area gets wiped out by a tidal wave, so the town's got an old-fashioned soaked-in-salt-water feel. Stroll the boardwalks, jet boat up the Umpqua River, or head south a few miles to Winchester Bay, where you can find great surf: big, hollow, cold, steep, treacherous waves of extraordinary power.

## OREGON DUNES

Miles and miles and miles of sand dunes. Snap your neck riding the hellaciously overpowered Charlie Manson-style dune buggies they rent to anybody who has a face and a driver's license.

Or rent crab pots and snag delectable Dungeness crab. You can take the pots and some chicken parts or fish carcasses for bait, go out to the dock at high tide, tie the line off your baited crab pot to a cleat or bull rail on the dock, plop the pot into the water, and wait a half hour or so before reeling your crab-filled pot back to the surface...

My naive 16-year-old daughter says that crabs actually "scream" as they are boiled to death. No way. When I drop them, plop! into that bubbly, steaming 220-degree water, they don't feel a thing.

Now, for some bird-watching. There are four sites between North Bend and Florence—at Horsefall, Eel Creek, Siltcoos, and South Jetty—where your eyes may behold the tundra swan, marsh wren, Canada goose, yellow-rumped warbler, red-tailed hawk, sanderling, long-billed curlew, dunlin, least sand-

piper, great blue heron, American bittern, green heron, Virginia rail, cinnamon teal, common yel-lowthroat, common merganser, belt-ed kingfisher, snowy plover, bald eagle, osprey, pine siskin, chestnut-backed chickadee, Swainson's thrush, wrenlit, Northern flicker, olive-side flycatcher, Anna's hummingbird, white-tailed kite, Northern harrier, violet-green swallow, downy wood-pecker, great horned owl, great egret, orange-crowned warbler, yel-low warbler, black-throated gray warbler, Townsend's warbler, hermit warbler, and, who knows, maybe even a robin or two.

## THE SEA LION CAVES

This 25-million-year-old cavern, 12 stories high and as long as a football field, is home to the wild Steller's sea lion and the rare pigeon guille-mot. Sight of the 2,000- pound-plus sea lions will hit you where you live.

## THE LOOKOUT AT CAPE FOULWEATHER

The world's most awesomely sited knickknack shop is perched 500 feet above the Pacific Ocean at the observatory four and a half miles south of Depoe Bay on Ottercrest Loop Road. It was at Cape Foul-weather in 1778 that the great English explorer Captain Cook first laid eyes on North America's Pacific Coast and "discovered" Oregon in the process.

**OKAY, ENOUGH. We're tired of writing the "Attention Deficit Syndrome Oregon Mini-Vacation Hard Points." Frankly, we just don't have the patience. Let's just get on to something scary.**

# THE TOP SEVEN BEST DANGEROUS WAYS TO RECREATE IN OREGON

## STORY AND PHOTOS BY ANCIL NANCE

What is it about us humans that we call it Mother Nature and Mother Earth? Have our mothers so mistreated us that when we watch a storm, we think, *Whoa, Mother Nature is really having a fit?* My experiences lead me to say Nature and Earth are no mothers I would choose. Talk about child abuse! Of course, a good part of the above is self-abuse in the search for risky adventure in recreation.

Danger lurks in any recreation that tempts gravity: climbing, kayaking, rafting, mountain biking, paragliding, surfing, bungee jumping, BASE jumping, skydiving, and motorcycling. Sometimes the danger is ignored until too late, and once in a while the danger is part of the calculations.

## BASE JUMPING

B stands for building, A for antenna, S for span (bridge), and E for earth. The big goal of BASE jumpers is to jump from all four in one day. To start BASE jumping without lessons is suicide, but if that is what you have in mind, Crown Point, a 500-foot cliff located east of Portland at the mouth of the Columbia River Gorge on the old Scenic Highway, is as good a place as any to earn the E. Atop Crown Point sits a domed building that was dubbed the "million-dollar outhouse" when it was built in 1917. Today it is a nice place to get out of the wind. The state parks and recreation department will arrest or cite you if they see you preparing for a jump. If you do get into the air and land safely, have an escape vehicle ready and waiting on I-84.

The First Interstate Tower in downtown Portland is good for a building B; then it's on to the antenna near Silverton A, and the bridge spanning Hoffstadt Creek near Mount St. Helens for S. Any high cliff will work for the E. Because BASE jumping is illegal, the successes don't get much publicity; only the failures make the papers. One jumper off Multnomah Falls slammed into the cliff a third of the way down, and after a few more bounces was left hanging by his parachute with broken bones and scraped skin until he was rescued. The wind swirls and rotors around in the monster grotto. Jumping, even with a parachute, from Multnomah Falls is very dangerous.

Once, coming back from paragliding the Columbia River Gorge, I saw many emergency lights clustered at the bottom of the aforementioned Crown Point. It looked like a massive rescue effort. It was. That afternoon a BASE jumper had attempted to get his E by running off the edge of that cliff. As at Multnomah Falls, wind rotors flung the jumper into the cliffs before he could safely parachute away from the rocks.

## MOUNTAIN CLIMBING

So many people slam to earth in mountain climbing that it is taken for granted. When fewer than ten people nationwide die climbing in any single year, it is a slow one.

Deaths on some expeditions are mourned, but not unexpected. *Accidents in North American Mountaineering* is required reading for mountain climbers. I pore over the reports hoping to see that all the accidents had causes I could explain or at least attribute to climber error, some mistake I would never make.

Loose rocks and avalanches, however, do not respect experience or skill. And human error in this sport kills. Stories of climbers rappelling into space, having neglected to correctly clip into their rappel rope, are legend.

I haven't been immune to dangerous mistakes. Once I was with a climbing partner on a small cliff at Smith Rock, Oregon. After the climb we rappelled down to find that the rope was somehow jammed above us. I thought, Why not simply climb the cliff again to get the rope, this time going up the rope hand-over-hand?

This worked fine until I reached the top, where the rope in my hands raised slightly, allowing the rope jammed underneath to run freely once more. For a second I saw the rope gain speed and whiz past me as I fell 30 feet, fortunately landing at the base of the cliff in soft dirt, not harsh rocks.

Another time I was with two climbing partners on ice-covered rocks near the summit of Mount Hood's east side. We were roped for a steep but short ice cliff, but we climbed in unison since steps were already cut and it looked easy. Then I heard someone yell, "Falling!" and said to myself, "Oh shit, this is it," as I reached in vain to plunge my ice ax into the rapidly retreating ice wall.

I knew we were on ledges above an 800-foot drop to the glacier below. Nothing could save us. In that instant I knew we were all dead. Then I woke up. I heard someone calling my name. I hurt all over. The rope was still attached to me, leading upward.

We hadn't died, and except for a few cuts and many bruises everyone was OK. Rocks and ice had snagged the rope that ran between the three of us, halting our flight. I crawled up to my two partners and we decided to wait for dawn in a sheltered area called the Eagle's Nest. At first light we began our descent, first along the top of Steel Cliffs, and then down the slope toward Mount Hood Meadows. Here I got a big inspiration.

Since it hurt so much to walk (it had taken us over an hour to walk a few hundred yards), I decided to glissade. The slope looked reasonable, covered with soft snow, and it was a joy to sit down. One problem was that we had only one ice ax left, but I thought that putting the spiked crampons in my hands would work to slow me down. It did. I yelled to my doubtful partners, "C'mon, it's greaaaaaaaat." Halfway through the slide I hit ice and began to accelerate.

Not as fast as falling, but almost. Then I began to spin, doing cartwheels. I thought: Here I am, going to die, spinning down this stupid slope after surviving a fall last night!

Seconds later I found myself in a tight ball at the bottom of a 3,000-foot slope. I blinked, wiggled my fingers and toes, and tried to stand.

Ouch. I sat down and waited for my partners. It took them 45 minutes, and they were glad to see me alive. They had last seen me as I was disappearing down the slope, over a couple of crevasses, and then nothing. They hiked down to a ski area, and the Ski Patrol sent a Sno-Cat up to carry me down the rest of the way. I ended the day with an air splint around my left leg because of a large gash. I took the splint off in order to drive home, since neither of my climbing buddies had driver's licenses, being only 14.

**If you want to have stupid, dangerous rock climbing stories to tell, try the harder routes at Smith Rock. It is in central Oregon, north of Redmond, near Terrebonne.**

**The potentially most stupid route in Oregon is Yocum Ridge on the west side of Mount Hood. Climb this in the winter and you are in the record books. Boxcar-size chunks of ice fall from this route, sometimes with people on them, so be careful.**

## BUNGEE JUMPING

A good bungee jump requires a good bridge. Forget Oregon. Cross the Columbia River and go to the upper reaches of the Lewis River in Washington. The bridge is a private one, so you need to call Casey at (503) 520-0303 to make arrangements. The leap from this 200-foot bridge is the highest legal leap in North America.

## HANG GLIDING

Early hang gliding was so unsafe that few pilots are left from the early years. Years ago, Reed Gleason, a hang glider pilot, flew from the summit of Mount Hood. It was hard. The glider comes in a long bag and weighs more than 50 pounds, so not too many people could carry something that big to the summit.

Reed couldn't carry his glider to the top, but he talked a strong man into doing it for him. . . on a bet. The strong man didn't think Reed was brave enough to fly from the summit, so he agreed to carry the glider up to the top if Reed promised to fly off. He did. Now the top of Mount Hood is in a designated wilderness area, and aircraft are forbidden to land or take off. As much fun or as dangerous as it may be, you cannot fly off Mount Hood. Unless. . . .

Unless you put a paraglider in a backpack and hike up in the middle of the night. A paraglider is lighter than a hang glider because it requires no metal tubes. It has an arc-shaped wing with guidelines hanging down to a harness in which the pilot sits, steering the craft through the air to an appropriate landing area. A paraglider is no more mechanical than a canoe. Mountain paraglider pilots have flown from the summit of all the Cascade peaks from Mount Baker to Mount Shasta. Some of the danger is being arrested by U.S. Forest Service guys with guns.

When I and two other pilots flew from the summit of Mount Hood a couple of years ago, we hiked up early in the morning, flew off at dawn, and landed well out of the wilderness area at the Nordic ski center parking lot near Highway 35. Visiting pilots have flown the mountain from just below the summit.

The walking wounded are increasing in numbers among the ranks of paraglider pilots. Narrow escapes abound. While flying at a coastal location I was hammered by unexpected rotors and forced to make a landing very close to the ocean's edge. When I landed, the beach was exposed, but only seconds later I was up to my waist in saltwater. Luckily the surf threw my water-filled wing up onto the beach and I was able to draw it farther to high ground. In the San Francisco area a pilot experienced a similar landing, but for some reason he sat down, couldn't get free of his wing, and was dragged back to the water and drowned before rescuers could cut him loose.

Another time I was flying over the ocean beach near Cape Meares when I decided to go a little farther out to the lighthouse, before heading back to the beach. My glide ratio was such that I just made it with 15 feet to spare, this time landing on dry rocks that were above the surf line.

Ultimately, it is always a contest with gravity, and any air sport is dangerous, because gravity always wins. My worst paragliding accident happened when I made three pilot errors: I didn't check the wing pre-flight, I didn't wait for more suitable wind conditions, and I didn't keep my hands on the controls. I launched in gusty conditions, gained altitude, then reached with both hands to adjust my flight recorder. As I did so, a change of wind collapsed my glider. I quickly reached for the controls, but went down before I could regain control of my wing.

I slammed into the ground and bounced. My fibula snapped just above the ankle, and the rest of me adjusted to this abrupt halt with a great wheeze and a loss of air, but I did not lose consciousness. A padded flight harness and seat prevented a broken back. It's been over a year now, the bone has healed, and though the cartilage flattened in the ankle joint is not rebuilding, I am back in the air.

**For the best paragliding flights, I'd choose Anderson's View Point near Tillamook for a good ridge lift on a northwest wind. For the best thermal soaring, contact Phil Pohl in Bend at (541) 389-4086 and he will introduce you to the joys of Pine Mountain.**

## SURFING

Besides a long attention span, dangerous sports usually require being in good physical shape. So

there it is, about 1 p.m. and the tide is going out, making it easy to get out to the breakers. Swim, swim, swim, swim. Shark stories start running in the brain. Swim some more.

I think about that guy down near Reedsport. A few years ago a great white shark took a bite out of his board and him. He lived to tell about it. This isn't suicide, then. Swim, paddle, paddle, sort of look like a seal from underneath. A shark is probably color blind, can't see this is a green board, probably looks dark, my hands look like flippers. It could happen, but doesn't. No menacing fins to match the *Jaws* theme strumming in my ears.

But where are the breaking waves? Been paddling and getting tired a long time now. Is anyone nearby? Can't paddle much more, gotta get back. Tide still going out. At least I'm not near the rocks, can't get thrown on them from here.

Need a tow, shouldn't have come out so far on the first day of the season, out of shape for sure. Yes, surfing is dangerous.

Sharks are the least of it. Surfers have suffered from exposure, exhaustion, being thrown on rocks, crushed in turbulence. You have to be in shape to paddle and fight the waves for hours on end. The water here is cold, wet suits required, big fires on the beach a necessity.

**The best surf site changes day to day, even hour to hour, with the waves, but the most reliable ready-to-tear surfing spots in Oregon pretty much boil down to Indian Beach in Ecola State Park or Short Sand Beach in Oswald West State Park.**

## KAYAKING

Kayaking is similar to surfing. Some whitewater paddlers take their kayaks into the surf to practice handling. Wet suits and big fires on the shore are practically required in this sport also. Dry suits are worn on the really cold days, paddle jackets on warmer days. Kayaking starts with learning to sit in a very tippy craft. Then you learn to tip over and come right back up again, a maneuver called the Eskimo roll, and a bunch of other strokes to get you forward, backward, sideways, and stopped.

Rivers are rated so that a novice doesn't make the mistake of getting in over his head, or hers, and staying there. In a kayak you can play on and under the water, do window shade rolls, flips, nose and tail stands, spins and stalls. The rivers with high difficulty ratings offer more for the expert, but beginners can get in trouble on less gnarly rivers by doing what comes natural, namely, leaning away from a large wave. The hardest thing to learn after the roll is to lean into a wave using the paddle as a brace. I took lessons, learned the basics, and luckily have made it down several nice rivers. The Rogue, Deschutes, White Salmon, Wilson, Sandy, and Umpqua Rivers all have moderate runs.

But I still tip over and roll back up. . . that is just a part of kayaking. The danger is not knowing when to stop getting on more and more hairy water.

There are waterfalls I would never go over, but that entice expert boaters every year. The high water of springtime is fraught with danger: new logjams, faster currents, sleeper logs; and every year an expert boater or two dies challenging them. At about eight pounds a gallon, water is very heavy, especially if your kayak is full and has pinned you against a rock or under a log. You cannot get free. Rescue workers have to extract you, hopefully before you sink under for the last time, lips sucking air, eyes wild with terror. You get that close just once and you back off—you don't see death; you just see how fragile life is. How insignificant and tiny you are. It is still a sport, not attempted suicide. Your T-shirt may say Make It Look Like an Accident, but you are only kidding.

**The best boat run for kayak or raft is the Umpqua River from the former resort at Steamboat. Pick the water level to suit your thrill quotient.**

# MOUNTAIN BIKING

Most accidents are avoidable. Just stay home. Accidents and bikes seem to go together. It is so easy to fall off a bike: go fast down a hill, try to stop, misjudge your speed, and off you go. Could break your neck. A friend of mine did. He survived several first descents of Class V whitewater rivers in rafts and kayaks. He survived some very nice climbing routes. He didn't survive going too fast on a bike.

Oregon has fantastic trails and logging roads open to mountain bikes that can be ridden year-round. On the coast, near Cannon Beach, Onion Peak thrusts over 3,000 feet into the air less than three miles from the beach. Close by are Angora Peak and Sugar Loaf Mountain, almost as high. The roads to

these peaks are guarded by large yellow gates, so no motorized traffic gets near the tops. Leave your rig at the gate, climb on your bike, and start pedaling. There are miles of untamed roads. From the summit passes you can see south to the Nehalem River and north to Astoria. The terrain is wild and knobby, with white snags of former forest giants poking through the new growth of Douglas fir trees. The basalt cliffs are dark with moss, shadows, and loose rocks. Nascent coastal streams crash over steep cliffs and then slip through forest grottos before sliding under Highway 101 and into the Pacific. Days could be spent on the endless roads, but usually a few hours will wear down all but the most fit biker. Anyone who ventures without a complete repair kit, food, water, map, and raingear is asking for trouble. Take a cell phone in case of an accident, like say you're going too fast, hit a piece of basalt in the middle of your track, tap your front brake by mistake, and go flying over your handlebars. If this sounds like fun, check in with Mike Stanley at Mike's Bike Shop in Cannon Beach. He knows what you need to know.

**The best mountain bike workout is Fire Trail 3 off of Leif Erickson Drive in Portland's Forest Park. It makes a great circuit with Fire Trail 2 or Saltzman Road as the balls-out downhill return trip. Coming down the fire trails in Forest Park is a real treat, but you can get more speed down Saltzman Road—gravel and dirt all the way.**

# ROAD TRIP

## BY BILL WICKLAND

EDITOR'S NOTE: Before he was 30, Bill Wickland was a shark in advertising, smoking a Cadillac and driving around in a big cigar. Then came the revolution: hippie chicks with thousand-color eyes, purple wedgies. Visionary Bill ascended from hype to editorship of Oregon's second underground newspaper, the *Stoneygonian*.

Since then, ladies' man Wickland (2,500 girlfriends and counting) has been everything from a cab driver to a car salesman. Now, while completing his first novel, *The Company of Women*, he is serving time as a merchant seaman, but most of all Wickland is a liver of Oregon life, a whiz at hanging out in the best nooks and top crannies.

E arly on a mid-September morning, I took off for the coast to escape 90-degree heat in Portland, and to see family and friends. I headed out Sunset Highway, destination Rockaway Beach. A four-lane highway to Tillamook County, then it is twist and turn through the woods and down the coast.

My intention was to catch little Oregon 53 at Necanicum Junction, wiggle southwesterly through wine and bovine country, and hit Mohler above Nehalem Bay. That's the road on which I first tested radial tires, on an MG-A, and those tires saved me from rolling right into the Nehalem River.

But just out of town I saw signs indicating construction on the Sunset, and up jumped Oregon 6—the Wilson River Highway—which leads to the back door of Tillamook. I hadn't followed it in more than 20 years. It hasn't changed much. I was in dense forest much of the way, with fishing camps and old mom-and-pop tackle and bait shops. At about where the south fork of the Trask crosses under the highway the first time there is a sign: Next Gas 45 Miles. What a beautiful concept.

Then I was in a forest that felt reborn and there was another sign: PLANTED IN 1955, TO REPLACE THE TILLAMOOK BURN. As a Boy Scout, I had replanted trees in the burn in the early '50s.

From the junction to Tillamook I passed a heavily laden old pickup, and was passed by a new 4x4 driven by a local who knew the roads. I drifted along in a reverie—until suddenly I was in the pastures of Oregon's Switzerland, home of world-famous Tillamook cheese.

Then came the ocean breezes and a little fog, then Garibaldi, and the next thing I knew I was pulling up next to my sister Barb's Airstream. One hour and 43 minutes after leaving town. Nobody gets to the beach in 1:43 any more.

Rockaway Beach is not much changed since I went to Camp Magruder there in the late '40s. I doubt the bowling alley has been painted since. Barb took me to Bosio's in Garibaldi for an unusual eggs Benedict. The hash browns had veggies under them, like a potato quiche or potato omelet.

As one who gets his sugar rush from scotch or Yukon Jack, I'm not one for desserts, but Barb made me try one before I left town. I can still taste it.

On the estuary where the Miami River enters Tillamook Bay in Garibaldi there used to be a huge lumber mill. There now sits Judy West and Rick Rogers Old Mill Restaurant, a big, airy place with lots of windows looking out over water. Barbara ordered us the marionberry tart with vanilla Tillamook ice cream. That dish gets my highest score for anything—three jesuses: jesus, Jesus! Jeez-US! Trying to make it last, I allowed the Tillamook to melt a little and it became an impressionist expression of red royal roses against high cumulus clouds. Really—and I was cold sober. Tillamook ice cream is the coup de wahoo.

In the glow of the Old Mill treat, I set off to see my mom in Lincoln City. I take US 101, Tillamook to Neskowin through Beaver, Hebo, and Cloverdale. On a warm autumn day this is a heady experience—treating one to valley, vale, dale, and den. When Swiss immigrants got here, they said, "Whoa, Nellie! and "Cheese it!" Certain aromas belong in certain places. I would not savor cow patties in my studio, but a mixture of cow, horse, and goat flop in the air is perfect in dairy country (the horses are for fun and beauty, and the goats keep the tenacious wild blackberries at bay; the cows make Tillamook vanilla ice cream).

The beach shows up about four miles short of quiet, fairly private Neskowin, then it is back into the trees and over the dramatic Cascade Head before dropping into Lincoln City, home of the world's shortest river.

The next morning I took my mother to breakfast. Sylvia's 91. She likes her evening TV, brandy, and crosswords, and doesn't start her day until near noon. Usually we go to the Salmon River Cafe at the north end of town. They take pride in a light-wheat homemade bread and specialties conjured with spices and unusual fruits and vegetables, plus an extensive wine selection.

The most expensive dinner item, at $10.95, is sautéed oysters, garlic butter, and butternut squash risotto.

But my mom and I go to get her an egg, sunny side up, and fresh jam for the toast. The egg comes perfect every time.

**Salmon River Cafe, 4079 'B' Logan Road, Lincoln City, (503) 996-3663. Get your own silver, pour your own coffee.**

After seeing my mother home, I ran off down the coast to see friends at Boiler Bay. We walked down to Depoe Bay for dinner and lots of booze at Gracie's, known formally as the Sea Hag.

Right across the street from the ocean, the Sea Hag is the perfect place after a long hike in the blowing mist—warm, solid, and a bit dim, with everything you want behind the bar. Toward the back is a firepit, beyond that a small dance floor and a little stage for weekend live music.

Through a doorway is the actual restaurant, lighter, brighter. Tables for families and friends. Gracie spends a lot of time in there, her big smile and warm eyes making everyone feel like a special guest. I've known Gracie for 30 years, and she just doesn't get any older.

The seafood doesn't either. Gracie's copyrighted slogan is "So fresh the sea hasn't missed it yet." You can spend $25 for lobster thermidor, but most offerings come in at about $12. Like the clam chowder, which is served in an onion roll shaped into a bowl and baked.

The flagship extravaganza is the Friday night seafood buffet. Sports fly into the airport a few miles up the coast just to partake of this $18 lavish spread. The oysters are raised in nearby Newport Bay, on ropes. That way they don't wait for tides; they just eat. No sand or gunk in them. Gracie pops them into a convection steamer with no breading or seasoning, and cooks them just long enough for the oysters to open a tiny bit. You enjoy them in their juices.

You can get a great steak at the Sea Hag, but why?

Best to take the dessert home, so you can get over the meal before enjoying it: a tart of marionberry, "invented" in the lush Willamette Valley's Marion County.

I like to eat in the bar, with a double Yukon Jack rocks, and halibut fish and chips. I could be eating in southern Spain, and I'd still think about the halibut at Gracie's. Perfect every time.

Nighttime here, you'll find a lot of locals. After a couple of belts, everybody is local.

Weekends, when there's live music, Gracie goes behind the bar, picks up spoons, and accompanies the musicians by "playing" the booze bottles. I'm not sure about her musical talent, but her pleasure in doing it lifts everyone like a tsunami.

I asked the saxophone player what it is like to play a room where the owner will jump in at any time. "I play gigs all over the country," he told me. "But I can be someplace like Reno and say 'Sea Hag' and someone will pipe up, 'That's where Gracie plays the bottles!'"

**The Sea Hag, Highway 101, Depoe Bay, (503) 765-2734. Credit cards, smoking, no espresso.**

The fading plywood sign outside John's Family Restaurant in Dundee says that the place is world famous. But in case you've missed the sign, John's is the place for breakfast for fearless eaters.

When I'm coming back to Portland after a wild night at Gracie's, John's is about perfect—an hour and a half from the beach, and an hour short of Portland, on the right-hand side of the road, at the top end of Oregon's wine country.

Average speed there on weekends is about seven miles per hour. You can turn right into the flow, but don't expect to turn left.

Closed by 2 p.m. every day, John's is a breakfast and lunch house, but serves only breakfast on weekends. People literally come from hundreds of miles around.

John offers homemade Hungarian (Vida) sausage as a luncheon special and there are five steak 'n' eggs specialties, including my second wife's favorite, chicken fried. When I was on the phone with John the other day, I heard a customer yelp in the background, "This is the best New York steak I've ever had."

**John's Family Restaurant, 109 Highway 99W, Dundee, (503) 538-1522. Credit cards, no alcohol, no smoking, no espresso.**

Next: east. I drove to Bend to see my big brother Lee. I took

Oregon 229 from Kernville through Siletz to pick up US 20 near Toledo. The 229 is twisty and winding and slow and sometimes bumpy, closely following the Siletz River through heavy logging country on the edge of the Siletz Indian Reservation. Some very wealthy folks have discovered that the two-lane road (it is the "other highway" according to legend, the legend on the map) is little traveled. But the homes and the hunting and fishing lodges and docks sometimes visible at the end of the posted "members-only" lanes fit into those little vales and riverbanks as if grown there.

US 20 goes all the way from shoreside Newport to Boston, Massachusetts, although part of it is now I-90. Three routes go east over the Cascades following the north, middle, and south forks of the Santiam River, and join just short of the springs of the Metolius River. I followed 20 up the middle Santiam, through Sweet Home (where I once edited the weekly *New Era*). The middle fork isn't as straight and doesn't have as many passing lanes as the other two routes, so you can just toodle along engulfed in forest and foliage, then be startled by a sudden vista over a clear-cut or down a deep canyon to the sparkling, streaming Santiam below.

Just beyond the Metolius I drove by elegant residence golf resorts into the popular town of Sisters, largely "restored" to a late-19th-century facade, crowded by a huge bluegrass festival. I could smell the high desert sage and see cattle, horses, and llamas as I rolled through Tumalo and into booming Bend.

❋

Leaving my brother's in the morning, I was on my way home, rolling out of the high desert on US 97 from Terrebonne to Madras and US 26 to Government Camp. It was already 80 degrees outside and I was eager to get back to the clouds over Mount Hood. I could smell the sage and juniper. The juniper forest in central Oregon shares the "largest" title with the one in the Holy Land. The burning bush was likely a small juniper; almost all sap, they burn in a glorious fashion, as far as brush and forest fires go.

Near Terrebonne is Smith Rock, world-renowned for rock climbing, but also wonderful for walking along the Crooked River at its base or climbing up to the irrigation canal on the bluff. Where the Crooked River runs under Highway 97 is a gorge that defines gorgeous. Get up around Madras at the right time of the year and one of the world's largest mint crops will make you feel as if you are in a "Little Nemo" candy-cane dream from which you do not want to awaken.

Out of Madras, Highway 26 rises sharply to a high open plateau, mesas on the right and snowcapped peaks on the left, and 11,235-foot Mount Hood straight ahead. Then everything disappears as you dive-drive straight downhill for five miles to cross the Deschutes River at the entrance to the Warm Springs Indian Reservation. Up sharply again to another plateau, you can run flat out to the Simnasho junction, leaving the high desert behind, and enter the Douglas firs and pines which, at the northern edge of the reservation, become Mount Hood National Forest.

I drove right into a cloud at 60 cool degrees at Blue Box Summit. This was not fog at 4,025 feet. It was a cloud. Now dense forest. I started skiing at Government Camp as a boy 48 years ago and it still thrills me to drive through it, even if I don't stop to smell the snow. It is downhill from there. Forty years ago I drove down the mountain drunk in a snowstorm at night, bellowing at the Norse god Odin to keep my dad's Dodge on the road. Now I am thankful, sober in the daylight, that it is four lanes all the way down through Rhododendron, Zigzag, Wemme, and Brightwood.

At the foot of the mountain you are still 30 miles from Portland, but it feels like home.

❊

## NAMING THE SHELLS

Sand dollars in shallow waves
tumble the light,
drop like small moons
in foam along the shore line.
We fill our pockets, knot
flapping shirttails into sacks.
Stiff as turtles or crabs,
we rasp as we step,
loose sand in the dollars
shifting with stars.

For years we watched commonplace
forecasts fulfill themselves,
a calm surface with scattered
offshore storms, an overcast sky,
a wind that died at dusk.
This pattern, measured daily
by high and low tides,
led us to accept a stingy
claw or clamshell spear
hidden in wet sand. We honed
our expectations to fragments
and ignored the salty spume
that links us like brothers
to the moon.

Now this show, this tumble,
this gift, begs a response.
Naming each shell
after a part of the body,
*liver flank tibula*,
we make it ours, *femur
spleen eyelid blood.*
Not being medical students
we run out at *heart*,
and since we have stacks
left to name, we call them
one after another: *heart, heart,
heart*, and hear in our voices
the pulse of the tide.

—JUDITH ROOT

# CAPE LOOKOUT

by ANCIL NANCE

Any place where Oregon is eroded by the Pacific is my favorite place, and the beach and sea-cliff areas of Tillamook County are best of all. From Neakahnie Mountain in the north to Cascade Head in the south lies an incredible variety of things to see and do.

The hiking trails take you from crowded beach to isolated forest, and the paragliding sites are tops for ridge soaring. I've spent hours in the skies over Cape Lookout flying with gulls, hawks, and eagles. I've launched from a cliff above the sand and risen over 2,000 feet. My longest flight was over three hours and 40 minutes. I only came down because I needed water. I flew within 150 feet of the beach and then climbed up to 1,500 feet in a matter of minutes.

I used to hike the Cape Lookout trail two miles out to the tip and scramble down the forbidden cliffs to the great cave under the westernmost point. Crawling carefully in at low tide, I'd explore the cave and imagine getting trapped and drowned by a freak wave. It makes my heart beat faster to recall the moment when a wave half-filled my view out the cave to the horizon. The dark tunnel leading back to the light became smaller as the water rose in the trapped channel. "Is this the one?" I'd wonder.

A few hundred miles of trails and logging roads can be ridden on mountain bikes, and if you throw in the seemingly endless stretches of bikeable beaches there is enough open coast real estate to keep me peddling for years after I am dead.

The coast highway is a wonderful stretch for road bike riding, especially the Three Capes route next to the ocean near Tillamook, where the motto seems to be "You can smell our dairy air." Maybe this is why the population doesn't grow very fast, though not for want of human beings—the Tillamook Cheese factory ranks fifth or sixth in the state for number of visitors, right up there with Crater Lake and Multnomah Falls.

As a kid I'd hike out to Cape Lookout and poke around the wreckage of a World War II bomber that crashed there in the fog. Only a few scraps of aluminum remained, but ghosts could be felt during the evenings on rainy days. Now the ghosts may have a home at the Air Museum in Tillamook, where there is a huge blimp hangar filled with old warplanes.

Here at Cape Lookout, we modern pilots soar with the gulls above the site where airmen died in the fog. Somehow it all seems to fit together, and it is the sense of continuity, not always that spooky, that makes this edge of Oregon my favorite place.

※

POOR FISH

upon the slimy boat
the ancient fisherman
paws coldly at his privates
as the lights flash on & off

while we lie here together
sucking madly through our gills

this scene
has happened

& no one is the wiser
not even the blond dagger
of a lightbulb in the cold.

—MARTY CHRISTENSEN

# THE Coast

## BRIEF ENCOUNTER:

# Cannon Beach

by DAVID NOONAN

Once upon a time Oregon was just a rectangle up near the corner of the map and the ocean wasn't the ocean at all, it was the Jersey shore, a quasi-urban boardwalk wonderland where you could get a great sausage sandwich and shoot BB guns and win a carton of cigarettes and maybe even hop around in the waves awhile if you could manage to tear yourself away from the bumper cars.

Then I went to Oregon, and though I was only there for three days, my ideas about fundamental things like continents and oceans and stars and man's relationship with nature were changed profoundly and forever. I also bought a sweatshirt.

I went to Oregon to meet a man who couldn't move. His name was Lance Meagher, and he lived in Cannon Beach in a house on a hill overlooking that small town and the Pacific Ocean beyond. Lance was immobilized by ALS, Lou Gehrig's disease, and I wanted to interview him for a book I was writing about the human nervous system and neurological medicine. Lance, a physician, was well known in ALS circles for a number of reasons, including his plan to fly solo around the world in a single-engine airplane; he'd had electrodes implanted over the visual cortex of his brain so that he would be able to operate the plane by moving his eyes across a computer screen. His eyes, his mouth, and his left knee were the only parts of his body he could move.

He was a remarkable man dwelling in a remarkable place, and

it was that combination of man and environment that made such an impression on me. Physically powerless, unable to breathe without a respirator, Lance lived in perfect, ironic harmony with the hyper-powerful forces of nature that surrounded him.

The first time I saw the Oregon coast, I thought to myself, "Now this is what the ocean is supposed to look like." It was one great beast hurling itself against another great beast, big land and big water pounding on each other, continent and ocean meeting. In fact, until I watched the cold February Pacific beat on the forested shoreline just north of Cannon Beach, I didn't appreciate what a continent was. Though I had seen the Pacific before—I had even driven the coast of California from San Francisco to Los Angeles—I'd never developed a true sense of the landmass (the mass of land) that was my home. But there was something about Cannon Beach, something in the way the waves crashed and the sun set and the stars appeared and hung so low, something in the misty seam where the sea met the sky, that spoke of the spooky edge of things. Caught there between the great swell of North America at my back and the looming gone-ness of that big deep ocean stretching out before me, into the west, into the night, I finally grasped the crunching tumble of geologic time, the eonic beat of plate tectonics. For the first time, I actually rode the ever-shifting surface of Earth. And riding with me, of course, were those crazy big rocks down there in the surf, Haystack Rock and its companion

rocks, that gang of rocks, big silent creatures, ancient beings, enormous and quiet and serious, deep in eternal meditation, dignified stone cats who went to the beach one day five million years ago and decided to stay forever. I was tempted to do the same.

Indomitable Lance, who could form words with his mouth but didn't have the wind power to make sounds, spoke via his nurse, who could read his lips and his gestures, "I believe the mind is what is human," he said to me, dismissing the notion that his useless body was a burden of any kind. Lance is dead now, and though I spent only three days with him nine years ago, his courage and wisdom continue to inspire me. He was terminally ill, but he never stopped dreaming about the future or planning for it. He never made his flight around the world, but I have no doubt that he would have if he hadn't run out of time.

To me, Lance Meagher, quiet and motionless, was as much a force of nature as the raw and powerful Oregon coast itself; his absolute refusal to accept limits of any kind was and is the purest possible reflection of the place he called home. And that is Oregon to me—the unconquerable human spirit in sync with the timeless beauty and power of nature.

P.S. My Oregon sweatshirt is just a gray sweatshirt that I bought in Cannon Beach. It doesn't have any writing on it. I'm the only one who knows it is an Oregon sweatshirt and I like it that way. I don't know why, but an unmarked sweatshirt seems like an appropriate Oregon souvenir, maybe the perfect Oregon souvenir. You figure it out.

**COLD HARD FACT**

| OREGON'S BEST PLACES ARE, IN REVERSE ORDER: |
| --- |
| 10) GENOA |
| 9) STROHECKER'S |
| 8) SASSY'S |
| 7) ASHLAND |
| 6) PENDLETON ROUND-UP |
| 5) EASTSIDE PORTLAND |
| 4) ODELL LAKE |
| 3) GOOSE HOLLOW INN |
| 2) TIMBERLINE |
| 1) WAYNE MORSE'S GRAVE |

# JOHN STRAWN'S HIP-POCKET GUIDE TO THE BEST GOLF COURSES IN OREGON

### BY JOHN STRAWN

Then out upon the green I walk,
Just ere the close of day,
And swift I ween the sight I view
Clears all my gloom away.
—WALT WHITMAN

Golf is famously addictive—I mean, is it any coincidence that casual users of heroin have borrowed the term "chipping"?—and as with any fixation, it can start innocently. I was looking for diversion when I was delivered instead into the callused hands of obsession.

The first time out it was Bails, Larry Colton, Tommy Mac, and me. Three ex-jocks—Colton a former big-leaguer with a ruined pitching arm, Bails and Tommy Mac both college hoopsters, and me, whose hormonal destiny was an enduring pubescence that squelched my roundball ambitions (and left me astonished as I continued to grow until, at the age of 30, married, and with two school-aged daughters, I finally reached my full size of just over 6' 1" and 200 pounds). But now I had dunked for the last time, Colton had long since squeezed off his ultimate slider, and Bails and Tommy Mac were strictly set shooters. Needing a new sport for middle age, we turned to golf. We already wore bad clothes.

We were on the first tee at Rose City, one of Portland's four (it now has five) municipal golf courses. Seventy years before, in the downtime between automobile races, Rose City provided a setting for the once-popular diversion of locomotive crashing. A promoter laid a mile or so of track, aimed two steam engines at one another, fired up the boilers, set the throttles, and ran for cover. After the Rose City head-on, the locomotive carcasses lay rusting for years, while a little group of pioneering golfers took advantage of the open space, buried some tin cans, and started a golf club. Our golf games promised to resonate to the melody of smashed steel.

For instance.

I've got a death-grip on the driver from my rental set, and I'm trying to grab the ground through my sneakers so I can swing really hard. I've just watched Bails send his tee shot 280 yards, tracing the trajectory great players impart—the ball looks as if it starts out low, then gains altitude, like a second-stage rocket igniting, before rounding the top of its arc and slipping toward Earth, bounding forward as the spheres collide. Bails, a photographer who made his real living as a contractor—art not paying what it should—had leather palms and cabled forearms and a golf swing as graceful and balanced as a butterfly settling on a blossom. Forgoing the wiggles and waggles most golfers use to find the repose that will liberate their swings, Bails planted his feet, glanced down the fairway, then turned slightly as he brought the club above his head, building torque like a trip-hammer. He launched the

ball with such unexpected vigor that I had to search for it, jerking my head to the sky like a chicken looking for a hawk. Bails had been a schoolboy champion in California and could shoot in the '60s, but he was volatile and subject to crashing waves of temper, so his scores rarely matched his expectations. But physically he was as gifted as a golfer can be. Larry Colton, who had eyes like Ted Williams, announced the distance, and we murmured respectfully. Bails grunted and reached for his peg.

Larry, next on the tee, stood on the wrong side of the ball. He does everything right-handed, except swing a baseball bat or a golf club. Larry's first clubs were hand-me-downs from his left-handed dad, and he was still using them 40 years later. The clubs in general looked as if they'd been assembled by the night shift at a Soviet auto plant. But Colton could break 80 as a kid, playing with his Uncle Al at L.A.'s Riviera Country Club, and could not have cared less. He assumed the gift of golf would quickly return—after a few warm-up rounds to restore his swing, he'd be scoring as well as ever.

Tommy Mac was, like me, a beginner. Tall and gentle, Tommy spoke in a quiet voice, and his shooting touch with a basketball was velvet. I assumed that he would pick up golf quickly. Wrong. Tommy held a golf club the way a fifth-grade boy holds a girl in dance class—he didn't know what to grab where. Good golfers are loose and flexible so they can generate speed in the club head. Tommy was so rigid the club head didn't get moving much faster than his hands, which meant that this big, strong, athletic guy could barely hit the ball past his shadow. His first tee shot careened to the right in a lazy slice, like a listing drunk.

I stuck a brand-new Top-Flite on top of a red tee, backed off a couple of feet, wound up, and swung so hard I corkscrewed in the ground, like Reggie Jackson swinging through a Nolan Ryan fastball. The ball sat undisturbed. The second time I missed, I smashed the club against the ground. Jesus! I had Bails's temper and Tommy's talent! Why couldn't it have been the other way around?

Over the next four hours, I missed the ball about as often as I hit it. Two sensations persisted from that inaugural round. First, I felt shame, laced with chagrin. That's part of what the Scots who invented the game wanted its devotees to feel. Then, miraculously, on the 13th hole (they've since reversed the nines, so if you're playing Rose City today, I'm talking about the fourth hole), I caught the ball perfectly

flush and drove the green (it's a very short par 4). I now had experienced the second of golf's primary emotions: hope.

The next day, I bought my first set of clubs.

That was in the early spring of 1982. Tommy, Larry, Bails, and I started a regular game Sunday at dawn. In late June in Oregon, dawn breaks really early, so we were on the road at 4 a.m. We drew an increasingly large circle around Portland looking for places to play. At the center were Portland's great munis: Eastmoreland, Rose City, and Heron Lakes (then only one course, called Delta Park, but now two fancifully named courses, the new one known as Great Blue, while our original favorite's been rechristened the Greenback).

We played Broadmoor and Colwood, near PDX, and then, as the arc of our exploration widened, cruised to the suburbs to take on Meriwether and Forest Hills. We ambled south to McNary and Salem Golf Club, or north, leaving Oregon, to Lewis River, Three Rivers, or my personal favorite, The Cedars, a course with a wonderful setting that's suffered years of neglect and poor management. (But these last three are not Oregon courses, so forget I mentioned them.)

Our end was about what you'd expect for a boys' club. Bails was playing poorly one morning at Eastmoreland, though still better than anyone else. Locked in his misery, he walked ahead of the rest of us, while Larry got madder and madder. "Look at him," Larry said, pointing at Bails.

"What?" I said. I hadn't really noticed.

"It's rude," Larry said.

By the time Tommy finished putting on 9, Bails had crossed the street and teed off on 10. That was it for Colton. He went to his car, loaded up his clubs, and peeled out of the parking lot, rolling down his window and shaking his fist as he passed.

"Grow up, Bails!" he shouted.

But none of us have.

My golfing odyssey eventually took me even farther from home. I studied golf course architecture and the techniques of course building full-time, even enrolling in a seminar on golf course architecture at the Harvard Graduate School of Design.

The United States has more golf courses than anyplace, about 13,000, the majority nine-holers. And the thirst for golf's delectable cocktail, a mixture of equal parts conviviality and misery, with vitriol for a chaser, drives American golfers to buy self-help books and magazines in astonishing numbers. An old Texas teaching pro named Harvey Penick, tutor to Ben Crenshaw and Tom Kite, assembled a little book of aphorisms that became the best-selling sports book of all time.

Americans will pay almost any price for a good golf game, short of actually practicing. The Japanese, on the other hand, practice endlessly, even though many will never set foot on a golf course. They're virtual golfers, with beautiful driving range swings, the counterweight to America's prodigious legion of duffers who play with the grace of a tractor-trailer plunging into a gorge—and that whenever they please.

In Oregon—doubly blessed with great biology and tolerable society—public golf reaches its American apogee. We can pretty much play year-round, especially in the southern part of the state, where it's drier and generally warmer than in the Willamette Valley. And even around Portland, where the rainy season can linger past logical tolerance, it's possible to play golf any month of the year. But not every year.

It is claimed that the second-oldest course west of the Rockies is on the north Oregon coast, at Gearhart, about 70 miles west of Portland. Portland's first muni, Eastmoreland, was built at the end of World War I. (Eastmoreland was also an early example of a golf course used to market real estate. The developers of Eastmoreland gave the land to the city. The land was marginal for housing anyway, because it butted up to the railroad tracks and was partially swampy. But it produced a great golf course.)

Recently, Oregon has enjoyed a boom in golf course construction. In August 1996, the United States Golf Association's Men's Amateur Championship was held at Pumpkin Ridge, in Cornelius, the best of the state's new courses. My list of favorite courses includes new as well as old. While I have restricted my choices to 18-hole courses, I'd recommend the state's abundant supply of nine-hole courses to anyone. Agate Beach, Sunset Bay, Vernonia, and the "valleys"—Olalla Valley, Illinois Valley, Elkhorn Valley—all are quirky, amicable, and inviting.

Here are my ten favorite public access golf courses in Oregon.

### 1. GHOST CREEK, PUMPKIN RIDGE, CORNELIUS.
Designed by Robert Cupp and John Fought, Ghost Creek complements Pumpkin Ridge's private course, Witch Hollow. These courses provide the finest golf in the Northwest. See what can be accomplished by a good modern golf course architect given a good site. Ghost Creek played like a mature

course on opening day.

### 2. EASTMORELAND, PORTLAND.
The city's greatest muni, even though a long-time superintendent spent decades trying to turn the golf course into an arboretum. Eastmoreland has more trees—and more kinds of trees, including a small forest of araucarias ("monkey puzzlers") between the 17th green and the 18th tee—than any golf course on the planet. It also has abundant wildlife, the Rhododendron Garden, and the subtlest greens in the state. Designed by Chandler Egan.

### 3. TOKATEE, BLUE RIVER.
Fifty miles from Eugene up the McKenzie River, Tokatee is the quintessential Cascade Mountain course, winding through tall firs and opening up vistas to the surrounding mountains. One of the greatest bargains in golf. Designed by Ted Robinson.

### 4. SANDPINES, FLORENCE.
Sandpines is the perfect place to discover the difference between a links-style course and a parkland course, because it combines elements of each in a brilliant synthesis. The prevailing summer winds, unfortunately, can make Sandpines very difficult to play. Designed by Rees Jones, younger son of Robert Trent Jones.

### 5. EAGLE POINT, MEDFORD.
The newest of Oregon's great courses opened

for play in the summer of 1996. Both designed and owned by Robert Trent Jones, Jr., Rees's older brother. Eagle Point combines commodious fairways with demanding greens in a setting that rivals Tokatee. The best public course in southern Oregon.

### 6. BIG MEADOWS, BLACK BUTTE RANCH.

Central Oregon is rich in golf courses, and there are rivals to Big Meadows as the region's best public access course—the North Course at Sunriver, certainly, and Widgi Creek, perhaps—but Big Meadows wins for me, followed by the Ridge Course at Eagle Crest. (Central Oregon's best new courses— Crosswater, designed by Bob Cupp, and Broken Top, by Tom Weiskopf and Jay Morrish—are private.)

### 7. GREENBACK, HERON LAKES, PORTLAND.

Easier by far than its companion course, the Great Blue (and also cheaper to play), the Greenback is my favorite of these two, not least because you can play it in four hours, while I've never gotten around the Great Blue in less than five. Designed by Robert Trent Jones, 1971.

### 8. MEADOW LAKES, PRINEVILLE.

A great environmental success and a good golf course to boot. Meadow Lakes is the effluent spray field for Prineville's wastewater treatment plant. The water it returns to the Crooked River is cleaner than the water it removes. Awarded *Golf Digest*'s first-ever Environmental Steward Award. Designed by Bill Robinson, 1994.

### 9. RIDGE COURSE, EAGLE CREST RESORT, REDMOND.

The Ridge Course is worked carefully into its surroundings, and is beautifully maintained. Designed by John Thronsen.

### 10. TUKWILA, WOODBURN.

The members' course of the Oregon Golf Association. Like Eastmoreland, it is a public course anchoring a real estate development. The golf course winds through working filbert orchards. Rich in wildlife, including resident foxes. Designed by Bill Robinson.

**TOP NINE OREGON VIDEOS**

BY
D . K .
H O L M

Oregon, being only a thousand miles from Hollywood and featuring lush greenery, vast deserts, an ocean, and a dearth of unions, has served as a location for several major, and many more nonmajor, motion pictures. Yet in all the hundreds of movies and USA World Premiere Movies shot here, only 9 will ever enter the pantheon of true greatness.

In essence, this short list of masterpieces provides an operator's manual for Oregon. Within these frames, one learns how to clear a narrow-gauge train track, how to stage a student riot, and how to escape from a mental institution. In our realm, what else is there?

## 9. The General (1927)

Buster Keaton's silent comedy masterpiece was shot around Forest Grove, and for many years the shattered remnants of the film's climactic action scene—the train, bridge, explosion—lay in a gully. The florid landscape of a barely populated southern Oregon stood in for America during the Civil War as Keaton's character sought to retrieve his beloved train—and his fiancée. Working within the more sunny climes of the south, Keaton would often stop production to mount a quick baseball game in whatever empty field they happened to be shooting near.

## 8. Portland Exposé (1957)

Producer Lindsey Parsons knew a story when he saw one—a cinematic masterpiece, in the case of Portland vice operator Big Jim Elkins. Directed by Harold Schuster and written by Jack DeWitt, *Portland Exposé* tells the tale of a Corvallis restaurateur (Edward Binns) whose foray into Portland goes sour when he is threatened by hoods, among them Frank Gorshin as a sex maniac goon. Occasional exterior footage gives a glimpse of Portland in the late '50s.

## 7. Ring of Fire (1961)

The prototype of the drive-in movie. Efficiently directed by Hollywood hack Andrew L. Stone, *Ring of Fire* captures the beauty of Oregon's pre-clear-cut landscape, while defining the art of the $5-a-carload Saturday night drive-in special. David "The Fugitive" Janssen as a sheriff, Oregon favorite Frank Gorshin as a punk hood, and a slowly building forest fire, all shot in southern Oregon.

## 6. Paint Your Wagon (1969)

Clint Eastwood sings "I Talk To the Trees." Need anything else be said?

## 5. Drive, He Said (1972)

Jack Nicholson's directorial debut (he doesn't appear in the film) blends his well-known obsession with basketball with the last feeble gasps of the days of rage. *Drive, He Said* centers around a basketball star brooding about the efficacy of selling out while all around him friends are smoking pot and trying to beat the draft. Filming in Eugene (filling in for a mythical Ohio town), Nicholson dragged his cameras into the middle of an actual riot near the student union at the University of Oregon.

## 4. One Flew Over the Cuckoo's Nest (1975)

This faithful adaptation of Ken Kesey's popular novel uses many of the actual locations mentioned or implied in the book. Jack Nicholson, as McMurphy, brings his anarchic spirit to the dispirited denizens of a state mental hospital. Though the film is set mostly in the green confines and corridors of the nuthouse, director Milos Forman does stray to the coast in a few scenes, which, seen today, show how much things can change in a mere 17 years. Kesey's other readable novel, *Sometimes a Great Notion*, was also filmed in Oregon in the early 1970s and starred Paul Newman.

## 3. National Lampoon's Animal House (1975)

You want rebellion? Stay out of the 1960s. Instead, drop into the late '70s, when *National Lampoon*, the once-funny humor magazine, inspired a slew of "animal" movies, in which college students and teens live in hovels, try to get laid, flout authority, and engage in endless food fights—apparently the only antidote to a gradually Reaganizing world. *Animal House* (shot on the University of Oregon campus) also begat *The Blues Brothers*, thanks to star John Belushi's exposure to blues guitarist Robert Cray, who was then playing Eugene nightclubs. It all happened in Oregon, the cultural epicenter of the world.

## 2. Mala Noché (1986)

A great movie shot from street level with picture-postcard vistas. Relish the view of the Willamette River between the Hawthorne and Morrison Bridges, the cluttered corners and cobbled surfaces of Southwest Second and Ankeny. Based on an autobiographical novella by local poet Walt Curtis, *Mala Noche* is the story of a store clerk on Skid Road who develops a crush on a young illegal Mexican. Gus Van Sant's low-budget film, artfully photographed in noir-ish black and white, shows beautiful long thoroughfares at night, street lamps illuminating rainswept asphalt, rundown Chinese restaurants, and bare rooms in cheap hotels. The real Portland.

## 1. Brainsmasher: A Love Story (1991)

Now, finally, we have it: the best film made in Oregon.

Recently, Portland has played host to many filmmakers, from Alan Parker (*Come See the Paradise*) to Bill Forsyth (*Breaking In*). The state as a whole has borne witness to the spectacles of Lee Marvin singing (*Paint Your Wagon*) and River Phoenix seizuring (*My Own Private Idaho*). But of all the scores of films shot here, mostly TV movies for the USA Network, your average film buff will probably nominate *Drugstore Cowboy* as the best. The movie is accomplished, visually interesting, funny, and coherent; has some great acting; and uses well several recognizable Portland locations. No question, it's great. There are, however, those who find supreme pleasure in a more subterranean cinema. That's why true connoisseurs of Portland cinema nominate *Brainsmasher: A Love Story* as the best film shot in Portland.

Directed by Albert Pyun (*Kickboxer 2*), *Brainsmasher* has a lot not going for it. It stars Andrew "Dice" Clay, perhaps the most hated performer in the short history of stand-up comedy.

Clay plays hero Ed Molloy, a bouncer roped into helping a model named Sam (played by Canadian-born actress Teri Hatcher in her pre-*Superman* days), who is fleeing a band of Chinese martial artists (they hate being called ninjas) who are attempting to claim a rare flower that will give their master all the power in the universe. Did I mention that it was a comedy?

Several stand-ups-turned-actors—Tim Tommerson and Charles Rocket among them—make goofy cameo appearances. But best of all, *Brainsmasher* uses Portland locations to their best advantage. For example, the Guild Theatre, a popular art-house cinema in the heart of downtown, is metamorphosed into a strip joint. The auditorium in the beautiful Pythian Building is converted into a disco. And the beloved MAX light-rail line that cuts through the city is used as a vehicle for an elaborate chase sequence-cum-love scene. The much-despised Clay gives a sullenly subtle performance, and Hatcher, eventually forced in the dance club to don thigh boots and a tank top, is sexy and funny. Oh, nominating this movie won't make the city fathers happy at all. But hey, *Brainsmasher* is the optimum Portland film.

# PLACE$ TO LIVE

New in town? Carpetbagging? Oregon possesses six of the best places in the United States to dig in for the long haul. They are:

**1) PORTLAND'S WEST HILLS:** Elevated home to Oregon's top swells. Woodsy, plush.

**2) GRANT PARK:** Tremendous neighborhood of old-fashioned mini-mansions—houses that look as if they should appear on postage stamps.

**3) LAKE OSWEGO:** Best suburb in the United States. Long houses amid tall trees. Beaver Cleaver never had it so good.

**4) LINCOLN CITY:** A new Beaverton, except right by the ocean. Thanks to the short-sightedness of the state's land barons, the Oregon coast remains the largest chunk of undeveloped coastline in the United States. Finally, however, someone has had the common sense to pave this paradise for parking lots and to tack up a huge factory-discount mall by the sea.

**5) SISTERS/BEND:** Wide open spaces, dry, real hot or real cold, beautiful forests, great skiing, excellent traffic jams.

**6) EUGENE:** The liberal Nazi capital of the world. Home to New Age Stepford wives and guys wandering around in Birkenstocks and Pendleton shirts who look like logger-poets but who you know just stepped off the airport commuter from Long Island.

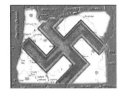

# OREGON WACKO:

## A CONNOISSEUR'S GUIDE TO THE BEAVER STATE'S FAR LEFT, FAR RIGHT, AND FAR MIDDLE: SKINHEADS, COMMIES, SURVIVALISTS, NEO-NAZIS, JESUS FREAKS, FREE LOVERS, AND REPUBLICANS

### By Jim Redden

*"We need to continue the ban on gays in the military. In the military we kill and shoot people—and we don't need their lifestyle hindering us."*
—SARA PAULSON, 1993 MISS OREGON

Oregon is America's Living Museum of Fringe Political Movements. Here thrives virtually every extremist group that ever rallied against the Establishment—from Birchers to Communists, from Black Power Muslims to White Pride Nazis. Lively folk who stage regular meetings, picnics, and protests.

## THE BEST OF THE LEFT

Oregon still has several Communist parties, including splinter groups of revolutionary Maoists and feminist followers of Leon Trotsky. This shouldn't be surprising, given that Portland was the birthplace of John Reed, dashing seminal U.S. Red, author of the renowned story of the Russian revolution, *Ten Days that Shook the World*—and the only American buried in the Kremlin. (Most Oregonians assume that Reed College, the elite ultra-liberal private school in southeast Portland, was named after John—played by Warren Beatty in *Reds*. It wasn't.) Although some liberal groups seem to ebb and flow in response to U.S. foreign policy moves, a number have remained constant, including:

# Radical Women

The ideal of a communist state as a worker's paradise is alive and well with Radical Women, Oregon's top Marxist cell. Largely lesbian, Radical Women operates out of a tidy suite of offices in the most yuppified part of Portland, but advocates pre-Gorby socialism and is affiliated with the Freedom Socialist Party, a splinter Communist Party organization that sides with Trotsky over Lenin whenever Trotsky versus Lenin questions arise.

But ideological purity has a price. Radical Women would make even *I Led Three Lives*'s Philbric nuts. The group always insists that it be represented on liberal coalition steering committees, but then usual-ly quits in protest over arcane issues of Redness that none of the other Reds can even understand. Still, Radical Women is the only Communist organization that offers a monthly discussion group featuring vegetarian snacks.

# THE FAR-OUT RIGHT

Oregon is a famously progressive state that nevertheless is crawling with right-wingers, most far more radical than the Newt Gingrich crowd. They include survivalists, gun nuts, and an assortment of self-taught constitutional experts. Among them:

# The Posse Comitatus

If ever a right-wing organization lived up to the media stereotype of uneducated, overweight, illiterate

# THE REVOLUTIONARY COMMUNIST PARTY

"Mao more than ever" is the slogan of the Chi-Com inspired RCP, the only *respectable* far-left group still advocating the violent overthrow of the U.S. government.

RCP cadre distributes copies of their weekly newspaper, *The Revolutionary Worker*, in local record stores and coffeehouses. Each issue documents the abuses of the collapsing capitalistic system—which somehow manages to continue oppressing us masses, despite its many flaws.

The RCP is most notable as the inspiration behind P.O.W.E.R., a wacky Portland multiracial rap duo that released a CD entitled *Dedicated to World Revolution* in 1994. Produced by RCP adherents Che and Krys Kill, *DTWR* combines Marxist diatribes with pounding rap beats. The duo puts the RCP revolutionary philosophy across by cleverly rhyming words as "racial purity" and "national security," but runs aground with such pairings as "sausage" and "hostage."

P.O.W.E.R. may have also compromised its impact by advocating, in the liner notes, that fans follow a P.O.W.E.R. ten-point program, which Che and Krys never got around to writing.

hicks, the Posse Comitatus is it. Founded in Portland in 1968, the Posse is a loose-knit collection of hillbillies and back-to-the-gold-standard advocates, united in the unbelievable belief that county sheriffs need their help. According to the Posse, elected sheriffs are the only people authorized by the U.S. Constitution to enforce the law—with the help of God-fearing, law-abiding, Jew-baiting citizens like themselves.

Convinced that elected officials have no legal authority to pass laws, group members occasionally travel to the state capitol in Salem to serve "subpoenas" on state legislators. The slightly official-looking documents usually alleging "treason" and betrayal of the country are replete with typos, run-on sentences, and obscure Biblical terms. A pox on these clowns.

## The Christian Patriot Association

Headquartered, no joke, in Boring, Oregon. Founded and led by an immense, bearded redneck named Richard Flowers, the CPA runs a bookstore, publishes a newsletter, and operates an unregistered bank called the National Coin Exchange for those who don't trust traditional financial institutions.

CPAs think America is about to fall victim to a vast conspiracy of mostly Jewish bankers operating through the United Nations—the UN being a satanic plot developed more than 200 years ago by the Illuminati, that most secret of secret societies. So secret, in fact, the CPA has yet to identify a single member or place of business—thus proving how diabolical the Illuminati really is.

## The American Front

For reasons which should perhaps be obvious to everybody, but which no one understands, lots of young Oregonians became racist skinheads in the late 1980s, producing several skinhead organizations—including East Side White Pride in east Portland (natch) and Preservation of the White American Race (POWAR). But the only one to stand the test of time is the American Front, founded and oper-

## The Unorganized Militia

Are you an able-bodied male between the ages of 18 and 45? And a resident of Oregon not currently serving in any branch of the armed forces? Then congratulations—you're a member of the "unorganized militia," a statewide, constitutionally mandated paramilitary organization that can be called up by the governor to defend the state against all threats, foreign and domestic.

No. Really. That's what it says in Oregon Revised Statute 396.105, approved by a vote of the people in 1961 and amended by the Oregon Legislature in 1989.

ated by a California transplant, Robert Heick.

The fast-talking son of liberal parents, Heick founded the American Front in San Francisco, primarily to piss off that city's staggering number of liberals. The group staged White Worker Day rallies on May Day—the traditional day of Communist celebration—before Heick was driven out of town by violent opponents. Moving to Portland in 1990, Heick organized the White Worker Rallies—an irony, since he himself was unemployed. Through flyers and newsletters, Heick asserts his group is neither left nor right, but is the champion of the "Third Position," struggling in the name of "revolutionary racial nationalism"—whatever that is.

## THE RADICAL MIDDLE

It's nuts to think of light-years-from-the-mainstream political movements only in terms of left or right. Many of Oregon's most visible activists fall way outside these parameters. They range from dope-smoking rednecks to suit-and-tie-wearing anarchists, all united in the belief that the government that governs least governs best.

# Ace Hayes

If you want to see a living, breathing wild-eyed conspiracy nut, drop by the funky Clinton Street Theater along bohemian Clinton Street in southeast Portland on the first Wednesday of every month.

That's when Ace Hayes, a cabinetmaker by trade, conducts his wildly improbable Secret Government Seminars—a free-for-all, open-to-the-public forum for exchanging every kind of conspiracy theory ever invented, and then some. Onstage, behind a table piled with obscure and largely impenetrable books, Hayes holds court. Like a doting college professor, he guides discussion left and right—everybody united by a belief that *they* are running the planet. Whoever *they* are.

Hayes is never at a loss for words. Diving into the texts before him, he never fails to find a quote or citation supporting whatever theory is being presented, even if it directly contradicts the theory that just preceded it. Frequent topics include the Kennedy assassination (*they* killed him), the Iran-Contra affair (*they* trafficked in drugs and weapons), and Whitewater (*they* are behind it). All seminars are taped and replayed on local cable access; in addition, Ace oversees publication of an irregular newsletter, *The Portland Free Press*, whose slogan is "Tell the truth and run."

BAD GIRLS

"O.J. Simpson has his image back.
I have done everything anyone has asked
of me. What I want is a chance to skate
again. I want my image back."

—TONYA HARDING

by
Karen
Karbo

Tonya Harding is not the first woman to disgrace our noble state. In fact, she is part of a not-so-proud Oregon tradition—the most recent *femme fatale* in an illustrious line of girl miscreants and troublemakers. Here are some of her sisters in ignominy.

## ELIZABETH DIANE DOWNS

If anyone deserves to take a spin in the chair, it's Downs. Convicted of shooting her three children with a .22 pistol, killing one and disabling the other two for life, she is currently serving life plus 50 years in a New Jersey prison.

Apparently unfazed by her conviction in the mid-1980s, Downs kept busy. She fell in love with an Oregon cop, with whom she wanted to have another child (!), escaped—briefly—from prison, appeared on *Oprah*, wrote a book (*Best Kept Secrets*), was the subject of another one (*Small Sacrifices* by Ann Rule), and was portrayed by Farrah Fawcett in a made-for-TV movie. All in all, a much more productive life than she might have led as a nonfelonious mother of three.

## JULIE LEONHARDT

Leonhardt is the Clatsop County district attorney recalled in a special election for allegedly framing two Astoria cops and trying to fix traffic tickets for her then boyfriend, a convicted felon who became her husband while under investigation for trafficking in explosives and switchblades. She was a Multnomah County deputy D.A. at the time.

## KATHERINE ANNE POWER

An accomplice in a 1970 Massachusetts bank robbery that resulted in the slaying of a Boston policeman, this 14-year resident of Lebanon, Oregon, worked under an assumed name at M's Tea and Coffee House in Corvallis before surrendering to the FBI in 1993.

Prior to her life as a revolutionary, she was her high school class valedictorian and winner of a Betty Crocker Homemaker Award. Katherine Anne adds a touch of class to the sisterhood. She got to wear the title "fugitive" in front of her name, outlasted the FBI's Most Wanted List, and prompted any number of articles analyzing Oregon as a place where on-the-lam wackos and ex-Weathermen could safely, underground, pass into middle age.

## GRETA RIDEOUT

The Lorena Bobbitt of the 1970s, Mrs. Rideout shocked the nation by bringing rape charges against her husband, John, an unemployed cook. At her husband's trial, Mrs. Rideout testified that Mr. Rideout chased her through a field, dragged her inside their apartment, and raped her while their two-and-a-half-year old daughter looked on.

Although this encouraged a re-examination of the old idea that a married woman is her husband's property, alleged rape victim Greta shot herself—and the country's newly raised consciousness—in the foot when it was revealed she was goading her husband about the affair she was having with his karate expert prison guard brother at the time of the rape. She shot down the impact of her case again when she and her husband were reconciled three weeks after he was acquitted.

## MA ANAND SHEELA

Personal secretary to the Bhagwan Shree Rajneesh, arrogant arsonist, and surly perpetrator of immigration fraud, Ma Anand Sheela apparently spearheaded a conspiracy to kill then U.S. Attorney Charles Turner and tried to poison the pop-

**DON'T DRINK THE WATER, SHEELA**

ulation of The Dalles in what would have been the first murder-by-salad-bar case in the history of jurisprudence.

Sheela hated us as much as we hated her, and she managed to humiliate Oregonians locally (she called them rednecks in the press) as well as nationally (the Bhagwan had *how* many Rolls-Royces?) Commentators and columnists wondered what was in the water out here. Sheela did make a singular contribution to public health by exposing the fact that those sneeze guards found at the salad bars of many restaurants are useless.

## RACHELLE "SHELLEY" SHANNON

A would-be assassin of doctors who perform abortions, whose act seemed to start a national fad, this 37-year-old resident of Grants Pass fired five rounds at Dr. George Tiller of Wichita, Kansas, hitting him in his arms. In a style worthy of Shawn Eckardt, Shannon was apprehended hours after the shooting as she turned in a rental car matching the description of the vehicle at the scene.

## DIANE WALDEN

This 40-year-old Portland day-care worker and mother of two kidnapped 13-year-old Peter Jay Rudge and carried on a cross-country love affair that ended when the two were found in Atlantic City.

It was the May-December aspect of their relationship (assuming a seventh-grader is capable of such a thing) that set the tongues of the nation wagging.

It was the revelation that the two had a "song"—Bryan Adams's "(Everything I Do) I Do It for You"—and a wardrobe of matching outfits that made the country gag.

It was Walden's sworn testimony that the couple never had sex (even though they spent weeks and weeks alone and allegedly slept together) that had the country sighing and saying, "What do they expect? They're from *Oregon*."

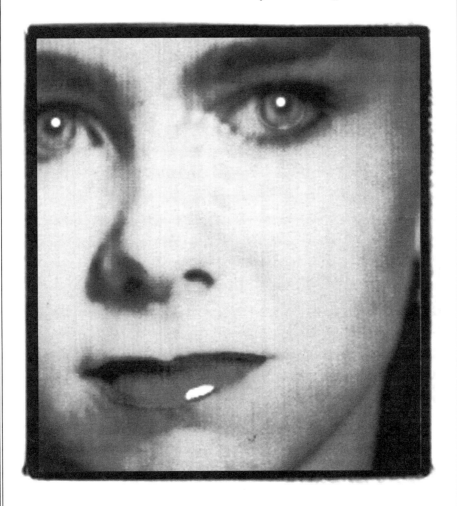

# PAUL ALLEN'S FIVE-BILLION-DOLLAR TRIVIA CONTEST

Hi, Paul Allen here. You know me, I'm the sidekick billionaire to Bill Gates. We founded Microsoft and I made $7.5 billion on the deal. The other day it occurred to me, who needs that kind of money? So I've decided to give a cool $5 billion away to the first WILD LIFE reader who can answer all of the following questions correctly:

1 Of the following four groups, which one recorded "Louie, Louie" first? A. Paul Revere and the Raiders B. The Wailers C. The Kingsmen D. The Zen County Hate Ranch

2 When Portland was founded, the men who were in charge flipped a coin to name the city, choosing between Portland and which of these? A. Jim B. Boston C. Santa Fe D. Hong Kong

3 The Peyton-Allen murders took place near which of the following? A. Rocky Butte B. Yaws Drive-In C. Forest Park D. Memphis

4 Which Portland high school has turned out the most NFL coaches? A. Jesuit B. Washington C. Jefferson D. Central Catholic

5 How many black dentists are there in Corvallis? A. One B. 88 C. Zero D. None of the above

6 What was Clark Gable's name when he lived in Portland during the '20s and '30s? A. Irv B. Manny C. Mugs D. Billy

7 In the team's first season in 1970, the Portland Trail Blazers had two first-round draft picks. One

was Geoff Petrie. Who was the other? A. Sidney Wicks B. Mikal Gilmore C. Walt Gilmore D. Gary Gilmore

8 On the famous Mel Renfro-Ray Renfro-Terry Baker Jefferson High School football team, who played first string both offensively *and* defensively? A. Ray B. Mel C. Terry D. Good old Ancil Nance

9 Remember when thousands of Oregon hippies went berserk here during the American Legion convention? Where did then Governor Tom McCall get them to go to cool off? A. Seattle B. McIver Park C. The Pacific Ocean D. Nowhere. He didn't like the American Legion either.

10 Of all the anti-war radicals running around Oregon during the 1960s and early 1970s,

who was never full of shit? A. Joe Uris B. Don Chambers C. John Bartells D. Mike McCusker

11 No, actually, Joe. I was just kidding. You too, Don, God rest your soul. Hint: What comes after C and before Z?

12 Which of the following sportscasters was born in Portland? A. Hannah Storm B. Curt Gowdy C. Ahmed Rashad or however you spell it D. Brent Musburger.

13 How tall is *Oregonian* owner S. I. Newhouse? A. 6'8" B. 5'2"

14 Former Portland State football coach Mouse Davis made a national name for himself developing a highly successful type of offense. What's it called? A. Run and Shoot B. Pick and Roll C. Drink and Drive D. Homies Go Long

*Dear Ms. Information:*

A two-part question: **1)** When I was a kid I dropped acid, protested the war in Vietnam, then went to the disco, had a couple of Harvey Wallbangers, came out, and, wow, it was 1997, I was 46 years old, and half my pals were granddads. What happened? **2)** What is the best bar in Portland to kick back, sip a few Dead Guy microbrews, take my digitalis, and lose my IQ in 20-point chunks watching brainless hard-body college girls strip naked to the classic crusher riffs of Ozzie and Aerosmith?                    BEAR BELLADAYWIC, PORTLAND

**ANSWER:** 1) Nothing. 2) Sassy's.

# OREGON'S

## TOP 10 BANDS

by William Abernathy

I f you are "into music" in Oregon, you are either: a) a hippie; b) into line dancing; or c) a resident of Portland.

It's been said that Canadians are united solely in their determination not to be accused of being Americans. If any blanket statement can be applied to the Portland rock scene, it is this: This is not Seattle. But so what? Seattle is history. It has been, in the word of one record company executive, "harvested."

Seattle bloomed huge largely because for years, skinny white-trash kids could edge-dwell off the economic lard sprayed from the whirling gears of the Reagan/ Boeing military-industrial machine. A punk could play in a band and beg, borrow, or steal enough to keep in secondhand clothes and a mostly dry pad. And you could still swing a dead cat without bonking into a major-label A&R toad.

We're not the next Seattle. Portland is the Second City of the Northwest. We don't have major league football, baseball, or hockey franchises because they don't make big foam-rubber hands with two upturned digits. But it's true: "We're Number Two! We're Number Two!" So, while everyone was fawning over El Grunge-o Grande up north, Portland was busy keeping itself amused all on its own. No rock stars, fame, or celebrity 20-gauge lobotomies. Just rain, a supportive crew of stalwart locals, and some wonderful music.

These bands are listed here

because I like them, and because they have contributed significantly, in my not-so-humble opinion, to advancing the Portland music scene. They run the gamut from the rather elderly to recent vintages, and from garage to hardcore, to genres that rock critics haven't come up with glib terms for yet. So don't kid yourself into thinking that I'm even trying to be objective as I list my top ten local bands.

**1** The tribal elders of the scene are the rock 'n' roll grandparents-who-shred in **Dead Moon.** Fred and Toody Cole play guitar and bass, and Andrew Loomis hits drums with a pleasingly Neanderthal flair. Fred and Toody used to run a delightfully grimy little music shop in downtown Portland called Captain Whizeagle's, done in by one of our myriad downtown improvement projects. Now they run a guitar shop in Clackamas called Tombstone Music. They have the same funky old monophonic record lathe that the Kingsmen used to cut "Louie, Louie." They still record their expert primordial Northwest punk sound in mono, and wouldn't sign a record contract if you held a gun to their head. Like a lot of Portland acts, they're widely alleged to be "big in Europe."

**2** Portland's first accepted Total Music Genius was Greg Sage.

With his band, the **Wipers**, he blazed a trail many bands still follow. He sang songs about being nuts, alone, and wanting to kill himself, and in addition to heapin' helpin's of self-pity, he wrote really excellent punk rock songs. Pre-Nirvana Kurt Cobain would drive, hitch, or crawl to get to a Wipers show, and went on to write songs about being nuts, alone, and wanting to kill himself. If it weren't for the long shadow cast by the Wipers, there might never have been grunge. In the early '90s, Sage moved to an Arizona desert retreat known as the Zeno Compound. He is said to be waiting for the mother ship.

**3** Portland's big contribution to punk was **Poison Idea.** They produced a furious, hard-edged, hardcore sound--and also wrote really solid tunes. They were also really fat. Guitarist Pig Champion peaked at around 500 pounds, while frontman Jerry A flirted routinely with 300 pounds. They got sick of being Poison Idea and broke up in 1993, went on to undistinguised side projects, and regrouped for a couple of gigs in late '96.

**4** **Crackerbash** I believed in with all my heart. Frontman Sean Croghan would get up there onstage and play his guitar and sing and sweat buckets. There was nothing fake about him. Drummer Ted

Miller and bassist Sean Fox are now in the campy-cool Satan's Pilgrims, a hellafun surf group, while Croghan is a solo act and also plays in Jr. High. They had "it" for quite a little while. Girl trouble in the band is widely rumored to have broken them up in 1993.

**5** Hazel is really cool. Onstage they have a lot of fun, and when they're offstage, they think a lot. Guitarist Pete Krebs does much of the band's songwriting. He also plays solo, and in the company of older bluesmen about town. Hazel drummer Jody Bleyle is also in Team Dresch, a marauding band of lesbians who make a lot of noise and tour the country in search of your daughter. Hazel also has this dancer guy, Fred Nemo, who is an endless source of mirth and terror, and who guarantees that the band will never be snapped up by a major label. The first thing industry hacks say when Hazel plays is "great sound, but who's that weird guy on the stage in the tutu with the beer pitcher on his head?"

**6** The Spinanes were a two-piece. Now they're sort of a one-piece, that is, if they even exist right now. For their first few years, Rebecca Gates sang and played guitar, and Scott Plouf hit the drums really hard, just like his older brother did for the Wipers (supra). Without a bass, the Spinanes schooled a lot of people on the importance of good songwriting, and on the strength of the guitar as an instrument. After their second album, Plouf joined Built to Spill, and Rebecca . . . well, as goes Rebecca, so goes Spinanity. She's done some solo stuff and some larger band stuff with the Spinane name. Whatever happens, at least you know the songs will be good.

**7** Heatmiser had a knack for writing songs which burrowed deep into your cerebral cortex and, when you least expect it, the tunes still jump up like a suppressed memory and will not leave you alone. Two guys in the band, Neil Gust and Elliott Smith, write devious psychological warfare experiments masquerading as excellent songs, and Smith has one heck of a solo career on the side. Heatmiser resides in that stylistic pigeonhole known as "pop-punk," but they say their next record is going to be "really different."

**8** Pond is three guys. Two are from Juneau, Alaska, and one is from Boring, Oregon. They make really exuberant rock with an Eastern, psychedelic edge. They were the first Portland act to sign with Seattle's Sub Pop label. Pond put out two really good Sub Pop albums, the first of which did well, and the second of which, arguably better, went nowhere. Pond thus became the first Portland band to leave Sub Pop.

**9 Thirty-Ought-Six** was my favorite Portland band, ever, a loud three-piece with tremendous everything. Their sound was heavily overdriven, with soaring vocals lording over the roaring din. What I liked about Crackerbash, I like about Thirty-Ought-Six. True believers and real craftsmen, passionate about their music and the world around them, or at least the ten feet immediately in front of them. They put out one album on Jody Bleyle's Candy-Ass Records label, and a second on Mute America. Both totally rip, dripping with passion and fury. They were the kind of live act that was capable of putting fear in my heart. I like that. Unfortunately, the candle which burns brightest burns fastest as well, and the lads in 'Ought-Six have gone their separate ways.

**10 The Dandy Warhols** are a full-on fluff-pop band cut straight from 1970. They wear the neatest clothes (when they have clothes on), have the cutest keyboardist, and put out songs utterly lacking the angst-driven, confessional tone of so many Northwest bands. Their theme song? "He-e-e-y La-a-a De-e-e Da-a-a!" They do, however, put out good fluffcore, and if you're into Brit-Invasion and Velvet Underground-derived tunes, or just need a little soda pop between weightier bands, they're just the ticket. The Dandies scored a huge deal with Capitol, so they should be carpet-bombing the airwaves in your neighborhood shortly.

You might also keep an eye out for the likes of Heavy Johnson Trio, King Black Acid, Gern Blanston, Atomic 61, Forehead, Svelt—and the cream of Eugene, the Cherry Poppin' Daddies (who are a lot cooler than the frat parties that they tend to pack). Also notewothy are Portland's queercore bands, like Sleater-Kinney, Team Dresch, Vegas Beat, and The Third Sex. They've advanced the cause of queer-identity music by creating a sound that, in addition to being empowering, is actually good. Will any of them become big rock stars? Probably not. Most will soldier on for a few years, maybe a decade, and then "grow up." Tinkerbell will die, and they'll start worrying about mortgages. But meanwhile, the scene lives on, more or less vitally, and the rest of us will be able to enjoy some darned fine tunes.

# MicroBrews

## OREGON'S TOP TEN CRAFT BEERS
### BY WILLIAM ABERNATHY

❶ **Deschutes Brewery Black Butte Porter**—the smoothest beer you could ever ask for. It's dark enough to make people think you're serious, but with its deceptively light body and moderate hopping, you'll find yourself halfway through your glass before you put it down. Go to Bend, where this beer is brewed, and visit the Bond St. Brewpub, where it is served. Order a pint of Black Butte, which is even better than the bottled product when enjoyed at the source. Buy a six-pack of Black Butte, and waddle down to the Deschutes River, which runs through the middle of town. Watch the flow of the river and have a Hermann Hesse moment.

❷ Brewed by brewmaster John Maier, **Rogue Brewery's Mogul Madness** is one of the most aggressively brewed beers civilians can lay their hands on. Maier uses no fewer than six different varieties of hops in this strong ale, which is, alas, available in the winter only. At all other times of the year, you should put their Shakespeare Stout ale to work on the back of your throat. Go to the Rogue Ales Public House in Newport, Oregon. Smell the sea. Admire the majestic arch of the Yaquina Bay Bridge. Drink the stout, or the Mogul, if you can wrap your hand around it. Have your attendant bring your stretcher, and make sure he tips before you leave.

❸ As the oldest craft brewery in Oregon (founded in 1984, when the dorky affect of a capital letter in the middle of your name was considered good marketing), **BridgePort Brewing** has long cranked out a beer whose familiarity had, for many years, bred my contempt. My mistake.

BridgePort's ubiquitous bottled product, **Blue Heron Pale Ale** is a BMW 7-Series in a field of hopped-up Dodge Chargers. While most Northwest pale ales will reach out and pound your head into the concrete with a vulgar display of brutish hopping, BridgePort's Blue Heron sings you to the rocks and shoals with a poised, sedate, and maturely brewed ale. Blue Heron strikes a judicious balance between all components of a pale ale, creating a tremendously satisfying light copper-colored drink, a beer for all seasons. The best site to savor the Heron is at the BridgePort Brew Pub in Portland. Ask the beertenders for Blue Heron "on cask." Take your pint out to the loading dock/beer garden. If the wind is blowing from the south, you'll be driven back inside by the heady waft of the fish-fertilizer factory next door. Otherwise, sit back and enjoy watching cars bog down in the unpaved and heavily rutted street. Perhaps someone you dislike will break an axle in the decaying rail switchplate in middle of the road. Hope springs eternal.

## ❹ Widmer Brothers Brewing

is the largest craft brewer in Oregon, largely due to the sales of a noxious faux-Bavarian atrocity called Hefeweizen—on tap in virtually every bar in the state. In keeping with the Bavarian style, the beer has a wheat-malt body, unfiltered and lightly hopped. In an utter desecration of the style, however, the Widmers employ a yeast with no resemblance to a proper weizen yeast. Redolent of sulfites from still-active yeast, thanks to one of the shortest fermentation times around, the ale is usually served with stench-suppressant lemon wedges. You only notice these things, of course, if you pay any attention, which the yuppie-twerp beer sippers who put this beer on the sales map never have. So dominant is Widmer Hefeweizen in the Northwest beer market that competitors who've endeavored to make weizens properly have lost their shirts, because the public has been "educated" on weizens brewed by the Widmers and by their many craven imitators. For all the havoc Widmer's full-court press has wrought on the hapless weizen style, the yeast that is so tragically wasted on wheated mash comes into its own in Widmer's comparatively unknown Alt beers. The Widmers' Alt is really good, true-to-style, and possessed of a full malt body with a good hit of residual sweetness. To be certain you can find some, you'll have to go to Widmer's tony Gasthaus brewpub at Widmer H.Q., a restored waterfront flophouse.

❺If you'd like to taste something approaching a real hefeweizen, you'll have to look south from Widmer. I know of only one Oregon brewery making an honest year-round effort to brew a real hefeweizen, to wit, **Wild River Brewing Co**. (with breweries located in Grants Pass and Cave Junction). Though I take exception with the hopping, which I believe to be a hair too eager for this delicate, light-bodied style, all the right components are present in this hefeweizen. Head Brewer and beer connoisseur Hubert Smith pits a proper weizen yeast (saccharomyces delbrueckii, for those of you keeping score at home) against a 55 percent barley, 45 percent wheat mash, yielding a lightly cloudy ale with the sweet undertastes of banana and clove, which are the mark of this classic Bavarian style. Though the ale is unfiltered and only lightly brighted, a considerable portion of the dead microbes find their way into the sewer rather than your glass, meaning no lemon wedge is required. With Wild River's breweries weighing in at svelte 7- and 15-barrel capacities, and (in proper Bavarian style) both being located way the hell at the bottom of the map, Wild River ales can be hard to find, although they are distributed all up and down the I-5 corridor, including in Portland. The best place to taste the ales, of course, is at the source, in either Cave Junction or Grants Pass. If you're lucky, Hubert will be there. Talk to him about beer, and you will rapidly come to feel like a rank malt-moron. As you glean an education, continue to drink his beers, and you will realize that his encyclopedic knowledge of brewing techniques, styles, and history has been put to good use. Wild River's hefeweizen is the closest you'll ever get to Munich without having to peel your buns off the bar stool.

❻The best cask-conditioned beer I've experienced was unquestionably **Full Sail's India Pale Ale** at the Harborside Restaurant's Pilsner Room in Portland. Cask-conditioned ale is a tricky affair. Unlike "traditional" American draft beers, cask-conditioned ales are not force-carbonated. They are drawn from the cask with a "beer engine," a hand pump that gingerly coaxes the beer out of the cask, rather than cattle-prodding it out Yankee-style with compressed carbon dioxide. The beer is lightly carbonated, solely as a result of the natural fermentation of the yeast, a process that can continue even in the cask. Zymurgy in motion. The Pilsner Room (a waterfront restaurant attached to the Hood River-based Full Sail's Portland "pilot brewery") takes pretty good care of their casks, conveniently located all of 20 feet away at the front of the brewery. Full Sail's rendition of the India Pale style is the product of the brewing genius of John Harris, who formulated many of Deschutes Brewery's fine ales before heading up to Portland to work for Full Sail. His I.P.A. will make you aware, once and for all, what hops are all about. India Pale Ale was originally intended to travel in barrels around the Cape of Good Hope for delivery to His Majesty's troops serving the Raj in India, and to still have enough socko flavor left in it when it got there to make it worth drinking. The merciless hopping of Full Sail's I.P.A. is sufficient to achieve a hop satori, the imported British Kent Goldings and Challenger hops transcending their hop bitterness with a sweet floral quality that makes brewers want to go read Byron and romp in the meadows.

❼ The tiny **Hair of the Dog** brewery is no pushover, making ales of rhino-stopping intensity. Run by a couple of confessed "beer geeks" in a Southeast Portland warehouse,

Hair of the Dog brews from some old converted Campbell's Soup cauldrons. As of press time, they only make two beers, both of them bottle-conditioned Belgian-style ales brewed strong enough to drop a charging Cape buffalo in his tracks. High in both sugar and alcohol, these beers are best savored in a seated posture. The better of the two, the Adambier (after the Adambier's tenth bottling, the BATF issued one of its random proclamations requiring Hair of the Dog to relabel it as just plain "Adam") is basically an Altbier on steroids. Double all the quantities, and then ferment the hell out of them (each brew is allowed to condition in the bottle for at least six weeks), and you start to get the idea. Sort of a sweet, liquid Marmite. Don a smoking jacket, pour the Adambier into a large wine glass, and savor it in front of a roaring hearth. Read Melville. Nod off.

❽ I've never been a huge fan of **McMenamins** beers; nevertheless, the phenomenal success of Oregon's most successful flagrant

Deadheads is undeniable. Rejecting the large, centralized breweries in which other Oregon brewers have invested, the Brothers McMenamin have cast seven-barrel brewpubs throughout the Willamette Valley and in Seattle and Vancouver, Washington. Each micro-brewpub has some latitude as to how its beers are prepared, and consequently, the Hammerhead Pale Ale you drink at one McMenamins may bear little more than a family resemblance to the Hammerhead you drink at another brewpub. In terms of scenic value, it's a jump ball between their Cornelius Pass Roadhouse (a beautifully restored farmhouse near Hillsboro) and their Edgefield Village complex (a beautifully restored former county poorhouse near Troutdale). Brewers in the chain give the nod to Cornelius Pass as the best McMenamins brewery. Cornelius Pass has a wonderful beer garden in back. Apply bug repellent, order a Terminator Stout, and watch the bats come out to feed over the adjacent industrial park. Edgefield Village is second only to Busch Gardens as a Disneyland of beer, containing multiple bed and breakfast rooms, meeting rooms, dining of both the hoity-toity and casual varieties, a movie theater, an outdoor amphitheater, a vineyard and winery, the largest brewery in the entire McMenamins chain, and (oh

yes…) a pub in which to swill its fermented efflux. You can enjoy "the Village" any way you like, as long as you don't get too close to the medium-security county jail next door. The glint of the razor wire in the setting sun, though, makes a Terminator enjoyed outdoors at the loading dock an experience not to be missed.

❾ The Northwest has been afflicted by a great disease of late—the epidemic of fruit beers. All beer starts out life as a mash of malted barley—sort of a sweet barley tea, with natural sugar drawn from the germinated, roasted, and cracked barleycorns. That's where maltose comes from. But, as anyone exposed to applejack or the Boone's Farm fruit wine line is aware, there's more than one plant out there that can give your yeast the sugar it needs to make alcohol. And so, in response to the needs of fey beer drinkers, brewers have prostituted themselves with a sorry stable of fruited beers, generally light-bodied, unsubstantial ales with a heaping dollop of fruit extract tossed in during the boil, or (worse yet) after fermentation. There are lemon beers, pineapple beers, apricot beers, raspberry beers, beers made with hathcupberries (I've never heard of hathcupberries either, but there's a beer brewed with them), apple beers, blueberry beers—I've even tried garlic beer. (Presented the opportunity, pass it up. It tasted like *eau de l'armpitte sicilien.*)

Look, beer is like oral sex: if you find the basic taste offensive, dousing the works with some god-awful fruit syrup is a fundamentally sleazy and dishonest means of making it palatable. Confess your sin: Mint condoms, strawberry douches, and Zima are your sorry lot in life. Go. Wallow.

Having said that, the best exemplar of the fruit beer ouevre I've encountered (I am hardly as well-versed in these sissified swills as I am in all-malt beers) is **Star Brewing's Black Cherry Stout.** Like one of those half-human, half-beast Greek demigods, it's got a robust, hirsute stout body and a nicely proportioned fruit taste grafted on top, bearing a more-than-passing resemblance to the original Belgian-issue cherry beers such as Kriek. Though Star is brewed in Portland, owner and brewmaster Scott Wenzel's inability to keep pace with the sales incentives (pronounced "petty bribery") of other breweries has made Star beers tough to find in the competitive Beaver State beer market, with a goodly portion of Star's production heading north to Washington. If you live in California, stay right there, and look around for Star in a 22-ounce bottle. Otherwise, you'll have to rummage around in Oregon specialty shops, or call your local distributor to find an elusive tap or retail market. Better yet, just drink an all-grain beer and quit fooling around with fruity beers.

❿ If you're hell-fired to drink a studiously inoffensive beer, and don't want to look like a chowderhead by drinking fruit ales or one of the eight million varieties of incorrectly brewed Northwest weizens, check out the Lucky Labrador Brewpub in Portland, and look into their summer seasonal rye beer, Quality Rye. It's lightly hopped, is a little sweet, and has a malt body that's made of about two-thirds pale-roasted barley and one-third rye, which adds a unique flavor. It's definitely different, and gives even a novice drinker a good idea as to what part of a beer's flavor profile is occupied by the malt. Of the other rye beers available in Oregon, Tugboat and Redhook, the former tends to clobber the subtlety of the rye with hopping, while the latter veers toward blandness. **Lucky Lab's Quality Rye** cleaves the twain. Since their beer is sold only on-site, you'll be enjoying it in either the barnlike indoors of the pub or the scenic beer garden, with its commanding view of the parking lot. Take it inside, chief.

SPECIAL
OREGON
DRINKER'S
SURVIVAL
SECTION

A GENTLEMAN'S GUIDE TO

BAR FIGHT

ETIQUETTE

OW!

OOOF!

In Los Angeles
you drive from
bar to bar, in
Seattle you walk,
and in Westside
Portland, you
ricochet.

**THE WISH** You duck! And the mirror behind you explodes, as the fat iron beer mug thrown at your head strikes it with a crash. Felonious Monk, president of the Satan's Infrastructure Motorcycle Gang, faces you across the bar at tony Genoa. A cruel smile plays across your face as you gaze at his 340-pound bulk. He has just insulted your date, the leggy, balloon-breasted ex-Rose Festival princess and Rhodes scholar Ms. Monique, having made light of her million-dollar book contract to do *the* definitive biography of Judas Iscariot.

"Monk," you say, raising your $13.25 triple snifter of Grand Marnier. "You look like three scoops of cafeteria mashed potatoes in those goofball leathers of yours, and right now I am going to have to pop your head like a great big zit."

You set your snifter aside and stride forward, lacing into Monk with your lightning-quick golf-ball-sized fists—

**THE REALITY** You duck! And the mirror behind you explodes, as the fat iron beer mug thrown at your head strikes it with a crash. Felonious Monk, president of the Satan's Infrastructure Motorcycle Gang, faces you from across the bar at Roamer's Rest, out there on the unexamined flats of East County. A look of petrified horror plays across your face as you gaze at his 340-pound bulk. He's just insulted your date—your boss's scuzzy little sister Fistula—and now you gotta do something. Either get pounded into the ground or get fired, one or the other.

What to do? Nontournament bar fighting, especially if you're yellow, can be avoided simply by steering clear of:

+ Establishments whose parking lots are filled with elderly, elongated "chopped" products of the Harley-Davidson Motorcycle Co.

+ Establishments whose long-haired patrons call you "brother" and want to play eight ball for twenty bucks.

+ Establishments frequented by both cowboys and Indians.

+ Establishments whose walls are papered with pinups from *Gent*, *Swank*, and *High Society* but whose real female patrons are outnumbered by the real male patrons more than ten to one.

Still, thank God, bar fights are often impossible to avoid. It's a cowboy universe. You get these muscle-bound drunk lunks all whacked out after their 666th game of Doom and nobody wants to dance with them or give them a kiss, and...

A word about bar-fight grooming.

Generally, less is more. Sturdy fabrics are best. A leather jacket, jeans, steel-toed logging boots or old-fashioned Clockwork Orange-era Doc Martens, and a half-dozen big, thick high school rings on each of your fingers provide a simple, elegant ensemble that's understated but effective.

And no ties. Unless you want to sponsor your own lynching. Also, keep your hair short. Otherwise your esteemed opponent gets two handles to your head. He grabs your locks and, quick as light, your schnoz meets his knee.

Finally, if you've been stomped recently, best just drink in your car. In barroom brawls, as in life, image counts. A face covered with scabs and fresh, weepy scar tissue doesn't cut it with the fist-fighting public.

As for training, it often pays to throw the blows with large members of your family or big friends in the privacy of your own home. Queasy about your bar-fight debut? Seek the company of your brawling betters (develop tight friendships with refrigerator-sized ex-convicts) or take a lot of bella donna.

Anyway, you've arrived at the bar-fight scene of your dreams. Now, what's the correct way to get things going? May I suggest two obvious openers:

"You, sir! Mind if I sleep with your date?"

Or, "Gee, I really like your hair."

As for opening blows, consider:

*The jab.* Strictly for purists. A strike meant to wound and enrage, not kill.

*Haymaker to the snot locker.* Considered the Pearl Harbor of opening blows. Not especially sporting, but effective.

*Head-butt to the solar plexus.* An all-or-nothing move favored by Samurai and diminutive hellions under 5'6".

*Toes to the beezer.* A classic. But you better be the ghost of Nureyev or nuts to pull it off. Very dangerous if you miss.

*Rabbit punch to the kidneys.* Only world-class scum even consider this one, but if delivered smoothly it will give you the satisfaction of knowing your opponent will think of you every time he takes a leak for the next three months.

## BAR-FIGHT WEAPONRY

Fillet of pool cue, beer-pitcher sandwich, eight ball between the front pockets...the world of bar-fight weaponry is heady and fascinating. Such sports aids can be invaluable to the chicken or otherwise faint of bar-fight heart.

A word about pool balls. Tipping the scales at about a pound and a half, these weighty babies can serve as rock baseballs. But what, you ask, about the pool cue? The less said the better. Pool cues should be used only as minor instruments of pre-fight coercion, or to lash and whack the tiny. Because to the enraged Mean Joe Green, a pool cue is just a toothpick on steroids. Good for maybe one swack before Mean Joe is tripping the light fantastic all over the parts of the body that exist above your ankles.

As for the beer pitcher, the experts are of several minds. I, myself, have found the standard- issue 32-ounce glass (as opposed to plastic) tavern model to be an effective conversation stopper.

**TO THE ENRAGED MEAN JOE GREEN, A POOL CUE IS JUST A TOOTHPICK ON STEROIDS.**

## Now, to the finer points of bar-fight etiquette.

RAINCHECKS. Say you're down at the Chainsaw Disco and you spot some monster feeb who absolutely makes you sick. So you shag up and say, "Okay, *kemosabe*, let's say you and I step outside for a little point-counterpoint."

And he refuses! Hard to believe, but there are people who—no matter how big, stupid, and angry-looking—do not see the necessity of motiveless bar fighting, people so gerbil-hearted that they will refuse to step outside and give you the

punches you so richly deserve.

My advice? Take it like a man. Don't hoot or holler, just leave him your card, return to your table, and await another night.

TEAM BAR FIGHTING. As you grow more experienced, you'll tire of the linear challenge of *mano a mano* and wish to enlist friends and enemies alike to tackle bar fighting at the "squad" or "mob" level. Boiling down inevitably to "our" guys against "their" guys, team bar fighting has a rollicking "shirts" and "skins" aspect and, at best, it can be like throwing your own private World War II. But organization is a hassle.

THE STRATEGIC RETREAT. Occasionally, it may occur to you that you are not going to win the fight. At least not without a breather. Not to worry, it happens to the best of us. Some yuppie Godzilla with a fist like a wrecking ball has got you butt to the rug. My advice? If there are tables or large chairs in the vicinity, scurry, roach-like, on hands and knees between them. Within moments you'll be (temporarily) safe amid a forest of fishnet stockings and checkered polyester. Even the most bloodthirsty opponent will be loath to come crawling down there after you. This is a tried-and-true tactic employed by the author on numerous occasions.

**CHICKENING OUT WITH STYLE.** The truth is, white guys have never learned to bug out with élan. Honkie cowards the world over rarely do anything but whine and snivel when exiting even the most benign and wimpy of barroom brawls. Chicken Afro-Americans, however, are masters of turning tail. Unlike his Wonder-Bread-eating-Volvo-driving ofay counterpart who's content to say things like, "I'll buy you a drink, give you five bucks, my whole wallet, my car, my girlfriend, if you promise not to beat me up," the savvy spineless black knows the rewards of aggressive hysteria: "Staywayfrommemuthafukka!orIbef orrippinyo'headoffanddropkickin'itt oVenus!" And before that whole sentence is out of his mouth, poof! the dude be gone.

My advice? Lie. "Beat it, I'm a cop" works for me.

## WOMEN & FISTS

And what, you may ask, about bar-fight feminism? Sure, a lot of you guys get all hotted up when milady's big mouth gets your butt pounded to street pizza in the parking lot behind some Gresham dive-and-dance or when La Poopsy's inconvenient flirting results in your face getting spread like Imperial Margarine across the brick back wall of the Ringside. But these are the '90s, and you do not want your better half deprived of her rights to bar-fight kicks under the law.

So girls, you are wondering: If I want to get mine, how best to be dressed?

My advice is: tastefully. Spring for one of those teased-to-a-bell-of-cotton-candy-bleached-blond-but-brown-at-the-roots bouffant hairdos, supertight jeans, stiletto heels, pink lipstick, and a set of that-was-me-with-my-knees-miles-apart-in-*Penthouse* fiberglass dagger fingernails. Paint them stoplight red. Also, use enough eyeliner and rouge to qualify your face as an oil painting, and develop an inability to pronounce the "g" in words ending in i-n-g.

If you intend to engage in pre-brawl political-social-economic discussions of the Susan Sontag stripe, go bra-less in a T-shirt with a printed message across your chest that reads something along the lines of Jane Fonda: American Traitor Bitch.

## A WORD TO THE WISE

**N**owadays most people either have a lawyer or, worse, are one. So before engaging in even the most routine bludgeoning, stabbing, shooting, or simple punching out of the lights, best require your opponent to sign a "Hold Harmless" agreement absolving you legally from injury, death, or embarrassment.

## THE WORST FOR LAST

**I** know that there will be those of you who will write and say, "Mark, you were too negative. If you can't write something 'nice' about bar fighting, don't write anything at all."

So it saddens me to have to conclude with the admission that 99 percent of all barfights are nothing like those you see when playing *Killer Kung Fu Fists of Dismemberment* or *Super Menendez Brothers* at the local video arcade. Or even like what happens on reruns of *Starsky and Hutch*. There are few roundhouse rights; hardly anybody ever gets a chair broken over his head. No. Most bar fights are brief, slashing, disorganized melees, sparked by scared, violent, aggressively stupid people who understand only two things: pain and incapacitating punishment. That's why you'll need to be red-hot

in the kick, scratch, bite, and gouge department.

So, my final advice? Learn to fight like a girl.                          –M.C.

## BEST ALL-TIME OREGON BAR

Erickson's. The primal huge and magnificent Oregon wild place. In the heyday of Paul Bunyan, loggers vowed they'd rather see Erickson's, with its lights on, than view the Grand Canyon or the Chicago World's Fair.

Bar, fixtures, and mirrors were the best money could buy. There was a concert stage. The free lunch was prodigious, a standard item being half of a roast ox. Soft bread for sandwiches was cut one and a half inches thick. Round logs of sliced sausages filled huge platters. Pickled herring swam in a large bucket of brine. Beer was five cents. Hard liquor a quarter.

The handiwork of Gus Erickson, who announced over a bottle of red- eye one Saturday night that he was going to build the biggest and best saloon in the world, Erickson's was constructed in the late 1800s and originally housed a Cuban mahogany bar 680 feet long, over twice the length of a football field. *Picture that.*

Erickson's featured an all-female orchestra, can-can dancers, gaming tables, whores, and a religious convocation. Today you can still see the outlines of where the cribs used to be, each a tiny room meant to accommodate a prostitute and her john.

Three-hundred-pound Jumbo Reilly kept order at this Cathedral for the Working Man, a saloon, according to the *Oregonian*, to serve the loggers, the miners, the railroad men, and the sailors—men so virile and huge and muscled they were a titan breed set apart.                  –NANKER PHELGE

63

*Nothing I ever do that's worthwhile ever takes longer than ten minutes.*

—FRANK PETERS

The old men—cancer victims, booze hounds, surgeons, and an Indian chief among them—are hard at it under the bright lights of Portland State's gym. The ten-time national champion, the East Bank Saloon's American Athletic Association team, 182-3 in tournament play, is scrimmaging against itself. The ball *thunk, thunk, thunk*s down the court in the big hand of the "team owner," six-foot-five Pudgy Hunt, while on the sidelines, ex-Portland Mavericks baseball manager, ex-candidate for governor, and ex-con Frank "The Flake" Peters observes what a snap total world domination really can be. "First we destroyed everybody in the United States, then we destroyed Australia, South America, Russia, and Europe. Then we went back and did it again year after year after year after year and, believe or not, at least during the championship games, a lot of our players were sober."

The team is the illegitimate brainchild, so to speak, of three men: Ron Koski, a sixtysomething retired

## LOCAL HERO

# MISTER OREGON

### FRANK PETERS

heavy equipment operator who has the hard drive and bright eyes of a 20-year-old; Pudgy Hunt, the Marlboro Man-like owner of the East Bank Tavern; and Peters, who, with Mel Renfro, Terry Baker, Mel Counts, and Steve Pauley, represented the golden age of Oregon athletics in the early 1960s and who was so innovative as manager of the Portland Mavericks that he had to hire a bodyguard to protect him from his own players.

❧❧❧

Excellent sports violence from TV monitors—crashing race cars on one, brawling "tough guy" white-trash boxers on another—beam a moony light over a forest of liquor bottles, microbrew beer taps, and pretty young women by the bar.

Standing at the buffet in his white toque and chef's jacket—the very same outfit he wore when he used to stand outside waving a sign that read Free Advice With Lunch—is certified chef de cuisine Frank Peters, creator of the Grand Cafe's monthly "Cooking Nasty and Eating Ugly"

(as well as host of an "Every Saturday Nite Lesbian Dance Party"). Peters's repasts have included whole roasted beaver, kangaroo steaks, reindeer at Christmas, a "testicle festival," ostrich hors d'oeuvres, fillet of alligator, and spotted owl. That the beavers were actually voles and the spotted owls were–what the hell were they anyway?–takes little away from the da-DA verve of Portland's most notorious sportsman.

Frank Peters. Described in *The New Yorker* in 1976 as "a platonic ideal of a baseball player...tall and rangy . . . [with] a horsey, handsome face and light blue eyes under blond eyebrows... His grin is both loose and sly." Add that he has since become a "lethal weapon" in karate and the description still fits.

Onstage tonight, King Kong Karaoke is being warbled by a hatchet-faced cowboy who sings so well that he could be Vince Gill, if Vince Gill bought his ranch riding clothes at J.C. Penney.

In the kitchen, a small sea of fried bacon. ("Why all the bacon, Frank?" "Because I need it.") Downstairs, more Miss Mays in the office are doing the books, and in the cooler is tomorrow night's repast, a wild boar—with a bloody bullet hole through its skull so that it looks more murdered than dead.

☞☞☞

Frank Peters has played on ten national champion AAU senior men's basketball teams, served as captain and coach of three, and was team captain and coach of two World Athletic Association championship teams. *"Nobody* beats us," he reveals, "during the regular season."

Sports have provided his true north. Peters was born in Corvallis, where his father played on the Oregon State football team that went to the 1942 Rose Bowl against Duke. All-league at Anaheim High School, he went on to play on the most renowned Oregon State basketball team of all, alongside Mel Counts—who became the first seven-foot white guy in the NBA—and Steve Pauley.

He quit college his junior year to join the Baltimore Orioles— then bounced around professional baseball for nine years ("You don't quit baseball; baseball quits you") before taking charge of the Portland Mavericks baseball team in 1975 after the previous manager was 86'ed for decking an ump. "No rules, no signs" was Peters's motto. A disciplinarian– "dope smokers to the back of the bus"—Frank led the Mavericks to glory in the face of serious setbacks. To quote *Inside Sports* magazine:

"Peters, in an effort to shake the Mavs out of a horrendous slump,

> **Frank drove a red Cadillac convertible and rode a Harley sporting hand-stitched saddlebags whose pouches he'd tailored to the size of a block of giveaway government cheese.**

decided to pick his starting lineup out of a hat. When Reggie Thomas was not chosen, the hard-hitting outfielder responded by producing a .44 Magnum and chasing the manager to his office. Barely beating Thomas to the door, Peters scribbled a hastily revised lineup: not only was Thomas included—he was leading off."

Facing teams rostered with the young Ozzie Smith and Pedro Guerrero, Peters populated the Mavericks with ace players, including his 79-year-old former high school baseball coach, whom he put on third base. Once Frank rotated the nine players through nine innings so that each player played every position—the Mavericks won the game. His team consisted of everybody from Jim Bouton to Kurt Russell. Under Peters, the Mavericks won 92 games and lost 69 and set an attendance record for Portland baseball. A year after Peters left, the team folded.

He opened Peters Inn in downtown Portland in 1972, cheers before *Cheers* for newly drink-legal baby boomers, the first sports bar. Then there was Peters' Habit, Judy's Push Cart Hot Dogs, Peters Super

Bowl, Satan's Disco, a *Clockwork Orange*-inspired Karova Milk Bar, and a Peters Inn in Seattle. He eventually employed 3,200 people—the hot dog pushcarts alone raked in $1,000,000 a year.

☙☙☙

I met Frank when I was 25 and the too-skinny bouncer-bartender at the American Museum, a dance hall/fistfight factory owned by former boxer Ron McCarty. McCarty, with his squared-off face and squared-off black glasses, resembled Clark Kent and ran his place in essentially the same way America fought the Vietnam War.

The American Museum was located on the corner of Third and Burnside, which then served as the Iron Triangle of Portland's thriving porn district. Across the street, Frank's Satan's Disco; to the east, a bottomless-topless sanctuary featuring an "all-nude revue." After midnight the creatures from Satan's Disco, including Frank, and the sweeties from the all-nude revue would infiltrate our regular, more uptown, clientele.

McCarty treated them all with the same feisty respect General Creighton Abrams afforded the Viet Cong. But behind the bar it was Us against Them. Our motto was "The customer is always wrong."

So it was good to have Peters handy. Frank wouldn't intimidate the clientele, he'd hypnotize them. A cue-stick-waving muscle-bound Martian would be raving about the "fuckin' Whizworts and pack-aloomers!" and Frank would simply fix him with his steely blue eyes and console him with "Now, now, messlespleck rootgorb the milmack," and the guy would settle right down.

Frank rescued me from thugs and an overdose of mushrooms and once when I told him my favorite nonfiction book was Jim Bouton's *Ball Four* the next thing I knew I was standing out in front of Peters Inn with Bouton himself throwing his patented knuckleball into my cold bare hands. Frank's office was like Scrooge McDuck's. Cash was stacked everywhere. Frank drove a red Cadillac convertible and rode a Harley sporting hand-stitched saddlebags whose pouches he'd tailored to the size of a block of giveaway government cheese.

His love life was radical. Women tended to regard Frank variously as a) an icky spider, b) a misunderstood guy caught between conflicting stereotypes, or c) an irresistible love god. While he was living at Portland Center in Fred Meyer's old apartment, Frank's gorgeous girlfriend Kate Fate—lead singer of Kate Fate and the Fingers of Doom (recording artists for Tombstone Records, "Records too tough to die")—put five bullets aimed "penis-high" through his front door after Frank, on the other side of the door, had pleaded, "Let's talk about it first," to her ultimatum, "Marry me or die."

She missed, and Frank was philosophical. "In the old days gunshots were just loud noises; now everybody takes them seriously."

Frank decided to run for governor in 1978. As an "independent." Endorsed by Tom McCall and presidential candidate John Anderson, he used baseball as grist for his campaign. (On Oregon's unemployed he said, "We'll use what we've got—some can hit and some can steal.") And he toured Oregon in a rented silver Mercedes carrying a Bible-like "wish book," in which the electorate could record their notions about the needs of the state. Supporting everything from solar heat to the Oregon Shakespeare Festival, Frank nevertheless faced strong opposition from people who thought he was crazy.

"I have to use reverse psychology to win," Frank said to me. "You'll go on the road with me. To write my speeches and guard my back. We'll hit the meanest redneck bars in the state and tell the people exactly what they don't want to hear. In farm country we'll be against corn subsidies. In mill towns we'll say hip-hip-hooray for the spotted owl. If we do our job right we'll have to fight our way out of every place we open our mouths. All you'll have to do is hold everybody off until I can get to a phone and call the cops."

He showed me a "strategic list" of "the top bail bondsmen" in the state. "Bondsmen we can count on." As a special incentive Frank had arranged with the Oregon Bartenders Association to provide us an oasis of poopsies every 200 miles so that however battered, we would find "X-rated first aid" when we got out of jail every night.

"But Frank," I said, "I just got married."

"That's okay," he replied. "Then you can watch."

*It's better to be a good player on a great team than a great player on a good team.*
—FRANK PETERS

Stocky, curly blond-haired Ron Koski, who has been playing AAU since 1949, his right arm a cancer-ravaged and nearly rigid L, trots down-court. Only five-foot-eight, Koski played point guard 42 years ago for Portland State University. Left-handed and intense, he's all energy. During the master's games in Buenos Aires, Koski told his wife he was going out to get a dozen eggs and didn't return for two weeks.

The East Bank fast break is a fast

stalk; their attack is siegelike, more accurate than quick. They shoot from the outside, though it is a blast to see Pudgy Hunt suddenly turn into a 20-year-old as he explodes to the basket, then lays the ball into the hoop as delicately as if it were made out of glass. East Bank teams include 70-year-old Chinook Indian "Chief" Cliff Snider, who has the football stadium at Clackamas High School named after him and was Oregon Golf Coach of the Year in 1977; and another guy, addled by Parkinson's disease, who they fish out of a nursing home every time there is a critical game.

"We face teams of former college stars who train 300 days a year," Peters says. "When we hit the court we look, basically, dead. Then we go out and stomp them."

But how?

*Always pick your crime. Never let your crime pick you.*

—JAILHOUSE SAYING

Frank has been a good friend to me and I was sad when he didn't win the governorship—he got busted. He'd set up "indoor pot ranches" all over town. Living the good life, Frank rode around town on his racing bicycle with a deck of $100 bills tucked in a sock, not a care in the world.

Until he got one girlfriend too many. "The most gorgeous girl in the world, but one day she said, 'Frank, I have terrible news, I'm in love with another woman.' I meet the other girl. She was even *more* beautiful, so I said, 'Girls, we have the makings of a tragedy, but let's go back to my place and—'" Unfortunately, the love triangle got too hot even for Frank, "One got *really* pissed and went to the police. It turned out the one my girl was in love with was only 17."

Peters got busted for possession of 800 marijuana plants worth a reported $1 million. Forty-nine counts of drugs and girls. His bail was set at $4 million. After his "pre-sentence investigation" it was recommended that Peters serve 120 years. (In a letter to the judge, Frank's teammate Ron Koski pleaded that the team needed Peters, that 120 years sounded excessive, so why not four months instead?)

Frank pleaded guilty, got ten years, and doubtless became the first convict in Oregon history to *request* hard time in maximum security. "If you're gonna do time," he said, "you might as well do it right."

*I have seen the light and, believe me, it was very, very bright.*

—FRANK PETERS

So what is the secret? "We follow the big man," Peters explains. Not to put too fine a point on it, but one excellent East Bank management decision was to recruit six-foot-eleven Leroy Ellis, who had played on four NBA teams, including the Lakers 1972 championship team. Never mind that he was in less than mint condition. In 1993 Ellis, on the eve of a hip replacement, with Frank Peters playing point guard, led his 50-and-over team to its eighth consecutive AAU men's master's championship.

Tonight Peters is taking a break during a scrimmage at Portland State. After Frank went to jail, I worried. Maximum security? But he wrote to say that being in with the lifers meant being able to play on the best prison sports teams, and soon he had "a cell with more room and a better view than three of my four last apartments and that was in a better neighborhood than my last two." I called him at the prison and had to go through Frank's *secretary*, some effete biker Bluto who rasped, "Mr. Peters's office. No, Frank is coaching basketball until 12, then

lunching with the warden. Can I tell him whose company you are with?"

Playing the silver market from stir, Frank was able to get his sentence bumped down to 30 months. He said when he got out he'd have money to pay cash for a "real girlfriend" or a brand-new Mercedes, which would net him several "unreal girlfriends."

But that was then, this is now. I ask Frank to explain the success of his team. Leroy Ellis does not a dynasty make. Other NBA players are on senior teams, Artis Gilmore among them, and what Peters describes is less a team than an organism. "Some of us have played together for almost 40 years. We go all the way back to the Claudia's Tavern team of the 1960s. Each of us knows where the other one is, all the time. We beat teams far younger using mind over matter. They're quicker, but waste movement, circle a lot, and telegraph their punches. Also, we practice ten times as much as we drink. We never stop practicing."

Frank is no longer the dictator of anarchy that he used to be (his own employees once banned him from Peters Inn), but in basketball, global hegemony-wise, he's more focused. "I am 53 years old. I want another world championship. In fact, I want about another five."

—M.C.

## BEST THEFT OF AN INVALUABLE OREGON RESOURCE

# TIMBER GRAB

### OR

## HOW THE OREGON PUBLIC SCHOOL SYSTEM WAS BILKED OF ITS PRICELESS TAX BASE BY CARPETBAGGING LUMBER BARONS

### BY WILLIAM BOLY

If there was one thing that early settlers of Oregon minded about their new territory besides the eternal rain, it was the blasted trees that overran the countryside. Homesteaders wanted open land to raise their crops on, but four-fifths of western Oregon was covered by forest. But you couldn't eat wood, and without a railroad, you couldn't ship the timber anywhere.

As late as 1890, the vast tracts of Douglas fir and ponderosa pine that blanketed the state were mostly unclaimed. Not until 50 years after settlers began arriving in the Willamette, Rogue, and Umpqua Valleys did anyone began to act as though the dense stands of Oregon timber might actually be worth something.

In theory the forests were there for the people. Federal laws providing for the passage of public lands into private hands were designed to guarantee that each settler got a piece of the action.

But that's not how it worked out. By 1914 there was more privately owned timber in Oregon than in any other state in the nation, 70 percent controlled by 68 owners. Most owners were not even residents of the state. The money to gobble up all that land, even at the absurdly low $2.50 an acre the government charged settlers, came from back East, largely through lumber magnates who had reaped massive profits from the Shermanesque leveling of the white pine stands in the Great Lake states and the Upper Mississippi Valley.

Onward to unmowed pastures.

As usual, Frederick Weyerhaeuser got there first. In 1891 he rode through the Pacific Northwest with his friend Jim Hill, head of the Northern Pacific Railroad Company. Weyerhaeuser and Hill were neighbors back on Summit Avenue in St. Paul. What Weyer-haeuser saw in the region stupefied him. Forests as far as the eye could see that *commonly* carried upward of 100,000 board feet per acre, three times what he was used to calling a good stand in the Midwest.

Hill had the keys to this kingdom; his railroad was land rich, thanks to the indemnity furnished by Congress for the construction of the transcontinental line. For each mile of railroad constructed, the Northern Pacific received 25,000 acres of land.

Weyerhaeuser bought 900,000 acres from Hill outright at $6 an acre, and the rush was on. Hill had lots more where that first sale came from.

"I am one of the few men ever to make a million dollars honestly," said Weyerhaeuser with becoming modesty. Actually, he was one of the few men to make a *billion* dollars, period. With that kind of wealth, honesty could look after itself.

Weyerhaeuser owned about 5 percent of the standing timber in Oregon by the time he died—not bad, but small potatoes compared to his holdings in Idaho and Washington. Industrious (he worked a 7 a.m. to 10 p.m. day) and painfully shy (his thick German accent made him self-conscious on public occasions, which he avoided), Weyerhaeuser progressed from a failed dirt farmer to billionaire, illustrating a phenomenon of his time: the concentration of Northwest timberlands into the hands of a few.

Which was not the way the laws for dispensing this great bonanza read. According to the Timber and Stone Act of 1888, the General Land Office would sell forest land to the settler in quarter-sections (160 acres to the household, no more) at $2.50 per acre. In Oregon about a third of all privately held timberland, 3,812,000 acres, was transferred into private hands under this act. Nevertheless, nearly all the land ended up in the timber speculators' pockets.

How? For one thing, most settlers were dirt poor and would never have had the $400 to buy a claim in their own right. Itinerants were happy to step over to the land office and sign away their rights for a few dollars, or even the price of a beer.

Timber barons and their agents hired "dummy" entrymen to file on land that the baron's "cruiser" had already picked out. The "dummy" would claim the 160 acres, and pay for it with the timber baron's money.

When timberland was opened for the purchase in the Deschutes country near Bend, trainloads of claimants, organized by "Eastern syndicaters," came from Minnesota, Wisconsin, and Michigan to get their share. An unlikely group: 150 claimants were women schoolteachers on summer vacation—all expenses paid.

❖

S. A. D. Puter, the self-styled "King of the Oregon Land Fraud Ring," wrote his memoirs with the leisure afforded by a 17-month stay in the Multnomah County Jail and described a group of "dummies" he led out to "shear the pristine grandeur of these forests" near Prineville: "The concourse of vehicles resembled a Sunday turnout in Golden Gate Park, only, of course, the equipages were not quite so swell."

But fraud wasn't the only way to rip off the timberlands. There were safer, legal ways—railroad land grants, for instance. In Oregon, the greatest beneficiary was the Oregon and California Line, eventually acquired by Southern Pacific. This line ran from Portland to Sacramento, cutting through the densest stand of timber in the

nation along its route. Every other 640-acre section for 20 miles on either side of the tracks became Southern Pacific's property, making it the largest private timber holder in the United States, and Southern Pacific got 70.2 billion board feet of timber. Free.

Although Northern Pacific had only about 30 miles of track in Oregon, it gained over 320,000 acres of Oregon timber through a legal maneuver subsequently labeled "the greatest land steal in history". When Mount Rainier National Park was created in 1899, Northern Pacific won the right to exchange its land within the reserve for land in any state through which its tracks ran. NP had a million acres of land inside the reserve, most of it unproductive—the rocky slopes of the mountain, glaciers or burned-over or already logged-off sections. The few miles of track in Oregon opened up the entire state of Oregon to NP's timber cruisers. In S. A. D. Puter's words, "Mount Rainier National park was created for the special benefit of the Northern Pacific Railroad, so that the Hill corporation could exchange its worthless holdings for the cream of creation."

Another first-class swindle was the building of the military wagon roads. This was almost exclusively an Oregon phenomenon—about three million acres were parceled out as compensation for the construction of five roads in Oregon. Congress allocated 500,000 acres in this way to the rest of the United States.

Each mile of wagon road built received three square miles of Oregon turf in compensation. Unlike those for a railroad, however, the standards for road completion weren't absolute. For instance, the Willamette Valley and Cascade Wagon Road was commissioned to run east from Albany via the Santiam Pass to the eastern border of Oregon. Construction past the Deschutes was a farce. A road crew on horseback with a light wagon "built" 10 to 15 miles a day. Government estimates placed the cost of construction at $10,000. The company claimed it spent $45,000, but this figure may include the cost of bribing the governor's special agent to declare the road complete.

In return, the road builders received 861,000 acres of land. By 1910, 178,000 timber acres of this land grant were in the hands of the Oregon and Washington Civilization Company, a Northern Pacific subsidiary.

The Dallas Military Wagon Road took this art form to its logical extreme—357 miles were constructed in three months at a cost of $6,000. The road, running east from The Dalles to the border, exhibited a certain shrewd, veering tendency. The builders steered it up every valley on the way to the border, including the John Day, Willow Creek, Burnt River, and Malheur River Valleys, in order to maximize the value of the acreage gained. The land thus earned—576,000 acres—cost the Eastern Oregon Land Co. less than a penny an acre.

Then there was the Oregon Central Military Wagon Road. It ran from Eugene eastward via the middle fork of the Willamette across Salt Creek Pass, through the Klamath Indian Reservation. The Indians pointed out that Congress really didn't have the right to give away a piece of land twice, but Congress thought otherwise. The timbered section of this property ultimately descended to the Booth-Kelly Lumber Company. The Indian land was blocked off in alternating sections, but Booth-Kelly wanted even more, and proposed to trade its scattered holdings—110,000 acres of pumice and jack-pine thickets—for 85,000 acres of excellent Indian-owned ponderosa pine on Yamsey Mountain. The superintendent of the Klamath Indian Reservation, one H. G. Wilson, readily agreed, later arguing that it was a good bargain for the Indians because they got more land!

The crowning irony of the timber ownership story is that, despite an original federal grant of 4.32 million acres to support public education in Oregon, today the state owns hardly any timber. The 1.6 million acres remaining lies mainly in Malheur and Harney Counties, is semi-arid or arid, and produces only a few thousand dollars in income a year.

The state legislature sold the "school land" as fast as humanly possible. Laws were framed to make sale easy. Timberland sold at $1.25 an acre. Despite the familiar protection of the "actual settler" on the books, only those knowledgeable in the intricacies of the school land system could "buy in." A state land agent, Timothy Davenport, issued a report in 1896 concluding that "our laws. . . might be nominated very fitly 'land monopoly made easy.'"

Washington state handled its school lands with more foresight, retaining 78 percent of its original grant lands and continuing to derive a sizeable income from timber for school support.

In contrast, a study by William Robbins of Oregon State University concludes, "The depleted funds from school lands in Oregon undoubtedly contributed to higher taxes to support public education and may have had a retarding effect on the state's system of public education."

Oregon continues to pay the penalty. Anyone familiar with the legislature's repeatedly frustrated attempts at taxing private timberlands knows that the political clout of the big owners remains absolute.

PICKING   BERRIES

Heat blurs the morning,
mixes with dust the winos lift
as they shuffle in the rows.
The dust settles, indifferent as weather,
on leaves and berries, lips and tongues.
It finds the hole the throat is
and sticks there,
a bad memory that keeps you picking
until the berries fill the boxes
and boxes fill the flats.

Fat ladies weigh the flats,
pass the wine you drink
in the stringy shade. "Hey, swabby."
"Look out, buddy." Your calls float the air
hot off Damascus Hill. The warm wine
slides over bad hands at poker,
your mother's letter about the lump, the log
caught in Celilo Falls where fish pool
like girls whose lips pucker in every berry.

The sweet wine sticks in your throat.
You pick berries for another bottle
to wash the first one down.

—JUDITH ROOT

# URBAN DUCK DEATH

## BY DAVID KELLY

Our leader lived to kill ducks. Sadly, he ate, drank, and was merry until a stroke blew out half his nervous system. But in duck-murder-friendly Portland, David Kelly continues to hunt. This is his story. Read it now.

The Second Amendment isn't about duck hunting, according to the NRA, so maybe Oregon needs one that is. "Mallard breasts sautéed medium rare in onion butter, the pan then deglazed with a decent Burgundy and a dollop of currant jelly, and the sliced breasts returned just briefly to the sauce being necessary to the maintenance of any free state we'd care to live in, the right to murder ducks within a 25-minute drive of city hall shall not be infringed."

Having it down in black and white would make us feel better. It's hard for Oregon's urban duck hunters not to be paranoid here at the wrong end of the 20th century. As we slip into cold camo at 3 a.m. and tow our decoy carts across the sleeping city in a pleasant November drizzle, we are aware of cultural currents running against us. They have started to let unarmed birders near Sauvie Island Wildlife Refuge during the season. There have been reported sightings of dogs other than labs. The parking lot in front of Sam's Cracker Barrel, at the far end of the bridge to the island, has on recent occasion been

full of bicyclists in tights, even at dawn.

Worse, as this is written, the mayor of Portland—brilliant, charming, effective though she may be—is a nonhunter. Our previous mayor, Bud Clark, was partner in a duck hunting equipment firm, and we always assumed that some such credential was a constitutional requirement.

Yet few of us speak aloud of these things, lest we find ourselves slam-dunked for ingratitude. About 50 yards outside the city limits, which run down the middle of the Willamette River off Kelly Point, lies Sauvie Island, an eight-mile-long paradise as flat as Holland, home of Halloween hayrides, clothing-optional beaches, and 28 marshy lakes hosting up to 200,000 ducks, geese, cranes, and trumpeter swans.

To see these vast flocks darken the sky of an autumn dusk is to be transported back to Teddy Roosevelt's America. Right here. Right now.

Crouched behind the cornstalk thatch of a Sauvie Island duck blind, a thin gray wash of wind-whipped rain blurring the edge of consciousness, I find it easy to paint myself into a private Winslow Homer watercolor. My old slouch hat and tattered, faded coat. My faithful wet Lab at my elbow. The graceful double gun, which I ease up and forward, thumbing off the safety as a fat pair of greenhead Mallard drakes, feet hanging and wings cupped, seem to hover in front of me for one fatal mo—

*Blaaaaaaaaaaaaaaaaaaaaat!*

They vanish to hoots of snickering laughter from the next blind. A

20-foot-high letter T glides along the top of the Columbia River dike across Hunt Lake—the logo on the stack of the *Toyota Maru*, which has just alerted North Portland's long-shoremen to the arrival of another 400 Celicas for Hair Club members all over the West.

Portland hunting may not be rural but it's convenient. If my old Volvo won't start, I can get to my blind for a $20 cab fare. If Tri-Met would add five miles to the #17 bus line, which stops at Sam's, I could do it for 95 cents. In all the world only Venice, Italy, can match Portland for easy access to duck shooting; but the Venetian shoots are all private and you'll fork out a hundred bucks to some moldy aristocrat for a few damp hours in a barrel pretending to be Hemingway.

There are aristocratic venues here, too: clubs whose origins are lost in the mists of the 1880s. Given the right connections to the Beebes or the Corbets, the patience to wait for an existing member to drop dead, and hardly more than the price of an XJ12, you can access a rustic club-house, a flunky who hands you your birds plucked and freezer-ready at the end of the day, and shooting no worse than I am enjoying over on Racetrack Lake for $5.

But Sauvie is first and foremost a public hunter's domain, a muddy meritocracy. While the boys in the

band flip through their fakebooks to "Fanfare for the Common Man," let's pause long enough for me to admit that I myself take privilege where I can find it.

Back in the early Clinton epoch, when you had to be a differently-abled leftist dwarf to be Secretary of Anything, the Sauvie Island Refuge staff, who depend partly on federal funds, started to feel the PC pinch.

These good old boys are umbili-cally connected to their four-wheel drive King Cabs, and they don't get off the island much. They added a wheelchair-accessible stinking Porta-Potty to the refuge's considerable array of stinking Porta-Potties. They constructed some wheelchair-accessi-ble duck blinds as specified by the Americans with Disabilities Act, but left kinda vague how those wheel-chairs were to cross the hundreds of acres of rutted muck surrounding the blinds. They had few takers.

I am paralyzed on my left side and a founder-member of AHA, the Armed Hemiplegics of America (our motto: "Oops, did I do that?"). I can walk with a cane for short dis-tances. Sauvie Island staffers are glad to see me, and I them. I am a differ-ently-abled they can help and feel PC about without getting out of their trucks.

Nowadays I, my big bags of decoys, my gun, shells, lunch, dog, and hunting partner are all driven to within a few yards of whatever blind I have drawn, and picked up again at the end of the day.

Since I'm comfortably seated before most other hunters, I get a great view of their bowed figures humping gigantic bags of decoys along the crests of the dikes, or straining to haul carts laden with even more decoys through the dawn-lit muck. To think that if I hadn't eaten all those bacon double-cheeseburgers I might be one of them still.

All this heavy equipment reflects the fact that Sauvie is not only the best public water-fowling area in urban America but possibly the most competitive. You'll want to put out at least four dozen decoys, and spreads of over a hundred aren't rare. Even so, if you can't call, you'll watch other people shoot.

The guy in the next blind could be Joe Doaks or just as easily John Fazio, Voice Calling Champion. John uses no instrument but his own larynx to convince every boy mallard within a mile and a half that a feathered Julia Roberts wants to give him a blow job.

The shooting isn't quite up to the calling. There are many good shots,

*Sauvie is not only the best public water-fowling area in urban America, but possibly the most competitive.*

hunters who have long since convinced their spouses that the price of duck on the table includes an expensive trap gun and long, grueling hours at the gun club. But they are handicapped by having to share pond space with too many impatient slobs who "sky-bust" at birds flying so high they'd be hard to reach with a rifle.

The same scum often "short-stop" by tearing loose at birds you called from afar and which, after many wary circles, are getting ready to hang their feet over your decoys. Talks with state officials are ongoing as to whether to add sky-busters and short-stoppers to the limit at the rate of one a day and one in possession.

The state would probably make us use nontoxic shot to bag these people, to keep plumbism from building up in the red foxes and bald eagles who do most of the carrion eating on Sauvie. Though I'm with those who think steel shot means more wounding and fewer clean kills, I'm willing to be politically correct if the end result is local eagles and foxes tearing the guts out of down-but-not-dead short-stoppers.

As basically a one-armed man, I've

long since ceased to take shots beyond 30 yards. I do my water-fowling with an open-choked upland gun, a model 23 Winchester Golden Quail with an ounce and an eighth of 4s in the first barrel and 2s in the second. It is a much better gun than I am a gunner, assembled with the kind of tolerances you get when old guys in aprons and eye-shades put in dozens of hours of handwork with little files. It's engraved with scenes of birds and dogs, and has a superbly figured walnut stock and a gold inlaid quail's head. I bought it before I had teenagers.

Whenever I miss an easy incomer with it, which is often, I'm remind-ed that Rudy Etchen, the greatest American shotgunner since Annie Oakley, shot the same hardware-store Remington pump gun from his teens until he retired, a few years ago, well into his 80s. Asked the secret of breaking all those thou-sand straights, "It's not a matter of hitting" he told me. "It's a matter of refusing to miss." A practical, bare-bones guy who would have fit right in here at everyman's duck club.

❧ ❧ ❧

At Sauvie, hunting is allowed only every other day in most of the area. The price of admission is, fundamentally, waiting in line at a checkpoint in your car with a $5

bill. People come as early as possi-ble, often the previous day. There's a short "reservation" line of those who have won a sort of electronic lottery held each month during the season, guaranteeing them access to whichever of the 19 hunting "units" they have chosen. There is a longer "nonreservation" line of peo-ple waiting to take what's left.

Usually that's plenty, but in case you get up to the window and find nothing you want, there's a third option, which is to sign up on a waiting list for blinds where the lucky hunters limit out early and go home. You may get only half the day, but in a "hot" blind.

The lines, often consisting of people who have known each other for years, have in the past been a social scene with warming fires, bourbon toddies, romping dogs, excited kids on their first hunt, goose music overhead, and stinking Porta-Potties provided by the state.

Some people finish a day's hunt and get right back in the nonreser-vation line, living in their pickup campers for days or weeks. Last year one couple had a tricycle along for their toddler, and spent their vaca-tion in line, taking turns to hunt or babysit. She was the better shot, they said, he the better caller.

A seldom-enforced law says you can have only ten birds in posses-sion. The couple admitted they had

60 birds jammed in their freezer back home, and a couple of mule deer, but as ecological penance they were giving up their elk season, a potential source of four or five hundred pounds of lean red meat.

In recent years, and to the despair of the local farmers, Sauvie Island has nearly sunk under a surfeit of grain-gobbling Taverner's geese, a medium-sized Canada goose subspecies. The trouble is that a nearly identical Canada goose called the dusky, which winters almost nowhere else, is listed as threatened. The good old refuge boys check your bag carefully at each day's end. Shoot a dusky by mistake, which is easy, and your goose season in western Oregon is over. When a hundred or so hunters have committed this inevitable error, the season is over for everybody.

The state requires all potential goose hunters to attend a special class, at which a stuffed and mounted example of each bird is displayed. Side by side, under bright fluorescent light, the dusky seems, well, duskier. But 40 yards out, at 30 miles per hour in the half-light of dawn, it is less obvious.

My own rule of thumb: if a goose flies right into your blind and begs for euthanasia, it's an endangered dusky. If it sees the corner of your mouth twitch from half a mile away and turns south for Eugene, it's an abundant Taverner. Upriver on the Umatilla Refuge no such strictures apply, so that's where most of the geese we use at home to make our renowned Cassoulet St. Pierre come from. But unsophisticated country birds are beyond the scope of this page.

# ALICE IN BIKERLAND

### BY SUSAN STANLEY

Saturday, 1:40 p.m. Here's Crazy Steve, talking, talking. Talking about his teenage kids, so smart they tease him they gotta be adopted. Talking about his 13 months in Vietnam, talking about the Viet Cong tunnels.

At first, I can't understand why they call him Crazy Steve, except any true-blue biker needs a biker moniker. The tattoo—U.S.M.C.—should've been a clue. Turns out they call him Crazy because that's what Vietnam did to him. Those tunnels, he tells me, they went under whole villages, with exits and entrances all over the place. Some were little-bitty tunnels you couldn't even stand up in. Some were big, so big they could hold a whole battalion, or a hospital.

Sitting here in the high desert of central Oregon, the late May wind swirling the dust around like the devil, we're surrounded by bikers— men, women, and kids. Food concessions, a dozen or so, provide succor from heat and dust. A hand-lettered sign offers Buffalo Burgers $3.95 (¼ lb. 100% buffalo meat), Paul Bunyan Burgers $5.95 (cheese & onions).

Presiding damply in the small open trailer are two young women, Kelly and Kelley. One-E Kelly flips the monster burgers on the grill, face glowing, dark ponytail hanging in dank strands. Fixed atop her generous right breast in its snug black spandex exercise bra-top is a pin decorated with the image of a penis head sporting a bow tie and surrounded by the international circle-with-slash forbidden sign. A hidden battery makes the pin blink merrily.

"It means No Dickheads," One-E Kelly tells us with a cheery shrug.

We're here for the annual ABATE Fossil Run, a gathering of some 1,500 bikers and their families. ABATE stands for different things in different states. In Oregon, it stands for A Brotherhood Against Totalitarian Enactments. Totalitarian Enactments = helmet laws.

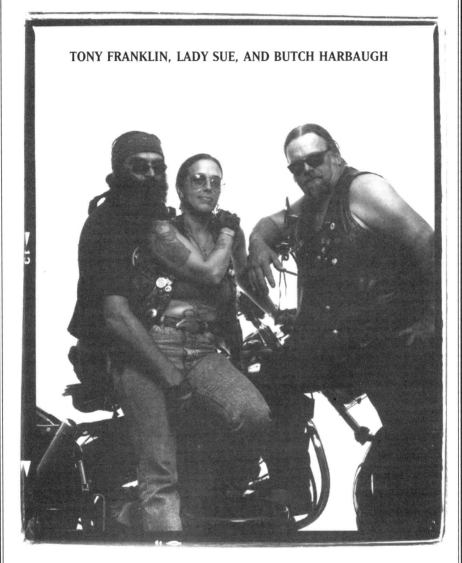

**TONY FRANKLIN, LADY SUE, AND BUTCH HARBAUGH**

At first glance, the crowd of bikers seems, oddly, to have much in common with, say, the Amish—dour folk who dress alike and fashion their hair in ways like their brethren. There's much leather, black and fashioned into vests and pants.

Patches identify clubs—what civilians usually label gangs. The Gypsy Jokers, for example, and Brother Speed. There are a number of types of clubs—the Cruizers for Christ, for instance, and a 12-step biker club called The Solution.

These are not the middle-class wannabes, or the Rich Urban Bikers sneered at as "Rubbies." We're talking Harley-Davidson motorcycles here, man, not Jap shit—not "rice rockets" like Yamahas, or fat-old-fart bikes like Gold Wings, the biker equivalent of, God and testosterone forbid, an RV.

Most of the women have long hair and, regardless of figure, display lots of flesh: leg, cleavage, midriff. Here amid the heat and the dust and the roar of starting-up Harleys—the *potato-potato-potato* sound so beloved and distinctive that Harley-Davidson is trying to protect it as a company trademark—wiry men with gaunt, careworn faces lean forward in earnest discourse with comrades whose enormous bellies sway over tops of Levis. Most sport beards. They wear bandannas and baseball caps, bills forward. Even on balding pates, the hair is long, either plaited or bunched back into a ponytail.

Tattoos—dragons, griffins, improbably endowed human females —wind around muscular biceps, spread across bare backs. Dainty rosebuds and butterflies adorn breasts and ankles. Patches adorn vests: *Helmet Laws Suck. Loud Bikes Save Lives. Jane Fonda: Commie Bitch.*

Fifty feet away from the food area, in a scene that could be from a century ago, ten children of varying ages splash and giggle on the shallow shores of the ice-cold John Day, while a dreamy-eyed mother, cold drink in hand, keeps vigil on the riverbank. A clot of biker men gath-

er in the shade of a tree, drinking beer and laughing.

Someone's boom box plays Steppenwolf's "Born to Be Wild."

❉

My husband is himself a biker, and a lawyer whose personal injury practice includes a sizable percentage of bikers. And while I don't share his enthusiasm for riding motorcycles, I'll take a *football field* full of bikers over a cocktail party full of lawyers any day.

Biking, it's the ultimate Real Guy Thing. To paraphrase Tom Hanks in that baseball movie, *There is no crying in biking.* Women have their own clubs: Women in the Wind, Leather and Lace, and others. But if you're going to tag along, if you want to climb into the men's tree house, expect to follow the rules: Don't horn into conversations between the men. Don't try to ride ahead of the man. Show some tit from time to time.

Not that bikers don't like their women ballsy. At a conference in Tulsa a couple years back, this tall, craggy-faced biker was ragging me about my refusal to ride. I know, and knew then, that he was just trying to impress the other bikers. Putz.

"Aw honey, you're just scared. Once you get over that, you'll . . ."

"Fuck off," I said pleasantly. "Just fuck off, OK?"

The other men laughed, warmly.
"You tell him, baby!"
"Don't you take no shit off him!"
"Stop buggin' the lady, man!"
*My,* I thought to myself, *I really like these guys.*

❋

Saturday, 7:30 p.m. Driving through the gloaming, through the gathering twilight, seeing the flashing lights of an Oregon State Police car ahead, we stop and an officer tells us that a motorcycle with two riders has collided with a deer. Both the young man and young woman are alive.

"Fortunately, one is alive because she was wearing this," says the officer, holding out a beanie-type helmet, its side viciously scraped by the road, its thin layer having kept her scalp, her brains, intact.

The pair lie together at the side of the road, the man comforting the badly hurt woman.

"I'm cold," cries out the injured woman, weeping. "Am I covered? I'm cold. I can't feel my legs. I'm thirsty. I'm cold." The man moves his body closer to hers. I return to our car and get out a bottle of Evian water, giving it to them.

**She is exquisitely pretty, the very image of a Renaissance princess, her long golden curls making a striking contrast with her short, tight slip dress imprinted with the images of human skulls.**

Out of the dark edges emerges another young woman. Can we give her a ride to the campground?

She is exquisitely pretty, the very image of a Renaissance princess, her long golden curls making a striking contrast with her short, tight slip dress imprinted with the images of human skulls. Sitting in the back seat of our car as we drive back to the campground, Our Little Princess gives us her tale of woe.

*I was driving with Derek and them to go to the campout and the cops stopped us for not wearing seat belts and when they called in on us the cops was told about a Failure to Appear on my record and handcuffed me and then Derek and them went on without me and the cops were so surprised that I could slip out of my handcuffs so easy see I got really skinny wrists. . . .*

She drapes delicate hands, dainty wrists, over the front seat, demonstrating.

*The Failure to Appear that was because my husband died in that motorcycle accident and so I was living on the streets I didn't have no place to go and it was winter and I was cold so I went into Mervyn's to steal a coat and they were not sympathetic but what was I supposed to do and when I told them cops a little while ago and I slipped out of them cuffs so easy they just let me go and do you have any cigarettes 'cause I'm rilly-rilly-rilly nervous do you have anything to eat?*

She cries then, great racking sobs with big fat tears to break a mother's heart. We give her a can of Diet Coke and a package of two Grandma's Cookies, the molasses ones with the white sugar frosting.

As we get closer to the campground, I'm feeling more and more happy that we stowed our bags with the wallets in the trunk. Stifling a dainty belch, she continues.

*Life just isn't fair you know nobody ever done nothing nice for me and boy-o-boy you guys' karma must be rilly-rilly-rilly good and you know Derek and them have my purse with them and in my purse is lots of money just lots of money and does it cost anything to get into the campground 'cause I know when I find Derek and them they'll be real happy to see me and give me back my purse with all the money but what'll I do if they won't let me in without any money?*

Then she cries some more.

Needless to say, the tattooed gents at the campout entrance are not about to let Our Little Princess in without the $20 admission. Nor are they moved by her tears.

Give them the twenty bucks, I tell my husband. He makes the most minute of shrugs and pays for admission.

*Nobody and I mean nobody has ever done anything for me in my whole life you guys' karma must be rilly-rilly-rilly good.*

She takes a breath, deep and shuddery.

*I'm gonna find Derek and them and get a twenty out of my purse and give it right back but just in case what's your name 'cause I'm gonna bring it to you don't worry I'd never try to Jew nobody not ever.*

Telling her mildly that he is Jewish, my husband hands her his business card.

Just then, she tells us to stop, scrambling out the car door shouting, *Derek! Derek! Derek!* at a man who clearly doesn't know her from Lady Diana, Princess of Wales.

✱

Saturday, 9:10 p.m. There is a huge bonfire, with people dancing around it to the cat-wail strains of "Honky-Tonk Woman" emanating from a boom box. The center of attention is Our Little Princess, the skulls on her short knit dress stretching bizarrely as she writhes to the music. Spotting us, she rushes to our side.

*Ohmigod I'm so glad to see you Derek and them they figure I'm a snitch on account of the cops let me go and they won't give me my purse with all my money but don't worry 'cause I'm gonna get that twenty back to you and here I am I don't even know where I'm gonna sleep tonight do you guys have an extra tent or something?*

In a word, no. We leave her whirling around to the music, the mass of golden curls painted red by bonfire flames.

❂

Saturday, 10:15 p.m. The Psychedelic Relics, tonight's headliners, play on a portable stage, standing out in sharp relief against a tie-dyed curtain backdrop.

With his shiny dark brown hair, beard, and beatific countenance, keyboardist Dave looks like Jesus, though in my Sunday school picture book, the S of G was not wearing a Harley-Davidson T-shirt and Levis. The lead singer has *Frisco Choppers San Francisco* printed in the shape of a swastika on the front of his black T-shirt.

Inside the drummer's big drum, a pillow in a tie-dyed case pulsates weirdly, like some hapless laboratory animal kept alive on life support.

In front of the stage a mustached man in his 30s, his glossy brown hair beautifully French-braided, dances, more or less, to "Wild Thing" while vainly trying to balance a can of Budweiser on his head.

He looks like Kevin Kline, mustache and all.

I am, how they say, in love.

He faces a woman who is attract-

**Just then, she tells us to stop, scrambling out the car door shouting, Derek! Derek! Derek! at a man who clearly doesn't know her from Lady Diana, Princess of Wales.**

ing quite a bit of attention. Blond curls (a wig? I wonder bitch-ily) cascade incongruously around her shoulders and worn, late-thirtyish face. Her fringed jacket of fawn-hued suede flops loosely over an abbreviated black leather bra.

Next to her, a skinny barefoot brunette in cutoffs and a black tank top dances alone. Eyes closed and hips awaggle, she rubs her breasts, her hands moving like crazed hamsters under the shirt.

The amplified musical din is like thunder, like jets flying directly overhead.

❂

Sunday, 12:20 a.m. A passed-around Harley cap has harvested a good $150 to reward the winner of the Fossil Run's Annual Titty Contest. At first, "Bear," a huge and benign man missing several important teeth, had trouble rounding up volunteers, but as the prize money increased. . .

The introductory onstage parade begins to amplified boom-box strains of "Born to Be Wild."

Contestant #1 is my favorite —a mid-twentyish blonde with a very pretty face, wearing jeans and a halter top.

Contestant #2 was the first, eager volunteer, long before any prize money was collected. Even fully clad, her huge, pendulous breasts hang wearily. She wears a baseball cap, bill forward, her dark braids pulled through the back strap.

Contestant #3 wears a bikini bra top, one cup white stars on a blue ground, the other red and white stripes. Above her Levis, a small gold hoop twinkles from her pierced navel.

Contestant #4 seems oddly prim, with long straight brown hair and glasses, and looks barely 18. She doesn't smile, not once, and doffs her top to reveal a small rose tattoo on her left breast, a large birthmark on her stomach, and much bright red sunburnt skin.

#5, an exotic, dark-eyed creature, is really good, with much well-practiced butt-wiggling.

#6, with her IT'S NOT PMS, I'M JUST A BITCH T-shirt, has a rose tattoo on her front, two more on her back, and looks somewhere between 30 and 40.

#7 has nipple rings, a big hit with

**Some bikers look like they haven't had a lucky day in their lives. They tend to have jobs, not careers. But bikers are always doing stuff like raising funds for crippled kids, or organizing food drives for homeless shelters.**

the drunken, swaying crowd.

#8 wears a bra of red lace which, upon removal, reveals a festive little Harley-Davidson logo tattoo, wings and all, on her right breast.

#9 doffs her black fringed leather jacket to reveal bra top and a ferocious sunburn. A silver conch belt is threaded through the belt loops of black jeans. A rolled bandanna is worn, Indian headband-style, across the forehead, and her hair is long and brown. As she does that male-entrancing humping-the-pole movement, I think, *This broad knows a set of pasties from a G-string.* Much music, heavy on the bass. *Boom! boom! boom!*

Much male cheering. *Ooooh, baby! Take it off! I love you!*

Much used-beer reek, along with something smelling like past-their-bloom irises rotting, forgotten, in a vase.

#10, a late addition to Titty Contestantdom, is being groomed by none other than Our Little Princess, who flips her own mop of unruly curls as she fluffs her friend's hair, whispering in her ear, before pushing #10 out onto the stage.

#10 whips off her top, revealing nipples as maroon as classy law-office carpet, the crowd goes *ooooooh!* as though witnessing a display of fireworks, and the man behind me begins reeling rhythmically against my rump. Is this is a pass?

The winner of Fossil '95's Titty Contest is contestant # 9, the pro-fessional-looking one with the ban-danna circling her forehead.

I seek out my favorite, contestant #1, and ask what she does in her, you know, real life.

"I'm a secretary in Portland," she answers.

Contestant #6, her IT'S NOT PMS, I'M JUST A BITCH T-shirt soaked with sweat, announces that it's time for the Weenie-Waggle Contest. Sparks from the bonfire ascend, stars shooting backward to the velvety dark-bright heavens.

❀

Take any unfamiliar group— racial, say, or religious—hang around them for a while, and you'll start to notice the differences. Crazy Steve, for example: gentle, funny, goofy, but stunningly cogent. Fast Eddie? He has a bike shop in Roseburg, and is a onetime social worker, a guy who's served on task forces with Governor Kitzhaber. Bagger Bob owns a silkscreen com-pany in Eugene, and communicates with other bikers on the Internet.

Talking with that tight, intense knot of guys over there—that's Howard Butts, the LaGrande plumber whose business card reads YOUR SHIT IS MY BREAD AND BUTTER.

Biking, it's poetry. Oh, I hear you, man. I've tried it and hated it more than anything I've ever done. I thought I was going to vomit right into the neck of my husband, he who was "packing bitch." But I hear you, man.

But here's the thing.

Some bikers look like they haven't had a lucky day in their lives. They tend to have jobs, not careers. But bikers are always doing stuff like raising funds for crippled kids, or organizing food drives for homeless shelters. In December 1995, mem-bers of ABATE of Oregon roared up Portland's Pill Hill to Doern-becher Children's Hospital, hand-delivering hundreds of toys to the ailing children—along with over $20,000 raised to provide wheel-chairs for poor kids.

If I were ever in real trouble, the kind that can't be cleared up with a phone call or two, the kind the police can't help you with, would I go to a biker for help? Believe it.

❀

Sunday, 2:35 a.m. The post-Titty Contest band is still playing. What kind of idiot band, I lie won-dering, accepts a gig playing at two

in the morning for hundreds of bikers who want to sleep?

✦

Sunday, noon. Packing up, we talk with a fiftyish biker, a square-shaped and hefty fellow, perhaps five-foot-five, whose few remaining white hairs are yanked back into that biker-guy ponytail. He tells of a recent adventure involving cops and tavern bouncers and loaded handguns. He wears swimming trunks of lightweight cotton, lime-green palm trees printed on a mauve background. His chest is bare, displaying tattoos: Mom. Becca. Delores. Merlynne. He likes talking about guns and cops. I mean, he *really* likes talking about guns and cops. In fact, he has an enormous hard-on that he keeps swatting like a pesky fly. In ten minutes of conversation, the little lime palm trees swaying in his personal breeze, he bats at his manhood 30, 40 times. Behind my dark glasses, I determine that this man is hung better than the great Harry Reems.

Here's to you, to all you Beccas and Deloreses and Merlynnes and Helenes, and all the rest who didn't rate a tattoo.

And here's to the men who love you.

## BEST BEDTIME STORY

The campfire is burning down to its embers. Tuck little Brandon, Allison, and Mustafa X into their sleeping bags, assure them that the bears in the dark woods attack tourists only once in a while, then treat the kids to. . .

# T  H  E

# BLOWTORCH

## by Katherine Dunn

Velma Smirl leaned on the kitchen sink and thought of her husband's clothes standing up and bulging, not with male flesh but with a thick and roiling tangle of rattlesnake. A pile of wrung clothes lay draining beside her. She let her hands rest, wrist-deep in the gray water. Its warmth soothed her.

"He's gone down there already," she murmured, her eyes on the fog-blanked window. "I know he isn't out here."

Her dripping, red hand smudged a clear swatch on the glass. Raw earth outside. She slid the cooling hand back into the water and squinted out at the woodshed. Congealing water moved across the window.

"No. He's gone down to the church and left the saw lying in the damp."

She let her fingers move slowly in the water. There was a peculiar cant to her spine as she stood at the sink, a comforting familiarity to the place where her pelvis rubbed the wooden rim.

"Mama!" someone was yelling. The voice was too far away to identify by a single word. She pulled the plug.

She slung the twisted clothes into a basket and hoisted it to her hip. The baby's crib stood against the wall in the entryway. A torn army blanket was draped over the end next to the door. She paused there to look at the huddled form. She watched the aimless sucking of the child's mouth and sniffed to determine that he'd not fouled himself yet.

"Mama!" The voice was closer. The warm wet from the clothes rose up to her armpit. She tugged at the blanket tent to keep drafts from the infant and reached for her coat.

"That voice has a full set of teeth. It's not one of the little ones."

She maneuvered herself and the basket out onto the back porch and closed the door behind her. Running feet.

"It's William." Benjy's stride is shorter and April wouldn't run for the Lord himself. She felt a heavy

crease forming between her eyebrows as she stepped off the porch.

One loud, close "Mama!" and William rounded the house with flying hair and red-blotched face. She was shouting before he could stop in front of her.

"What's the matter? Why aren't you in school?"

His long knobbed bones jiggled in front of her, his clothes subsiding around him. His blowing face heaved air into his chest, the pale eyes wrinkling up at her triumphantly.

"You give me. . ." he puffed, "a can of milk. . . ," his elbows and knees danced with the effort to breathe. "And six. . . six eggs. . . Daddy said so!"

"Ha!" The explosion of air from her chest startled her. She pulled the child close to her, trying to still him, quiet him so she could see into his eyes.

"Why aren't you in school? Tell me!"

The red was sinking away from the surface of his skin.

"Daddy said. . . ." His face paling around his pale eyes.

"What?"

"He said I could help him. It's his week to feed the test snakes and there's a new test coming."

"He said you could stay away from school."

"For the morning. I'll go back after lunch."

He was afraid now. She had squeezed the triumph out of him. Her mind skittered, reaching for a phrase that could wipe the look of the father completely from the boy's face.

"You go in," she said, her fingers clenching at the bones of his wrist, "and *mind* that baby. You be there when he wakes up and you mind the little ones. They're in the woodlot. I'll be back in a while to fix lunch."

"But Daddy said... he needs the milk and eggs."

"I'll take him what he needs. You go in!" There. The mouth had softened, fallen. The boy was a child again turning to the porch.

"And you mind that baby!" she hissed at his back. His narrow shoulders jerked up to protect the soft nape of his neck, exposed to her stare.

She took several steps in the wrong direction before she remembered that she still carried the basket on her hip. She stamped back to the clothesline and hung the garments hurriedly, shaking them out and jabbing them with wooden pins.

"I might just as well raise hell. It couldn't be any worse if he left us all." She threw the empty basket down and set her chin into her coat collar.

"There's the good saw lying out. He hasn't done anything in weeks. And now that boy. Ten years old and

they'd have him down there." She moved toward the road in an unseeing fury.

"Snakes! Tests! Filthy tricks and snakes to eat their time and let them act big. Eggs he wants. Milk. Where would I get an egg? He sends the boy, says in a loud voice in front of the others, 'Tell the old lady to give you six eggs.' Make them think he can spare six eggs. Church, by Christ! I'll give them church!"

A truck roared past her. She flinched at the blast. The bare limbs of the trees stood hard against the gray sky. She sighted the tin corrugations of the shed roof, then a flash of livid red from somebody's jacket. A small battered truck was parked in the gravel in front of the building.

Above the door hung a big sign lit by a bare bulb that was always burning. The square black letters spelled, The First Church of God's Test. She snorted at the words. The man in the red jacket was pulling a cardboard box out of the truck bed. He swung the box onto his paunch and turned toward her. His face was already set in a smile.

"Good day there, Mrs. Smirl," he said. The box swayed from left to right with his paunch as he walked. She watched the dainty creasing and flopping of his trouser knees as she followed him to the door.

The back of his neck was a solid roll of fat. He kicked the door open and swung the box inside, took a step, and then changed feet lightly to hold the door with the toe of his dusty shoe.

She stepped in. There was a green park bench and some chipped kitchen chairs arranged in empty rows. At the other end of the shed, the familiar spine bent inside a shirt that had passed between her fists a hundred times in the wash. Two men stood looking down at Smirl where he crouched behind the pulpit. His brush of pale hair dangled over his forehead. She couldn't see his face. The big man swayed down the aisle with the box.

She couldn't scream and shout after all. The words she'd saved to use now weren't right. There might still be something left that she wouldn't want to happen. The phrases and tones that she had ready fell back inside her. Sink dreams. She stood in the aisle with her hands clenched in her pockets.

"Here it is, Brothers," said the bog man. "Forget the snakes." He bent in massive ripples and lay the box on the floor. He lifted the flaps and spread them. Mrs. Smirl caught a gleam of dull blue metal. The men bent their necks and Smirl swung around, still on his haunches, his long knobbed fingers reaching into the box.

"He's made himself somebody here," she thought. "They stand back and let him reach into the box and he's only been coming here a few months."

The four men were crouching now. She saw their black-rimmed nails and heavy shadowed creases at their mouths.

"Smirl!" she said, and his head swiveled toward her. The set of his mouth tightened.

"I need to talk to you, Smirl," she said. She pushed through the chairs all the way to the door before she looked to see if he was following. He was plucking at the tops of his trousers, saying something to the faces raised to him from around the box. She let the door slam behind her. The winter-blasted trees were dark and still in the cold. The gravel of the parking lot spilled in thin tire trails to the highway. She stood with her hands deep in her coat pockets. Her knuckles wore at the thin seams and discovered the beginning of another hole. The door creaked behind her.

"Whatever I say now, at least I

> She couldn't scream and shout after all. The words she'd saved to use now weren't right.

didn't do it in front of them," she thought. "He ought to thank me for that."

His hand gripped her arm hard and pulled.

"Where's the boy with the food?" His voice chilled. She felt her eyes opening. "He's ready for me. He knows I'm mad." The surprise muted her. His face darted into hers. His voice went hoarse.

"By God! I'll whip him for giving in to you!"

The calm came down on her. It was their unspoken rule that only one of them could be angry at a time. There was no effort in the softening of her voice. "I'll talk of other things," she thought, and said softly, "What's that thing Orrie has in the box?"

His face slid a little. A certain weight of smugness pulling at the anger lines. His head jerked back toward the door.

"That in there is the Finger of God. Yes. The Finger. You don't understand that, do you? But it's going to reach out. There are some men," and he leaned toward her, nearly smiling, almost a smile except for the eyes that were filled with triumph. "There are some men," he said, "who can seek out and touch the very fingers of God."

His look turned her. That gloat of victory bragged that she was the vanquished enemy. Her rage spewed.

"You fool! I thought you just wanted to hang around and look big to all the others, but you're making yourself believe that you're some kind of holy saint. There isn't one of those men shouldn't be home doing some chores or out looking for work! Just like you! And when's our wood going to get cut? And when are you going over to ask the Martins for the ditching job? Those six brats of yours are supposed to freeze and starve so you can show yourself off to God? And then dragging that ten-year-old boy down here with you as if you didn't have a big enough audience. You want him rolling on the floor and praying those snakes will bite him? God's Test!" she sneered. "And you send him to ask me for eggs!" Gathering her venom she spit full into his raw face. His fist clipped her ear at the same instant, an absentminded blow. The real intent stayed in the narrowing of his eyes, the lips shaking.

"You're my test! I see it. I don't need those innocent rattlers in there. You're right. I sleep beside an eviler thing every night and wake up safe in the light of the Lord every morning anyway. That's it. You're mad jealous." He opened his mouth and laughed a fierce bark. She rubbed her ear slowly.

"Eggs for snakes," she whispered. "And keeping that boy away from school to fill him with sloppy Jesus talk and give him a yearning to be bit and poisoned and sick so the whole Sunday shed-full can see how brave he is! And holy!"

He gave her arm a final shake and pushed her away.

"Ah, I've missed him," she thought. "He's not paying attention."

Smirl passed a hand over the wrinkles of his naked forehead.

"That's pride talking," he said. "You'd rather be God yourself. Never anything higher than your belly and what goes into it and what comes out of it. You were never happy unless I was running chores for your belly. But I've escaped, and you can't stand that. And William's like me!" His long frame hunched over itself with laughter.

"No eggs," she said calmly. "No milk."

"You are the devil," he grinned back at her. "But you can't touch me. I've still got the rent money." His hand dove into his pocket, pulled out a gray bill, and wove the air with it. She hated his smile. He stepped back to the door, waved the gray bill at her once more, and went inside.

She stood staring at the door. Its hinges were just a trifle out of plumb. She turned to crunch out through the gravel to the road.

She cooked the last of the peas that night for supper. There was no bread. Smirl did not come home

and she sat glowering round the table seeing his face repeated on each small skull. She flopped open her dress to the baby and felt his strong pull at her breast.

She saw, even in the smallest jaw, the same line that set itself in the faces before her. "Mine too," she thought. "They look like him and I'm coming to look like him."

She looked at the pale flat hair that fringed William's averted face. She watched the busy plying of his cheeks and the ostentatious virtue of his spoon in the bowl.

"Trying not to attract my attention," she thought. "That's what being good is around here, not being noticed." She closed her eyes in the fatigue of bitterness.

Late that night, Smirl was still not back. Her anger was the same as fear and kept her awake. She didn't bother to undress. She scrubbed the tops of cupboards and the window frames, all the surfaces that she usually ignored. She stopped every few minutes and stalked to one of the black windows to stare out. She was doing that when she heard the unmistakable scratch and hiss of a match being struck. At first she thought that the sound had come from outside and she was frightened, riveted by her own caved face reflected in the dark glass. When the sound came again she closed her mouth with a click and marched out of the room. Up the torn linoleum-covered stairs, down the creaking hall of the upper floor. Her hand closed on the bathroom doorknob, turning and pushing simultaneously. She saw fingers snatch up a match from beneath the sink. "William." She had assumed it was one of the little ones. She'd caught Susie playing with matches under the porch. He crouched on the floor beneath the sink, his soft face tipped up to her, waiting. The clear tears poured smoothly down to mingle with the mucus that ran from his nose.

"What?" She leaned down to him. The stench of sulphur moved around her. She touched his damp cheek. A spray of small black spots on the linoleum. A broad smell of something else burning. He leaned his face pitifully against her hand and his whole body shuddered.

"What have you been doing?" Her voice broke and she felt no anger. The relief of not feeling anger melted her. She took him against her, her arms around the small bony shoulders, his wet face soaking her breast.

"I was. . . ," he began. His treble voice startled her. She had thought

of him as speaking with Smirl's voice. He was sobbing.

"I tried, Mama. . .but I couldn't. . .I couldn't." And the grief freshened, flooded. He rattled against her. She reached for a cloth to wipe his face, and rose to her knees to douse it under the tap. The sink held a puddle of floating burnt, wet matches and there were black streaks etched against the porcelain where they had fallen, still burning. She wrung the cloth and straightened up. She sat on the toilet seat and pulled William into her lap. Folding his body so that she could hold him, she washed his face where it lolled helplessly on her shoulder and felt hot tears dropping on her neck.

"You're no beauty," she thought. "But you're mine."

"Now tell me what you were trying to do besides burn the house down," she muttered into his wet ear.

"The test," came his soggy voice.

Her stomach clenched. "What test?"

"The new test. . .with the blowtorch. I'm not afraid of snakes. I could hold them any Sunday, just like Daddy. I know about snakes."

She wiped his face again and he

"You are the devil," he grinned back at her. "But you can't touch me. I've still got the rent money."

sat up. His pale hair lay in wrinkles, stuck up in jags. His face had red lines from pressing on the shoulder seam of her dress.

"But Mr. Orrie Childers said he was bringing a blowtorch. Somebody donated it to the church, and Mr. Childers said it was going to be the biggest test of all."

He held up his left hand to her, and began to cry again.

"But I couldn't stand it. . .the chosen can pass through…fire…But I couldn't."

The thumb was charred. The nail yellowed and coarsened, the black blurring every ridge and swirl on the pad to a swelling shine. The fingers curled, innocent, but the ruined thumb shivered, erect and separate. His nose ran and she saw his small face vaguely, far away from the fierce focus of the thumb.

"You did this?" She felt the saliva seeping from the corners of her mouth. "You did this to yourself?" Her hand seemed to grip his wrist too hard and yet she could not ease her hold. The skin at the tip of the thumb seemed to have lifted slightly, bubbled over the flesh. "The finger of God," she thought. The boy pulled away from her suddenly rigid shoulder. His pale face peeked anxiously at her. She rose abruptly, dropping him to his feet with his wrist still in her fist. She stood at the sink holding his arm as though

it were a stick. She pulled the plug, rinsed the matches down the dark drain, and ran cold water. She shoved his hand into the water.

"Soak that," she muttered, and let go of him. His face had closed. She didn't know him anymore. She didn't like him.

She found a clean cloth and a thin tube of antiseptic cream. Beneath the boy's silent face she wrapped the thumb. Neither of them spoke. His tears were gone, caught in the tightness of his jaw, in his covered eyes. She tied a loose knot in the bandage, stood back for him to go. His head passed just below her eyes. She watched his fragile shoulder blades stir the ragged T-shirt as he went into the darkness of the hall. She listened to the pad of his bare feet on the floor, heard the bedroom door sigh and the creaking of the bed as William climbed in beside his younger brother.

**M**rs. Smirl was still sitting blankly at the kitchen table when feet hit the porch a few minutes before two in the morning. The door swung and shut confidently. Smirl's long form moved against the edge of her sight. He was leaning in the doorway, looking at her. She kept her eyes on her hands. She refused to be the first to speak. She expected him to speak. But the moment thickened, gathered heft and color, without a motion or sound between them. Just as she was ready to break, at the instant her will was wavering and a soft word was finding its way to her tongue, Smirl moved. He strode out of the doorway and across the kitchen as though he had never paused. Her head jerked to follow him as he swung up the stairs. She heard his feet on the floor above and the shifting of the house to accommodate new weight.

She jumped up from her chair and went to the sink. The numbness dropped out of her. Running anger stung her fingertips and filled every limb with motion. She moved back and forth from door to sink. The white light emphasized the cracks in the walls. The holes in the linoleum rasped her feet through the soles of her shoes. The room conspired to aggravate her and the blood in her veins whispered hatred to her flesh.

"Not to speak! The boy up there rotting stupid and I was going to offer a soft word and a pleading because the silence went too long. And him not to speak. Not a word."

She reached the outer door and opened it. The house could not hold her. The black air had fallen into the frost zone but she didn't notice the cold. She filled the night with a heat that left no room for fear of darkness. She reached the highway without noticing, as though she moved faster in the dark, as though sight had been a burden to her. The flashing blindness of headlights swept her. She didn't cut off through the trees but waited for the gravel driveway before turning off. The lone bulb leaned over the sign. Her lips didn't bother to curl as she read The Test of God. No other light but the passing cars.

She slid quickly into the shadows of the building.

Rectangles of deeper darkness showed her a window. She dressed at its edges, tugged up and down. Her fingernails bent but the window stayed. She stooped and pushed her hands along the ground. Pebbles, twigs, freezing earth, finally a stick. She lifted it and whacked at the pane. The stick bounced back in her hand. Too light. She held it straight before her and ran at the window. The end of the stick, with her

> She reached the highway without noticing, as though she moved faster in the dark, as though sight had been a burden to her.

weight behind it, penetrated, and the glass fell down around it. She stopped, her breathing out of control. When she could think again, she reached in and fumbled with the latch. The window lifted easily, bumping against the frame.

She had one leg over the sill when the wind blew cold up her thighs and she stopped to laugh, leaned her face down to her knee and chuckled softly, grasping and muffling herself so a shrieking giggle would not break out.

"Like a kid up to some devilment," she thought, and if they caught me like this. . . ." A brief vision of how she would look in the glare of a flashlight, with her blue-veined legs awry and her old skirt halfway to her shoulders. The cold touched her and took away the laugh. She slid and scraped her way into the dark and stood on broken glass.

A few gray planes in the black showed her the directions of the room. She was halfway between the door and the pulpit. She stood still, waiting for her eyes and lungs to accustom themselves to the room. As her breath grew quiet she heard a faint slithering of paper from near the pulpit.

The snakes. She had forgotten them. A few were in a wicker trunk and the rest in nests of torn paper at the bottom of thick cardboard

boxes. And the torch was in a cardboard box. She recalled the blue glint, the metallic glow.

"I'll have to risk the light." She would not fumble among the boxes looking for the right one.

It was simple. She edged to the door, found the light switch, and flicked it. The room came up white and dull. She saw the right box immediately. The others had boards across the top held down by rocks or hubcaps. The blowtorch sat innocently, its flaps open, near the woodstove. A line of empty soda bottles stood on the floor between the box and the stove. The men must have sat here late to talk about the new wonder. "Maybe Smirl was giving a demonstration," she thought. "He'd set himself up as an expert."

She looked hard at the black stove and the red flicker that danced in the slit of its door. She realized that the room was warm. A large box behind the stove was heaped with kindling and split lengths. The weighted boxes ranged within a few yards of the stove. Her jaw clenched in a sudden flash of anger. Her eyes tightened.

"They bank that fire for the snakes!" she snapped. An image of the shed's exterior clicked in her mind. A woodpile. A big one. At least three cords, neat and tight. "They cut all that wood for snakes!" The thought scorched her. A knife of cold air twisted into the room from the broken window. She took one quick breath and lunged at the stove. The two buckets of sand beside it had obviously been used as spittoons. With a tight grin, she whipped up a bucket, swinging in the same motion to the door of the stove. She flung open the door and pitched half a bucket of sand into the red flames, snuffing them instantly. The rest of the bucket followed, and then the second one. Dropping the last pail with a clang, she grabbed up a length of wood and danced, leaping, to the windows. Smashing outward into the dark, one after another, she laughed at the black cold that sprang in through the jagged openings.

When all the windows were broken, she went to the box with the blowtorch. She lifted it up, grunted, settled it on her hip, balanced with both hands. She stumped to the door and rubbed the light switch with a shoulder. In the new dark she heard a thump from one of the other boxes. "Snakes striking," she thought. "Mad and stiff and jabbing their heads at the sides of the box because they hear me, or feel my heat."

She closed the door behind her so that no one driving by would notice anything wrong. All six windows on the side were gone. In minutes it would be as cold inside as out.

She went home the back way through the woods. But first she stopped at the outhouse in the clearing behind the church. She stood inside with the door flopped open behind her and held the blowtorch daintily between her thumb and forefinger before dropping it down the hole. A flashlight hung on a string above the toilet paper. She flicked it on and aimed it into the pit, searching intently for any part of the torch that might float. Gone. Sunk. She giggled softly to herself.

When she finally crept into the bed beside Smirl she felt complete, at peace with her fatigue. Even his warmth beside her was a pleasure. She smiled in the dark.

"I can burn that place down if I want to," she thought. The good ache of tiredness pulled her down. Her mind strayed into a lingering image of the terrific energy of snakes on fire.

# BEST OREGON ARTIST
## Ragnars Vieland

Let two pictures say two thousand words.

*Now that we've honored him, we regret to inform you that Ragnars has abandoned the state for San Francisco (hey, if you're that good, why stick around?).*

## BEST PERSPECTIVE

# TEN QUESTIONS FOR TOM BATES

nobody knows Oregon like Tom Bates. As editor of *Oregon* magazine, he was the first to develop a unified field theory of the state. A college basketball player and Vietnam War protester who grew up in the logging town of Oakridge and who holds a Ph.D. in history from the University of Wisconsin, Bates has a tremendous three-dimensional feel for our history, land, and strange collective psyche.

Long before Bob Packwood was shown to be a macro-cad, Bates exposed him more meaningfully in a feature story entitled "Senator for Life" in which Packwood was revealed as an ultimate 20th-century American political power broker. Bates made national headlines when he refused to let the Central Intelligence Agency censor 16 words in the feature "I Was Idi Amin's Basketball Czar for the CIA," written by an Oregon man who had served with the agency in Uganda. Bates went on to be a key editor responsible for revitalizing the *Los Angeles*

*Times* Sunday magazine. He is author of *Rads*, the story of the bombing of the Army Math Research Center at the University of Wisconsin, and currently a writer for the *Oregonian*.

Here goes.

**1. What has been the best thing that has happened to Oregon in your lifetime?**
Nobody discovered it.

**2. What is the worst thing that has happened to Oregon in your lifetime?**
They finally did.

**3. What is the most surprising thing that has happened to Oregon in your lifetime?**
Oregon has replaced California as the moonbeam capital of the world. We used to be known for the bottle bill. Now it's assisted suicides and absolute free speech. Yet many Oregonians are no longer willing to speak freely. A tasteless joke may get you fired.

We used to be famous for political mavericks who defied the vested interests and stood for peace. Now we're known for a senator who sticks his tongue in your mouth, and an Olympic skater who kneecaps her competition.

Oregon has become America's Denmark and East Portland has become Oregon's West Hollywood. There are 20 times the number of nude bars in Portland as in Los Angeles. It has given new meaning to the Beaver State.

### 4. Who do you regard as the most influential person to have lived in Oregon in your lifetime?

Klamath Falls film producer James Ivory (*Remains of the Day, Howard's End, A Room with a View*). In the age of mindless action-adventure films, he has kept the flames of humanism burning. Then Phil Knight. Who'd have thought putting a waffle pattern on the bottom of a running shoe 30 years ago could have evolved into a whole way of life? Around the world the Nike swoosh has product identification second only to Coca-Cola. Offshore Nike apparel factories have helped bring whole countries into the industrial age. That doesn't make Knight a hero, but let's face it, his "Just Do It" is Hank Stamper and the 1960s all rolled into one. And it has, not incidentally, made him richer than anybody, except maybe Bill Gates.

For runners-up, I like Wayne Morse and Tom McCall. In the dark days of Vietnam, Senator Morse was proof to the '60s generation that you could still trust someone over 30. If he and Senator Ernest Gruening of Alaska hadn't voted against the Gulf of Tonkin Resolution, the darkness would have been complete. As a politician, Wayne Morse set a tremendous example by acting honestly according to his perception of the truth.

McCall was a giant. He gave us the Oregon Story, which is the savings and loan of our idealism. He created the image of our state as a progressive haven. As governor, he gave the contemporary environmental movement its political start.

Then there is Neil Goldschmidt. By creating Tom McCall Waterfront Park and the Transit Mall, Goldschmidt made Portland the crown jewel of the Pacific Rim, the one city that really works.

Finally, Howard Vollum, the man who created Tektronix. If it were not for him, I wonder if there would have been the great software boom in Oregon and all the attendant economic expansion.

### 5. What is your favorite place in Oregon?

Odell Lake. Dive in. It's so cold it takes all your pain away.

### 6. If you could change anything about the state, what would it be?

Gresham, Tigard, and Lincoln City. Like clogged arteries, they need to be

BATES AS RADICAL, CIRCA 1971

bypassed so you can get to the coast or Mount Hood without slogging through miles of overpopulated commercial strips. While we're at it, let's run a tram from Government Camp to Timberline, soundproof Portland's Markham Bridge, give Sandy Boulevard back to the kids, move the Spruce Goose to OMSI, establish first-rate professional schools at Portland State, create a High Cascades World Park from Lassen to the Canadian border, and find some Oregonian to open an Italian restaurant that doesn't put sun-dried tomatoes on everything.

**7. Progress destroys. What is the most important thing you feel has been lost in Oregon during your lifetime?**
The city and regional magazines are mostly gone. And the salmon. When I was a kid you could practically just scoop a 20-pound salmon out of an Oregon river. Niceness is going too.

Our honk time is decreasing rapidly and I'm not sure why. We're just not as nice as we used to be.

### 8. How do you think Oregon has changed over the last 25 years?

Oregon has become a state of contradictions. A dead tree has more rights than a live fetus. You actually meet people who'd go to jail to "save" burned-down slag from salvage logging. We're placing all our bets on high-tech, the Silicon Forest. But you can manufacture computer chips about anywhere. Meanwhile, Oregon grows the best clear vertical grain timber in the world.

Rural Oregonians feel undermined by urban special interest groups. It's a classic showdown; city versus country, slickers versus bumpkins. As usual, the slickers have the better lawyers—and the big urban vote. All the underemployed, outvoted, overruled ruralites have are their thirty-ought-sixes and the Second Amendment. Some are out in the woods playing militia as we speak.

### 9. What worries you most about the future of Oregon?

Polarization. The culture war my generation began may have gone too far. I was talking to Andy Kerr, the anti-logging guy. He's from Creswell, downriver from my hometown of Oakridge, so we have a certain Emerald Leaguer rapport. Andy used to read the *Oregon Times*. He told me this horror story about spotted owls

and I realized he was quoting me from 1976. Informed by people like myself, Andy started a 20-year campaign to shut down the woods. Now Oakridge has no mills left, and about all the stores—except for the espresso bar—are boarded up, including my dad's.

### 10. What's the upside?

The mountains are still there—most of them, anyway. And we make some of the best microbrews, Poire William, and pinot noir in the world. And Portland is a cool city. A cultural campus is taking shape along the Park Blocks. The biggest singles scene in Portland is Wednesday night cocktails at the Art Museum. Northwest 23rd reminds me of a rejuvenated Melrose Avenue. Hollywood shops here for the ceramic tiles to furnish their Bel-Air mansions. Oregon brandies have replaced Armagnac in the better New York restaurants. The country's hottest ad agencies, sports apparel designers, and gourmet hardware stores are here. Filmmakers are moving here because the airline commute isn't any worse than driving in from Tarzana. We have maybe 200 art galleries. The critical mass is almost there for it to become a true renaissance city. All it takes is a few individuals of exceptional vitality to make it happen, and those people are already here. I believe a thrilling time is just ahead.                    –M.C.

Top Ten Portland Bars

here have never been ten great bars runnin' simultaneously in Portland. Not in my lifetime, an' I ain't lyin'. That's how we talk. Très droll don'tcha think? Oregon barflies—there have never been any like us, a whole state-full, and we have nowhere else to go because Montana doesn't have an ocean.

The value of a bar is in how extremely or variably you can achieve the state of "Thank God, I'm glad I'm here instead of at my house."

So relax.

Drink your drink. Ahhh, that's better. Nine times out of ten, one drink and it's time to go. You're not intrigued here, you don't belong. No hard feelings, pull a dollar out of your pocket, the oldest most wrinkled one is best; you don't want it anyway. No telling how many slimy old bums have fondled it, it's proba-

bly been the star attraction at a leper-colony sex show, it's probably counterfeit, leave it for the bartender. "Thank you bartender, one drink's my limit, gotta run."

Great bars are rare, discovered infrequently and with a kind of soporific glee. One magic night you happen upon a new place, but you've been in a million bars and...whoa, doggies...now that's a good drink. The corners of your mouth break ranks and race in opposite directions as that new song you like comes on the jukebox, the one you've only heard once on the radio, and the waitress is saying, "Love this song…" You look around and this gorgeous… creature with a sledge-hammer smile looks away, startled at being caught staring at you. . . ." Anyway, there are (just fewer than) ten best bars in Portland:

## 1. The Space Room

No better Bloody Marys anywhere. Spanish coffees. Mais oui. Saturn light fixtures. Beneath the bar is a full-length painting of the Earth from (you guessed it) outer space. Notice the regular blue-collar Joe sitting next to a blue-haired, dog-collared 21-year-old, who's chatting amiably with a friendly suit, all three swaying distractedly to Patsy Cline on the jukebox. A mom and two daughters run the place.

★★★ *800 S.E. Hawthorne Boulevard; (503) 235-6957.*

## 2. The Alibi

The quintessential tiki experience. What can I getcha? "Something. . . blue." Imagine mixing late '50s "Suburban Regency" (deep red velvet drapery framing overly large, slightly mis-hung mirrors, floral patterned wall-to-wall carpeting, gold accents, tuck 'n' roll and diamond-pattern padded vinyl booths) with B-movie South Seas Paradise gold-sprayed bamboo, palm trees, plastic tropical foliage. Plus giant carved tikis, bas-relief black-light tropical sunset painting, actually torch-shaped torchière. Works for me.

★★ *4024 N. Interstate; (503) 287-5335.*

## 3. Hung Far Low

Respite from Satyricon/fellini, where you will sit not six inches away from the guy were trying to avoid at S'teericon. This tiny bar, up a long staircase in a second-floor Chinese restaurant of the same name, is where a certain drummer gave detailed instructions on shooting up smack to actors and film crew of *Drugstore Cowboy*—back in the days before you could just ask a grade-school kid. Great drinks. If I may borrow from that Texan, Shot-fu. Waitress-fu. Decor-fu. Red-lighted Buddha. You'll be back.

★★ *112 N.W. 4th; (503) 223-8686.*

## 4. Mary's Club

Portland's oldest strip joint, the place to spend a heartbroken afternoon shelling out dollar bills to naked ladies, enjoying the classic black-light paintings, shooting pool on their much-used table. But don't be a scaredy-cat. Take a seat at the "meat rack" for an anatomy lesson.

Ever since I was a young boy, I've been fascinated by what girls looked like without their clothes on. Not until my mid-20s did I get over the stigma of entering a place where they would trade me the privilege for just... a few dollars. Many of the women who dance at Mary's Club are astonishingly beautiful, and I wouldn't trust any local male politician who denies ever having been there. My wife has even been there. Did I mention pool?

★★ *129 S.W. Broadway; (503) 227-3023.*

## 5. Rialto

A beautiful old-fashioned pool hall, with the best jukebox in the universe, off-track betting (go, horsey, go), and a few of the city's best bartenders. Good happy hour—that's when I work. Five to ten, Tuesday through Friday. You try and write for a living. Great drinks.

★★★ *529 S.W. 4th; (503) 228-7605.*

## 6. Berbati's Pan

Music, action, dancing, a sprawling playpen of a place. Intimate dining, two bars (one quiet enough for conversation), consistently good music, three pool tables—a good place to meet new lovers or lose old ones. Go early, stay late, cab home.

★★★★ *10 S.W. 3rd; (503) 248-4579.*

## 7. 1201

Cocktail culture. Cool new bands in an intimate setting. Artists, musicians, college students, lots of cat's-eye '50s housewife garb. Top honors for their promotional T-shirt which has "1201" on the front, and on the back a blurb from an *Oregonian*

restaurant reviewer: "The food's not that great."

★★★ *1201 S.W. 12th; (503) 225-1201.*

## 8. Satyricon/fellini

The granddaddy of the new music scene. At this clubhouse for the wild things, music every night features local bands, touring bands, art projects—most anybody who has the guts to get onstage. A hotbed of searing underground fun. Many patrons hang out there seven nights a week. Before I got married. . .well, we won't go into that.

Satyricon now serves hard liquor, and the haphazard toilet-in-hell dreary junkie nightmare decor has been scrapped, replaced by a more beguiling nightmare that retains the same great, dark vibe. Irreplaceable landmark nightspot. Deservedly internationally famous hangout. Recently expanded to include a restaurant named fellini, sporting a low-budget yet inventive menu. Go catch the next Pearl Jam, years before the rest of the world. History in the making on a nightly basis.

★★★★ *125 N.W. 6th; (503) 243-2380.*

## 9. Candlelight Room

Small, live jazz 'n' blues venue, jam sessions, loose, loyal crowd. Even your dad would fit in. Hell, he might even get laid.

★★★ *2032 S.W. 5th Ave; (503) 222-3378.*

I told you there weren't ten. Cheers.

As a merchant seaman, I go to bars and taverns all over the world, but first and foremost in every sense is the Goose.

I don't feel like a stranger there, at any time. Usually I know half the people in there by name, and a few for more than 20 years. Two of them I've known for 37 years, and I'm only 56 years old. A few people in there have known each other for 50 years.

The tavern opened as Goose Hollow Inn in 1967, after Bud's downtown Spatenhaus was demolished to make way for a civic center. It had been Anne's Tavern for many years, and before that, a fresh fruit and vegetable stand.

The nut-brown patina is from nicotine. Little improvements get made. About 15 years ago, when the interior drip-catching buckets grew in number to nine, a new roof was put on, and greeted with derision. In '84, when a deck was put on out front, we cried, "What's next, ferns and yuppies?"

Yes, we got yuppies. Just now I notice a new countertop, and the freezer door has been replaced. In a couple of years there will be a light-rail MAX line stop right out front.

**BEST TAVERN IN THE KNOWN UNIVERSE:**

# The Goose Hollow Inn

**BY BILL WICKLAND**

We dread that just to have something to grouse about.

There are people there I've "known" for 15-20 years and I don't know both of their names, or what they do. "What's your name? What do you do? What do you drive? What are you investing in?" You hear that only from recently divorced people in from the suburbs to find a new identity, and it gets them nowhere.

There is one wonderful word to describe the Goose crowd: eclectic. The Funk & Wagnall's definition of the word works here: *one favoring no particular belief or practice, as in philosophy or art, but selecting from all school or methods.* There are architects, bodybuilders, cabbies, taoists, educators, fornicators, geologists, hippies, iconoclasts, Jesuits, knuckleheads… it's easy to go on like that.

The local media used "eclectic" to describe us when, in '84, Bud ran for and won the Mayor's job in Portland. The word spread from the Goose to every quarter of Portland's establishment and anti-establishment that Bud was a decent, rational businessman who had never missed a payroll, paid well and gave benefits, and had very loyal employees. He got re-elected four years later after making city hall a friendlier place. Then he decided that eight years was enough. Now he's a part-time handyman at a place called Goose Hollow Inn.

Beer, wine, sandwiches, salads, soups, one pizza, snacks. They have gardenburgers now, but have never had hamburgers. No scotch. No hard liquor. I drink beer there as a way of paying dues for being there. Being there is what it is about, for me. Everybody has personal reasons.

I come back from a four-month trip to the Persian Gulf or somewhere and friends say: "Hey. Haven't seen you in a couple weeks." Bill Bolger moved to San Francisco maybe six years ago, comes up for a week or two every season, and some regulars think he still lives here. See, it doesn't matter; it's just good to see a friend who likes to chat and drink and doesn't care about your station in life, unless you care, and want to unload. Then we listen. Then we say: "Get a life."

There is quite block of us who are in our 50s, were in our 30s when the Goose opened. Most of us have been divorced at least once, and our kids got to know "the club" as kids, though in Oregon kids can't come inside.

The kids would play outside, in the trees, or on the porch next door. My son Stoneleigh was taught to throw Frisbees by a long-haired artist, P.C. And in this case, P.C. does not mean "politically correct." His name is actually Pat Cress, and that will be a surprise to some regulars who have "known" him for up to 20 years. My daughter Cydne wants to start a club one day called "Goose Tree Kids," and over the years has run into others who agree. "Where do I know you from? Oh, the trees at the Goose!"

In good weather, before the deck, there were often more people out back than inside, and they were like uncles and aunts to the kids.

We worried for a while that no younger people were coming in to replace us as we aged. I was sitting on the safe by the front door one evening when a young couple came in, milled around a while before being served, drank one down and exited. On their way out, I heard her say, "I knew you had to be 21 to get in here; I didn't know you had to be 40 to stay."

Now that Bud and Sigrid's gorgeous daughter Rachel has taken a role in the place, more younger folks are showing up. And who knows

*Goose hollow Inn*

CLOSE COVER · STRIKE ON BACK

1927 S.W. Jefferson
Portland, Oregon 97201

what the MAX line will bring?

If you show up as a tourist, just be relaxed and patient. Don't be *interviewing* people, but feel free to jump into almost any conversation; don't be offended by coarse or irreverent remarks, and don't feel bad if told you must be nuts.

Maybe that's the rule: you must be nuts. No, you must be *you*.

And don't be surprised if you see Jerry and Cathy Ericksen, in their fifties, up in a tree out back. It will mean that their son Chad is having his first beer in the Goose and they are complying with his wish to have that beer while his folks are up in the tree. In fact, buy him a beer. That's what the rest of us will be doing.

**GOOSE HOLLOW INN,** *1927 S.W. Jefferson, Portland, (503) 228-7010.* CREDIT CARDS. **"Best Reuben sandwich on the planet."** Off the menu, I crave ham and cheese with Reuben sauce. Beer and wine, including locals and exotics. Smoking allowed everywhere. Raucus selection of graffiti.

TAVERN RUNNER-UP

# THE LATE GREAT VAT & TONSURE

Plainly decorated, authentic simple English food, Americanized enough to taste good. One of the neatest basic taverns anywhere. However, it seemed for a while that the pale people who worked there were not tavernkeepers at all, but in some other business only accidentally adjacent to bar stools and beer taps. I suspected that key unseen sallow guys in the kitchen were coordinating the Vat & Tonsure to a higher purpose than service. Was the V&T a beard for outlaw science? The thin, balding young bartenders in their flannel shirts might be hackers with in-the-kitchen hot rod Macs sucking the digital guts out of the Pentagon. Or maybe protecting the on-the-lam inventors of cold fusion who, in the kitchen, were reinventing a cold-fusion machine that would … explain why nobody'd draw me a beer. Finally I asked the bartender why, and he replied, "Because last time your lawyer friend was here, I heard him swear." (I was there with the president of the Oregon Trial Lawyers Association.)

But a recent sea change. The V&T staff looks exactly the same, but is mysteriously friendly and attentive. Those wan guys in the kitchen? Maybe it was a cloning experiment.                                                —M.C.

# THE TEN BEST Restaurants

Oregonians, do you want to eat lunch or art? That's what Oregon's top restaurateurs have tried to decide. Me, I don't much care if the creamy slabs of veal in my *cima alla Genovese* has been prepared to look like a sculpture by Caio Fonseca, or if my Lark's Tongue in Aspic Club Sandwich is constructed to mirror Fallingwater.

Oregon has been the origin of four major excellent restaurant chains: Trader Vic's back in the 1950s; the Old Spaghetti Factory in the 1960s; restaurants developed by Bill McCormick, owner of Jake's; and Tiger Warren's Macheezmo Mouse. It used to be that major restaurants in Oregon were like monuments. Well-known, enduring, but few and far between. In Portland there was the original Tiki-swank Trader Vic's, the intimate Jerry's Gables, and the Ringside—still the greatest steak house anywhere.

Perched high on the West Hills was the elegant Hill Villa, out in the new southwest suburbs there was the Crab Bowl and the Original House of Pancakes, and on the way to Vancouver and right by the Columbia River there was Waddles—then and now possibly the world's biggest coffee shop. The Crab Broiler was a major landmark on the way to the coast—close enough to the beach that you could smell the ocean—and there was Bev's Steakhouse in Eugene, home to Bev's Steakhouse Special nationally known dragster.

Then back when Nixon was still president, Michael Vidor and John Rian hit Portland—two brilliant but very different bolts of culinary lightning. Michael Vidor was a bookish man who, when he opened L'Auberge in upper West Burnside, brought Oregon its first contemporary haute cuisine (read light sauces instead of heavy). Vidor set the standard that has been followed by every "artist-chef" restaurant in Oregon since.

John Rian's vision was more middle class, but just as smart. Rian developed the high-quality, high-volume steak and seafood house. A thoughtful, dynamic man who resembled the "Moon River"-era Andy Williams, he introduced mini-mass-production of lunches and dinners based on high-quality seafood and beef.

Rian's was the perfected prototype for everything from the low-end Beef 'n' Brew to the high-end McCormick & Schmick's. (Yes, Bill McCormick drew off his experience with Jake's, a has-been blowhole when he rescued it from the Sega Corporation and pumped it back to life by bribing local cabbies to steer tourists through its doors; and with the Refectory in Raleigh Hills, from whence had come the primordial steak-and-salad-bar equation.) It was that simple. Rian's menu was no more complicated than the Ten Commandments. I worked there when I got out of college. Waiters and waitresses were hired from the local cast of *Animal House*—boys and girls barely old enough to serve

drinks whose names we were maybe educated enough to pronounce. The kitchen ran off expertise—the dining room ran off enthusiasm. Three hundred and fifty dinners a night were no problem. And if the guy at table five got the woman at table eleven's TS/MR instead of the NYS/WD he ordered, in this dim light and with all the BV Cab Sav '69, who'd be the wiser?

Times have changed.            –M.C.

---

## I. GENOA

*The Best Restaurant in the Universe*

The chance for me to go to Genoa rarely occurs. Though it is a steal at $50 per person not including wine, I can afford it maybe once a year. Genoa is the best restaurant in the world (at least in my world) and under no normal circumstance would I consider going without my wife—as that would be the last time I could legally refer to her as such, what with her resulting divorce papers based on extreme mental cruelty and culinary abandonment. But when I got a chance to have my Genoa tab underwritten while she was in Arizona, I decided to risk it.

My reservation was at six; dinner for one. About three-thirty I started acting like a giddy prom date. I was freshly showered and picking out the tie I'd wear. I swear, I was actually choosing one. I don't have a lot of ties and I was eating alone... you with me? I looked in the mirror—I had an ear-to-ear grin that resembled rigor mortis on a guy who died having sex.

All dressed up and ready to go, two and a half hours before I have to be there. Why, there might be time for a cocktail.

What's that bar on the top floor of the big pink bank tower? Atwater's. I spend the next hour nursing a Stoli Sea Breeze before arriving at the gates of heaven.

Genoa inhabits a small, one-story building whose long display windows are blocked off above by two large, ambiguous pedestal urns holding dried flower arrangements. The restaurant is hermetically sealed from any intrusion save the front door. Through this portal, you are transported to a setting that could be anywhere on Earth.

"Hi. I have a reservation for six o'clock."

"Zorn?"

"So happy to be here."

"Ah... right this way." I am seated at the corner table by the entry to the lounge, a parlor really, where you are invited to retire for a break at any point, a place I go between courses to smoke. (A restaurant reviewer who smokes? Remember, dear reader, this is regional publishing.)

The lounge is charming, furnished with comfortable club chairs and small couches around low tables. This room is a real indulgence on the part of the owners, setting aside dining space for the comfort of their guests. This retreat is a master stroke, as the main room resembles nothing so much as a perfectly dressed stage, where Your Evening unfolds: patron, waitstaff, and repast interplay, and it can be a relief to step offstage for a breather. I found it a way to extend my precious time there. I'd just slip off, smoke cigarettes, and giggle, playing the mad lord ignoring his guests.

The star of tonight's drama, however, is the food. Rhapsodic. At turns revelatory, subtle, complex... exceptional.

The menu at Genoa changes every two weeks. So you could conceivably eat here 25 times a year and never have the same meal twice.

Dinner starts off with an aperitif, and I choose the sherry. To illustrate the level of service, last year my wife and I ordered two different aperitifs on our second visit here. The waiter presented our choices and went to attend another table. My selection was really delicious, and my wife grinned when she tasted it. From across the room, the waiter somehow picked up on this, and without a word went back to the kitchen, returned to our table, swept away Cindy's first choice, and replaced it with a second glass of the elixir.

Genoa celebrates the cuisine of northern Italy, and the waiter's hushed, loving description of each dish makes you feel part of a gleeful conspiracy of privilege.

"Tonight's antipasto course is *vitello tonato*, one of Piedmont's most famous warm-weather dishes: top round of Oregon-raised veal poached in an aromatic broth until rosy pink, then thinly sliced and served with a velvety sauce that combines tuna, anchovy, and capers." Well now.

I ask for a bottle of Ridge Farron Crest zinfandel. I had the good fortune of being invited to a staff wine tasting of zinfandel at Pazzo's last spring, and am enthusiastic about this rather dark-horse red. The wine cellars at Genoa are renowned for an exceptional selection of Italian wines. Genoa is credited with many reciprocal visits from many of the premier wine producers of Italy and is, further, in no small part responsible for the popularity of these wines in the Northwest. Tonight, I was dining alone and living for impulse. This California red is delicious.

The first bite of veal dreamily closes my eyes. You just can't chew slowly enough.

"Your soup course tonight," the waiter informs, "is *pappa di zucchini*, a traditional soup of Tuscany: a rich, savory purée of chicken stock and onions combined with ronde de Nice zucchini and its blossoms, and a drizzle of extra virgin olive oil to garnish."

"Soup ahoy," say I.

Soup is a delicate thing, easily compromised. The wrong balance of ingredients, too high or low a flame, and wham—dishwater. Genoa's *pappa di zucchini* is a marvel of robust clarity, suspending each contrasting note of flavor above the stock, not forsaking the delicacy of the blend. Magic.

"This fish course is *cazze con zafferano*: steamed Kamilche Bay mussels in the shell, with a saffron sauce that includes thyme, parsley, cayenne, cream, mussel liquor, and Cinzano Bianco, served with crostini."

Mussels always bring to mind my father, and a walk he and I and my little sister took on the beach at the coast. "Kids, c'mere a minute. I want to show you something."

I was maybe thirteen, my sister about seven. My dad was standing by a large boulder below the high tide level, a boulder encrusted with, well, crustaceans, of course. Hundreds of mussels and barnacles, overrun by tiny scurrying crabs.

My father started cutting the mussels away from the rock and shelling them, and making a grinning spectacle of noisily devouring live anything he could pry away. When my sister and I were past our initial bug-eyed revulsion and fits of laughter, he very seriously said, "If you're smart, you'll never have to go hungry."

So as I am eating this tide-pool delicacy, I raise my glass to him. The mussels are perfectly done, and the crostini disappear before the sauce is gone—so I order a small portion of bread to rescue the last fragrant splash. *Molto bene.*

The entrées tonight are swordfish, tenderloin fillet, or *anitra in pignatto con fichi*: "a tender, spiced confit of duck leg and a boneless duck breast grilled rare, served with a fresh fig poached in red wine and black peppercorns and sauced with a reduction of the wine, enhanced with duck demiglaze and cognac. Served with green beans."

I choose bird. Somehow, game just has that drama to it. The mad lord thing and that third flagon of red has put me in the mood for something medieval. "A-harrr, look lively now and grrrill me a wee birdy!"

Once again I am lost in gustatory transport; it is all I can do to open my eyes to target the next bite. The smoky cognac wafts above the plate lofting wisps of pepper-spiced fig. . . that Cathy Whims (the chef) can prepare something this rich and yet ephemeral attests to the notion of natural genius.

The dessert tray is gorgeous. But at this point I can picture eating only crème brûlée, the smallest portion of anything available. It does not disappoint. I wonder if they have some deal with the local wood nymphs to gather morning's first mist to whip into the custard. I feel as if I've eaten nothing at all. Which leaves room for the fruit course. From a cornucopia, I select some perfectly ripe figs. A wonderful complement to my second espresso with whipped cream.

*2832 S.E. Belmont; (503) 238-1464.*

–Zorn Matson

## 2. THE RINGSIDE

Small, usually packed, dark as a cave and unchanged since the heyday of the buzz bomb. Oregon's most legendary steak house. Waiters in tuxedos, a big black-and-white photo on the wall of football players in baggy-looking helmets crashing together on midfield.

The state's best steaks. Thick as bricks and served so hot it becomes apparent they are still cooking. You simply wait, listening, as your filet sizzles and crackles right there on your table in front of you until it reaches, say, medium rare.

Plus potatoes. Genuinely famous onion rings. Wonderful hot bread. The finest brown food anywhere.

Green, as in vegetables, is represented by the quartered lettuce heads that serve as salads.

For flesh eaters the Ringside has no equal.

*2165 W. Burnside; (503) 223-1513.*

–M.C.

## 3. JAKE'S FAMOUS CRAWFISH

Dead-center great restaurant muscle and awesome culinary range. Fresh seafood is the Jake's mainstay. But they present a huge selection of wildly varied items, so the first thing you may think is: These people have, so to speak, bitten off more than they can chew, menu-wise. Okay, then try something that looks both sort of obscure and tricky way down the page. Try the crawfish bayou burrito with avocado salsa at lunch. It sounds like some graduate of the local matchbook chef school's idea of nouvelle cuisine ten years too late, but it—like many other delights on the Jake's menu—is original and great. Fiery crawdads in Spanish rice, wrapped in a warm, soft tortilla. Most restaurants would headline a dish like this; at Jake's it's just one among the masses.

Sit at the bar next to the big potato in the flannel shirt (not Sub Pop–style flannel, but Pope & Talbot–style flannel) who, when the bartender offers him another drink, says, "Sure, if I'm going to go home and kick the old lady's ass, I guess I

better not do it sober," and order the salmon pastrami on rye, with horse-radish, tomato, and capers, or the surf clam sandwich with tartar sauce and french fries.

Try salmon at dinner.

*401 S.W. 12th Avenue; (503) 226-1419.*

–M.C.

## 4. THE VEGETARIAN BURRITO CART

Big, cheap, delicious, fresh tortilla bags of beans, guacamole, hot sauces (you can choose from many different kinds) cheese, and sour cream are the best gut-bomb health food anywhere.

*Recently spotted at the corner of 10th and Morrison.*

–M.C.

## 5. ZEFIRO

Excellent. But is it food or is it art? Food is arranged architecturally on the plate. The oysters on the half shell come to the table in a metal bowl, as big as a satellite dish, filled with ice on which the oysters sit like tiny islands. Lift this construction of metal and frozen water. Note that form (the metal and ice) outweighs substance (the oysters) by about 1,000 to 1.

Otherwise, down-home haute cuisine, e.g., pork shoulder on a mound of what? It looked like mashed potatoes to me. You can order a whole little village of tapas for $8.95.

*500 N.W. 21st Avenue (located across the street from*

*the main branch of the public library downtown);* (503) 226-3394.

–M.C.

## 6. WILDWOOD RESTAURANT & BAR

Like all great restaurants, Wildwood can be many places to many people. It's wonderful for a special dinner, ideal for a business or birthday lunch, and perfect for a quick meal in the bar. Truly excellent cocktails. The house margarita is not to be missed. The dining room is spacious and comfortable—ask to sit in the back if you're bothered by noise. The front area and the bar can really hum.

The entrées are generally exceptional, so why not choose several dishes, primarily appetizers, and share? The salad of greens, fried oysters, and pancetta on crepe is exquisite. The briny oysters make a winning combination with the salty meat, both perfectly cooked, arranged on a worthy bed and dressed in a delicate vinaigrette. Wildwood's special brick oven turns out chewy bread and pizzas that are everything yuppie pizzas should be: creative, interesting, and delicious.

*1221 N.W. 21st Avenue; (503) 248-9663.*
–AUDREY VAN BUSKIRK

## 7. THE GRAND CAFE

Okay, okay. There are at least 20 restaurants in Portland that serve more polished fare. The food at

Grand Cafe falls somewhere between what you might expect to find at Jake's and what you might expect to find as a prop in a *Saturday Night Live* skit. Care for a spotted owl cheeseburger? Or a big thick reindeer steak at Christmas-time? Or how about a little testicle stew? Chef Frank Peters creates major heart attack food. No little fruits and little vegetables and little meats or any artsy-fartsy nouveau swill—this is big, gory, inexpensive food that can probably, over time, plate your aorta and kill you.

Peters, who is sort of like a combination of Dennis Rodman—except shorter, older, and white—and Gertrude Stein—except taller, younger, and male—is Oregon's most celebrated amateur "senior" basketball player. When he isn't in the kitchen, he presides over Grand Cafe as if it were a literary salon—minus the literature. On any given afternoon you can find tables around the bar populated by jocks, journalists, and attorneys, with Frank there in his white chef's outfit riding herd.

*832 S.E. Grand Avenue; (503) 230-1166.*

–M.C.

## 8. MONTAGE

A great hall of a people's gourmet restaurant. Left over from what's left of the Portland left. Open from 6 p.m. to 4 a.m.; people start lining up outside just after 5:30, and the place is usually packed by 6:05.

Hoist a bottle of Green Death (aka Rainier Ale). Talk to your waiter. He'll give you the Marxist dialectic on motorhead. Select from a menu that includes everything from sea bass with crab stuffing to "spicy Spam." Order mussels and the waiters scream "Mussels!" to the chef. Notice the crone sitting next to you wearing the Food for People Not for Profit T-shirt.

Montage is best known for its macaroni and cheese at $3 a plate and it's. . . worth it.

*301 S.E. Morrison Street; (503) 234-1324.*
—M. C.

## 9. THE BRAZEN BEAN

Recreational sex and drugs are out. Cigar smoking and cocktail drinking are in. Way in. There's no better place to indulge than at this parlorlike smoke and spirit house. There's also a limited but delicious menu of appetizers, small meals, and desserts. Items include daily soups, chicken liver pâté, ginger chicken salad, a rich and creamy vegetable lasagne, and chocolate amaretto mousse. The soup plate comes with an array of neat cheeses and different breads, and the truly indulgent won't want to miss the Brazen Classic, chocolate fondue.

There is a big nonsmoking section, but despite the partitioning by plush, deep purple curtains, the whole place smells pleasantly of cigars, and it is the intimate smoking room itself that holds the most charm, with its richly colored walls, dim candlelight, close tables, and smoky air.

*2075 N.W. Glisan Street; (503) 294-0636.*
—A.V.B.

## 10. CAFE DES AMIS

One of the most romantic places in town. Classic French cuisine with Northwest influences. The fillet of beef with a port-garlic sauce never changes, and no one wants it to. This lovely round of meat is cooked exactly to taste and bathed in a rich, sweet sauce.

Poussin, with "40 cloves of garlic," is a traditional and often-duplicated chicken dish. But here it's done very, very well. Several tender cloves stud the plate, and the tender bird is infused with the heady aroma and flavor of garlic.

A special halibut dish arrived grilled and cooked in a light butter sauce—again, the secret is the ingredients and the cooking, not elaborate recipes.

*1987 N.W. Kearney Street; (503) 295-6487.*
—A.V.B.

## 10.5. LOTUS CARD ROOM

Uptown lowdown. The Lotus used to be a wino bar. Now it's a wino bar with a very good chef, a change reflected in the typical Lotus patron. Stopped in for a lunch of

tastefully bland crab cakes, gourmet baby food, and salsa-ed corn and salsa-ed black beans, thank God for the bourgeoisie and note that bum, with a purple exploded nose, like an apparition from a previous universe, rising from a table in back. See him gaze in wonderment at all the young stockbrokers who have replaced all the old alkies; watch him stagger, muttering, back onto the street.
*932 S.W. 3rd Avenue; (503) 227-6185.*

—M. C.

## THE BEST
# BREAKFAST
### BY BILL WICKLAND

If I knew how to prepare hollandaise sauce, fresh or even from a store-bought mix, it would cost me a new and larger-sized wardrobe every few months. I'd eat it on everything. When I treat myself to hollandaise, I do it on eggs Benedict, and I do it at the Brasserie Montmartre.

Their traditional Benedict is perfect every time. I don't ask for the O'Brien potatoes, but the fresh fruit is delightful. I suppose that their smoked Nova salmon Benedict is too, but in food I'm a creature of habit.

I love the Brasserie's location right downtown on Park Avenue, one of the two or three narrowest streets in

Portland. The place is huge, and except for the foyer on Park, it has no windows. Very high ceilings, a lot of art on the walls, and a spiral staircase leading to another high-ceilinged room downstairs. Massive columns were put in when the place was Zorba the Greek.

So you are in a Parisian bistro with Greek columns. Hey, it works.

Upstairs and down, the bars are elegant. I'd bet that if a whiskey maker changed its bottle color, the product might get moved to a different spot, to fit in just right. The centerpiece of the downstairs bar is a magnifico La Pavoni copy of a La Victoria Arduino espresso machine—rounded brass with an eagle on top. If you were to sample all of the espresso drinks, you'd be a wide-awake drunk for three days.

Art, music, magic, alcohol, and great food at moderate prices. I can get my Benedict until 2 p.m., or go down after 11 at night and have it with jazz, which is offered every night of the week. Mark Allen's magic is performed five nights. And while the cutlery is elegant, the only linen is in the napkins. Tables are covered with white butcher paper, and each table comes equipped with a jar of crayons.

Each spring an art contest is held,

from after lunch into the evening, and winning works are framed and displayed on the high walls.

My Benedict costs $5.25; the smoked salmon Benedict is $6.25. Pasta dishes, including Thai chicken and penne, are $7, a Caesar salad $6. You pay $6.50 for the chicken Dijon at lunch, $8.95 at dinner. Oregon snapper with crabmeat goes for $11, and you can pay $15.25 for yellowfin tuna or a New York strip steak.

BRASSERIE MONTMARTRE, *626 S.W. Park Avenue, Portland, (503) 224-5552. Credit cards, smoking areas.*

# THE BEST
# BELTS
(AS IN WHISKEY)

A decade ago, Northwest 23rd and 21st were a mix of old people, lower-middle-class families, and hippies. Then 23rd took off and got yuppified. Wives of doctors from the huge Good Samaritan Hospital complex started buying up the grand but cheap old Victorians and remodeling them. Then they needed places to shop and drink espresso, and pretty soon every restaurant had a theme, and the simple bars disappeared.

But now there is O'Brien's—a whiskey joint on Northwest 21st. It used to be a Christian reading room and thrift store. Now it has generous belts at low prices, good food, a beautiful bar, nice wood, pool tables, Oregon lottery-sponsored gaming machines, and skill machines like Asteroids. You can smoke anywhere.

Try the daily specials, like the Monday $2 burger. Thursday you get a prime rib dinner for $6.95. I like the Sunday spaghetti dinner with garlic bread for $3.95. They don't even call it pasta..

O'BRIEN'S, *519 N.W. 21st Avenue, Portland, (503) 223-5390. Credit cards, no espresso, easy atmosphere.*

—B.W.

### FATHER IN THE KITCHEN

Your left hand grips
the knife, pulls white
old knuckle scars.

Fingers hidden
in a fist guide the slicing
blade, set the quick chop,
steel to wood,
steel to wood.

It's only an onion.

Though in their barrel
they roll
like whites of eyes.

—JUDITH ROOT

EDITOR'S NOTE: *"JD" has been adapted from Mikal Gilmore's award-winning memoir* Shot in the Heart, *the story, in part, of his growing up in Portland as the youngest member of the ultimate dysfunctional family, one that produced his older brother Gary, a talented artist who was executed in Utah in 1977 for the murder of two Salt Lake City gas station attendants.*

## BEST MEMOIR

# JD

### by
### Mikal Gilmore

I have a story to tell. It is the story of murder told from inside the house where murder is born. It is the house where I grew up, a house that, in some ways, I have never been able to leave. And if I ever hope to leave this place, I must tell what I know. So let me begin.

I am the brother of a man who murdered innocent men. His name is Gary Gilmore. My first memory of Gary goes like this: I must have been about three or four years old. I had been playing in the front yard of our home in Portland on a hot summer day and I ran inside to get a drink of water. In the kitchen I saw my mother and my brothers Frank and Gaylen sitting at the kitchen table, and seated with them was a stranger. He had short brownish hair and bright blue eyes and gave me a shy smile.

"Who's that?" I asked.

Everybody at the table laughed. "That's your brother Gary," my mother said. "We've kept him buried out back next to the garage for a while. We finally got around to digging him up." Everybody laughed again. The truth was he had been at a reform school for the last year or so, and nobody wanted to explain him to me.

For years afterward, that's how I thought of Gary: as somebody who had been buried in my family's backyard and then uncovered.

In 1952, my family bought a house on the outskirts of Portland. In this case, the term outskirts is no exaggeration. The house, which was located at one end of a rural-industrial highway called Johnson Creek Boulevard, literally sat on a line that divided Multnomah County from Clackamas County. The line ran right through the bedroom in which my three older brothers slept. When it came time to decide which nearby school the boys would attend, a county official came out to examine the situation. He decided that the side of the county line the boys slept on would determine the school they would be assigned to. Gary and Frank ended up going to junior high in Multnomah County, and Gaylen wound up going to grammar school in Clackamas.

The house itself was one of those weather-wasted dwellings that my father seemed to have a mysti-fying affection for. It was a two-story, dark brown shingled place with an unfriendly-looking face, and it sat with one or two other homes between a pair of large industrial buildings that filled the night with an otherworldly lambent glow. Across the street lay the train tracks that carried the aging trolley between downtown Portland and Oregon City. Just past the tracks ran Johnson Creek—in those days a decent place for swimming and catching crawfish—and beyond, a large, densely wooded area. It was rumored that teenagers gathered at nights in those woods and drank and had sex in hard-to-find groves. It was also rumored that a gruesome mur-der had taken place there years before, and that some of the body

parts from the crime had never been recovered and still lay buried some-where among the trees.

In Portland, trouble was easy to find. By the early 1950s, Portland had been Oregon's largest and most important city for more than a century, though it was still groping to define itself. It didn't have the sort of history or ambition of other West Coast cities like Seattle, San Francisco, or Los Angeles—in fact, Portland was a town that pointedly decried ambition. The city's sense of conservatism was a car-ryover from its earlier days, when its original New England settlers had sought to build a place that would be a refuge of civility and comfort in the midst of the rowdy Northwestern frontier. That attitude of smugness held sway for generations, keeping the city hidebound and insular. At the time we settled there, much of Portland still looked and felt like a prewar town that did not want anything to disrupt its heart of fearful pettiness.

But the postwar sense of release coupled with all the new blood drawn here to work for the war effort had forced a crack in the Victorian veneer. Portland had changed its character. Along the

The police knew about these vice dens and tolerated them as long as there was kickback in it for them.

main drag of Broadway there was a strip of bustling bars and restaurants, and many stayed open all night. Inside these spots were a mix of Portland's rich folks and aspiring bohemians, plus a colorful smattering of would-be criminal types. Off Broadway, down toward the Willamette River, there were 24-hour movie houses, where the last thing anybody did was watch the movies. Instead hustlers worked the patrons, dispensing oral sex or hand jobs for a few dollars, or selling marijuana or harder drugs. There were all-night gambling dens and crowded brothels not shy about servicing teenagers.

The police knew about these vice dens and tolerated them as long as there was kickback in it for them. At the same time, they never let major organized crime get a foothold in the area, if only because they didn't want the competition.

The early 1950s saw the rise of juvenile delinquency—and by the middle of the decade rock-and-roll would signify the growing enterprise of youth rebellion. But my older brothers Gary and Gaylen did more than merely enjoy or consume rebellion, they brought it home. They wore their hair in greasy pompadours and played Elvis Presley and Fats Domino records. They dressed in scarred motorcycle jackets and brutal boots. They smoked cigarettes, drank booze and cough syrup, skipped—and quit—school, and spent their evenings hanging out with girls in tight sweaters or racing souped-up cars along county backroads or taking part in half-assed small-town gang rumbles. Mostly, they spent their time looking for an entry into a forbidden life—the life they had seen exemplified in the crime lore of gangsters and killers—and more and more those pursuits became dangerous and scary. I remember being frightened of them. They looked deadly—like they were beyond love, like they were bound to hurt the world around them, or die trying.

It is tempting to try to find a moment where everything went wrong—an instance that gave birth to my family's devastation, and especially to Gary's.

Gary had his view. The first year or so we lived on Johnson Creek. When he was about 12 and was heading home from parochial school, he decided to take a shortcut. He crossed over from 45th Avenue—the long, winding road that connected Johnson Creek Boulevard to the street where his school was—and made his way to the top of the hill that loomed about a block behind our house. Gary started down the hill and hit a thicket of brier bushes, full of blackberries. From the hill's top, the berry brambles had looked relatively small, but once Gary entered them he saw they weren't small at all. The briers had been there for years and formed a tangle of thorns that stretched up the hill's incline, as much as 30 feet above his head. The farther down the hill Gary went, the more dense the brush became, and he saw there was no easy path through the overgrowth.

He could have climbed back up the hill, but decided to push on. An hour and a half later, he was hopelessly mired about halfway through the brier patch. He thought about screaming, but it was unlikely anybody would hear him. He figured he could keep pushing on and work his way through, or he could die in his place. Hours later, Gary came out the other side, torn to pieces and bleeding.

Gary said the story represented the point at which he became aware that he could never get afraid. But I saw his face every day in the last week of his life. I knew how to look into his eyes, because I'd been looking into those same eyes throughout my own life, in my mirror. Those eyes would never lose their terror.

In Portland in those days, if you were a teenager interested in proclaiming your lawlessness or toughness, the hippest thing you could do was join the Broadway Gang. A combination of street gang and car club, the Broadway Boys—as they were also known—dressed in pachuco-style clothes and hung out late at night on Portland's main avenue, outside a restaurant called Jolly Joan's. Though some of its members occasionally stole cars, sold drugs, and ran prostitutes, the Broadway Gang was perhaps more obnoxious than it was genuinely dangerous. "They were just little street bastards," one of Gary's friends told me. "They used to raise hell downtown, you know, push people around. Every once in a while one of them might flash a switchblade. But they were not used except for show."

Gary longed to join this gang. After school, when Gary and his friends would meet at the swimming hole and drink beers, my brother Gaylen would boast that he knew that the Broadway Gang members needed guns. If Gary could supply them with a few pistols, he claimed, Gary could join their league.

Gary took on an after-school paper delivery route, for the purpose of finding homes that might have guns he could steal. He became familiar with the comings and goings of the residents—when they took dinner or left on vacation. He would look for an unlocked or easy-to-jimmy window, then would pry it open and climb inside. He liked those first few moments, standing in the stillness and darkness of somebody else's home, feeling the power of violation that he brought to their world. He soon learned that breaking into homes was a good way of learning other people's secrets—where the residents hid their money or dirty books or photos, what size brassiere the blond girl in his homeroom class wore, whether her parents were heavy drinkers or Bible freaks or both. He'd feel the intimacy of their underwear, he'd taste their liquor, he'd pocket some of their pornography. To Gary's disappointment, though, he never found any handguns in those homes.

> He soon learned that breaking into homes was a good way of learning other people's secrets

One night around Halloween 1954, Gary was waiting at the depot in downtown Portland for the trolley back home. It was close to skid row. Down the block there was a pawn shop, its window full of .22 rifles. Gary saw a Winchester semiautomatic he liked. A beautiful gun, but at a price much higher than he could afford. It was already past midnight. The streets were quiet, deserted. He was the only person within howling distance. He wandered over to a deserted building and sorted through its rubble until he found a brick and then came back and threw the brick through the window. No alarm went off, nobody reacted. He climbed in, grabbed the Winchester, then filled a paper bag with boxes of cartridges. He had cut his hand climbing through the window, but he didn't much mind.

Gary found a newspaper in the shop. He dismantled the gun—it broke into two parts—wrapped them in the paper, and stuffed the gun in a large shopping bag. Then he waited for the trolley and rode with his rifle and bullets back to Johnson Creek. When he got off the trolley, Gary walked into the woods and hid his gun and ammunition in a place where he so often hid the items he stole from the neighborhood's homes and grocery stores.

One night, as the Oregon sky was changing from indigo to black, Gary met his pals at Johnson Creek's swimming hole and showed them his gun. The small group made their way through the woods, over the tracks, and along the tracks to the Johnson Creek trolley station, which was located across the road and a few hundred feet down the way from our home. The station was a three-sided timber construction—a weather shelter, with an overhanging light. Gary lay on the track, with his friends behind him. He aimed at the station's lamp through a side window in the building. He squeezed the trigger and the lamp exploded. A woman came running out of the station as fast as she could. Gary kept shooting her way, laughing all the time.

Today almost nothing is left of the old neighborhood. The dingy brown house we lived in is long gone, as are all the other dingy houses in the immediate vicinity, torn down and replaced by sprawling industrial constructions. Maybe it's just as well. Johnson Creek was never much more than a strip of industrial wasteland. Now it's simply another ugly city boundary road people drive down as impatiently as possible to get from one barren place to another. About the only thing that survives from those days is the stretch of bramble bushes, growing down the backside of the hill above Johnson Creek. Those bushes look as primordial and fateful now as they did forty years ago. They still stand, an ugly relic of the moment a boy realized his life was a thicket, and that no matter how much he screamed, nothing would save him from his fear.

*Flaming Dad*

by Gideon Bosker

For generations, our fathers, our fathers' fathers, our fathers' fathers' fathers—and all the fathers back to Adam, for that matter—spent their lives as passive recipients of feminine culinary skills. But at some point during the quiet Eisenhower years, as nuclear families gathered around the grainy transmissions of a Zenith TV console to watch beatnik Maynard G. Krebs on the Dobie Gillis Show, this changed. Under sunny skies, with red-winged blackbirds chirping, and children munching Oreo cookies, modern working men shed their role as refrigerator vultures and ice box scavengers.

Although suburban homes sprouting across the country were equipped with all the kitchen conveniences anyone could have wished for, they also featured patio eating areas—nevermind the dirty umbrellas that stayed out all winter—where, in the bosom of his family, the post-war American male could explore his epicurean talents.

The daddy-dominated, patio gastro-bash was an exercise in gustatory *savoir faire*, a ritual signifying the man's ability not only to bring home the bacon, but to cook it as well. And who can forget those immensely satisfying, gut-filling meals of humble means? Hunks of watermelon, Kool-aid, sweet corn, green Jell-O molds, and Oscar Meyer wieners would fall off soggy paper plates and tumble into the grass, where they become either instant pet food or the buffet for an insect hootenanny, depending on the sucrose content of the slippage.

Sometimes no larger than ten feet square, the flagstone patio became the modern equivalent of the Neanderthal fire pit, a meeting ground, of the raw, the savage, and the cooked. Patio dining was not, however, without risks. Most of us can recall the treacherous, hair-singeing, backyard fire dances our daddies executed in the name of grilled grub.

The road to self-immolation, patio-style, was never a pretty sight. We can remember them as if they were yesterday. First, our Dads would direct parsimonious squirts of Wizard lighter fluid onto the coals, light a match, then silently pray for ignition. When this failed, as it almost always did, they would douse the dark nuggets with a steady waterfall of lighter fluid, desperately goosing the can to produce long, arched streams. Then a second match. As the coals caught, our fathers were suddenly transformed into fire dancers from Samoa. Patio-Daddy-O's would perform strange hops, skips, and jumps as they tried to dodge tongues of fire that leapt wildly out of the grill in search of the black, white, and red Charcoal Wizard cans they still clutched in their hands. "Hot potato, two potato, three potato, four ... "

*Best Indication why the author growed up all wrong*

# HOT ROD

## by Mark Christensen

I was almost 16 and had to have a car. Something along the lines of a 400-horsepower, nosed and decked, lowered and louvered honeymoon suite. I got a job at a car wash. Fired for snapping towels, I was hired to wave a big red flag atop a Sizzler steak house, and within two months I had two things in my corner: $350 and no common sense. The daily *Oregonian*'s want ads were a garden of earthly delights beaterwise, and I quickly fell in love with every other tarted-up piece of motorized rubbish in Washington County.

Hot cars were everywhere—my Dad was an eye surgeon and we lived in Raleigh Hills, a lush suburb of Portland with long low custom homes—and all around me my friends were buying or building great machinery. Like Bill Winfree's '55 Chevy coupe. White, elegant in its simplicity. Grace Kelly, but a car. In 1966, hot rodders were slapping on every kind of wheel and upholstery, jacking bodies up and down, painting their rides as many colors as you'd find in an oil slick. But Winfree's Chevy coupe was spare as ice. His genius was that, mostly, he'd just left it alone. The car had its original chrome and from the outside looked almost stock. Even his hubcaps were standard Chevrolet wheel covers mounted on only slight-

ly oversized blackwall tires. The only hint that this car was any different from its factory-minted brothers was the dual exhausts that protruded from either side in front of the rear tires, the white-knobbed Hurst shifter, and the Sun tachometer mounted on the dash. But under the hood rested a fuel-injected 283-cubic-inch V-8 constructed with a brain surgeon's care. For the first time I saw somebody of my generation actually do something that meant something. Namely, make art. Winfree made me reconsider everything I'd ever thought about hot cars.

Then there was Dick Donaca's '54 Ford, a machine as garish as Winfree's was conservative. Lowered all the way around, painted a fluorescent blue, chrome bulging and gleaming, it looked like a Czechoslovakian pimp-mobile but was quick as light. The Donaca's house was a wonderland: hot rods, motorcycles—eight or ten of them at a time—go-carts, a sleek yellow airboat with a huge German cross painted on the tail, model airplanes with tiny gas engines that looped and zoomed around the Donaca's backyard like big pissed-off mosquitoes. But the Donaca's long

*The problem I had with the car was I couldn't drive it. Not without a B average.*

suit was hot rods. Dick's older brothers had taken a 364-cubic-inch Buick V-8, torn it down, bored it out until its cylinder walls were no thicker than a traffic ticket, slipped in pistons as big as paint cans, installed a racing cam and three two-barrel carburetors, and shaved tolerances between moving parts nearly to the molecule. The result: 360 real horsepower. A cool joke to be played at somebody else's expense.

One night we were riding around and Dick slowed for a light and pulled alongside Heinrich Himmler's own Pontiac GTO. Jet black, jacked high off the ground, monster tires, Mickey Thompson mags, capped dump tubes standing like cannons below the front wheel wells. Dick, built like a tough pixie, had a sense of the ridiculous. "Watch this," he said, booting his accelerator. His exhaust pipes crackled.

The guy in the GTO looked over. "Pussy wagon," he said.

"Wa-wa-would you la-like ta-ta-ta race?" Donaca stuttered.

"Hardy-har-har." Rock-jawed, crewcut, maybe 20, maybe 40, he peered at Donaca's blue Ford as if it were something off the bottom of his shoe.

"Aw, ca-come on," Dick said. "I ju-

just ba-bought it from a gy-gy-gypsy and want ta-ta-ta see how it goes."

"Twenty bucks," the crew cut replied.

"Okey-doke," Donaca nodded. The light changed and the Ford exploded off the line with enough force to snap my neck. The GTO was lost in a billowing cloud of burning rubber.

The guy followed us into the parking lot at the McDonald's. Stepping from the GTO, he reached into his wallet, forked over a ten, a five, and a fan of ones. "What on God's green earth kinda engine you got in that thing, anyway?"

Donaca shrugged, "Beats me, pilgrim. I can't get the hood up to find out."

I had to have a car. Because there was more. One night I rode to a teenage nightclub in Beaverton with a friend and his girlfriend and ran into a pretty, bookish girl short enough to still be growing who had smooth hair the color of cut wood—the friend of a friend of a friend. Over the racket of "Woolly Bully," she said she "liked" me. Later we went out and parked in front of my parents' tall hedge. In my past, romance had plateaued at the word "no." But now there were no no's. One door opened up after another and soon I was in a room I knew nothing about.

I begged my father to let me buy a rust-gutted yellow and white '55 Chevy four-door with sheets of oil oozing from the blown soft plugs of its huge Ford truck engine, and nearly cried when I couldn't find an extra $100 for a '56 Ford coupe that was a steal even though apparently a hand grenade had gone off on the front seat. After all, what were STP and seat covers for?

Then I lucked into the metallic blue 1953 Chevy. Green-gray leatherette seats, a little Chevy six-cylinder engine, dual carburetors, a polished aluminum Offenhauser valve cover, an Iskendarian track cam, a split manifold with dual exhaust and dump tubes, a Sun tach, great big 8:20/15 tires on the back, a Corvette shifter, and a 3,200 heavy-duty clutch mated to a balanced aluminum flywheel. It was a wonderful machine and it took me only $1,000 and a year to turn it into a screaming piece of thundering junk.

The problem I had with the car was I couldn't drive it. Not without a B average. That wasn't happening. I wasn't a student. I'd sit in algebra unable to understand why I should ponder $35y (4s - b) + 44q (5m - 3) = ?$ when more important questions loomed. Like: If Nelson Rockefeller saw a dime on a floor, would he bend over and pick it up? (and to my English teacher: "Mr. Dietsche, does 'Question authority' begin with a *C* or a *K*?) Without a B average I couldn't drive the Chevy outside of my parents' driveway. So confined, I'd remove the caps on the dump tubes so that the exhaust would shoot straight out of the manifold, back the car up to the street, rev the screaming engine up to 4,000 rpm, dump the clutch, and send the Chevy hurtling through the breezeway and into the asphalt cul-de-sac in back. Then I'd slam on the brakes, bang the shift into reverse, back up, and—the rear tires screeching—do it over again. Until I broke the rear axle.

Fixing it wasn't fun. I jacked up the Chevy, pulled off the rear wheel, removed the brake, slid a greasy busted shaft from the dark hole of the axle housing. I wanted sex, not gynecology.

Briefly, my dad relented. I could drive the car, but could not have anybody else ride in it with me. I was walking again when he discovered that I had friends ride on the car, rather than in it, driving around with pals standing on the rear bumper clinging to the rear window post so they wouldn't fall off the back.

Okay, if I couldn't drive it, I could still change it. What to do? For one thing, I had to face facts: the car was jinxed. After having the valves ground, my pals Dave Mills and long tall Loog and I were torquing the cylinder head back on when Dave slipped into the car to light a cigarette. We had a study lamp for a trouble light and, holding the unhooked fuel line over the socket, Loog said, "I'll bet you got an electric fuel pump. Start 'er up, Dave." I said, "Are you crazy!" just as Mills hit the ignition. Gas shot from the fuel line onto the light socket and, whoosh. Fire everywhere. The engine compartment was blazing, flames were licking at the frame around the garage door. The three of us pushed the car out to the driveway and I began squirting it with a garden hose.

"That's not gonna do anything with gas!" Mills said.

"Then," I replied, "let it blow up." I was sure the gas tank would go any second.

Instead, Mills—a clean-cut boy who resembled me except that he had a chest and a brain—ran inside my house, dashed back out, and began heaving roostertails of flour all over the engine. I was astounded; in seconds the whole fire was out.

But water and flour and heat had made a bread that coated everything. The metallic blue paint was fried. The hood looked like the face of the moon.

Obviously, it was time to get realistic. Because my '53 Chevy with its minuscule six-cylinder racing engine wouldn't be blowing any Nazi GTOs off the road, that was a lock. I needed V-8 power against the day, month, year, decade, millennium I'd be on the loose again.

So, a plan. For I knew that while a great hot rod is a good place to get drunk, fucked, and possibly killed, it had to be created within an extremely well defined and traditional format—sort of like playing football in a hallway and, like football played anywhere, a conservative sport: success goes to he who makes the fewest mistakes. For all its bows to anarchy, a successful hot rod is almost always a device whose body, engine, and interior is organized around a series of related, dramatic, and enduring design headlines à la JFK SHOT IN DALLAS, LEE HARVEY OSWALD NABBED AS SUSPECT, LBJ SWORN IN—a confluence of taste, money, craft, and imagination. Building one was an endlessly self-referring business, every new hot rod an editorial on the one it supplants.

So picture this, it'll make you nuts: a brand-new big, black Chevy 409, bored and stroked, balanced and blueprinted and threaded with a big, fat Iskendarian roller cam, one that makes the nice *lubbalubbalubba* sound at the stoplights. For carburetion: monster dual Holley four-barrels on an aluminum high-rise manifold. Around the edges, Mallory ignition and a brand-new Sun tach. Plus a T-85 four-speed transmission and—wait!—I almost forgot. Back to the engine. Tuned Hooker headers and polished aluminum valve covers.

What else? Hurst shift linkage and Chevy factory Positraction, plus Traction-Masters. As for the exterior, why go overboard? I'd settle for American Mag wheels mounted on brand-new Firestone tires. Big 8:20s in back and less big 8:00s up front. That should about do it.

All I'd need was about $2,000.

At $1.10 an hour at the Sizzler I'd be flag-waving up on the roof into the next century before I saw that kind of money. Then, salvation. My friend Jimmy Huygens had a 322-cubic-inch Buick V-8 he said he'd sell me for $40. I was astonished. Wunderkind Dick Donaca's 360-horsepower engine right there. Or at least it would be as soon as I did all the things Dick's brothers had. Forty bucks was nothing. I slipped him two twenties, knowing I was home free at last.

Smoke erupted from Loog's wide mouth in a stony white cloud, popped back in, then began leaking in two sibilant streams up his nose. "You're porked," he informed me.

The Loog was even taller than I was and as skinny, mantislike, with fists as big as boxing gloves and a voice that sounded as if it were coming through an empty oil drum. Loog's interests ranged from cat burglary to interior decoration. At dinner, for the Loog, plates were bureaucracy. He ate from the pan and he knew few car problems that could not be solved with a crescent wrench, a breaker bar, a case of beer, a ball peen hammer, and the words "Reef on it."

Thus I'd been surprised when, slumped in a corner of my dad's garage, gazing at the six-cylinder Chevy engine hanging on a chain above the Chevy like a side of beef in a meat locker, Loog—an acrobat with Pall Mall Straights—blew one smoke ring through another and said, "Dig this, dog: five'll get you ten that car never runs again."

Getting the little six out had been easy, but getting the Buick V-8 in was not gonna be. The Chevy transmission, enclosed driveline, and rear end were not built to handle the extra torque of a V-8. So surgery was required. Like a whole new drivetrain. A chore I could perform as well as an ape doing algebra. A cool-looking local mechanic, who owned a pink Lincoln Continental with tail fins to rival the one on a 707, agreed to install a '57 Chevy rear end and axle in exchange for my Chevy six. Jimmy

*The brakes had to be constantly pumped or I could die at any stop sign. Thus, just two girls were willing to brave the Chevy.*

Huygens and I towed the engineless hulk six miles to the guy's shop, where he revealed complications in our bargain. Like $350 in extra labor.

He was able, however, to conjure a kind of primordial mechanical swamp under the hood of the Chevy that could facilitate rudimentary life of a V-8 engine.

I'll never forget push-starting the Chevy that first time in the rain at night in front of my parents' house and hearing the engine pop and hiss and explode to life, my eyes tearing with the sudden smoke that filled the car's recently perfect interior.

The machine lurched forward. I couldn't get my new Hurst shifter to hit second gear, and it was soon apparent the Buick V-8 needed a little work. Like new rings and valves. But so what? Who cared that the clutch slipped and would not adjust, that the Buick three-speed had a shifting pattern as tricky as a combination lock, and that the V-8 caused the little Chevy radiator to turn into a boiling tea kettle after three miles?

I had achieved, after all, V-8 power. Or would have if I'd had more than

85 pounds of compression in any of the cylinders.

I remained, however, optimistic, for I had a great ally. Jimmy Huygens was a smart mechanic, a smooth-faced boy with a neat haystack of straight blond hair who, walking, held his arms slightly bent at the sides as if he were wearing guns. He was possessed of a Cotton Matherish rectitude and real will. Months ago he'd been like me, just another inmate of bonehead classes designed for boys whose idea of promise was boot camp. Then Jimmy's banker dad offered to buy parts to build a hot rod if he, Jimmy, would improve his grades. A's every-where in one term. So I was confi-dent. Soon I'd have the car cherried out and beautiful girls would want to ride around in this, the first of my tin utopias.

Well, not many girls bought the dream. Like just two. For one thing, I had an exhaust leak so bad that blue clouds hung above the driver's seat in delicate layers. Romance with-in the Chevy was like trying to neck inside the gas chamber at San Quentin.

A bigger problem was the brakes. I had them rigged up with only an inch of play before the brake lever hit the Buick engine's fat steel bell-housing. So the brakes had to be constantly pumped or I could die at any stop sign. Thus, just two girls

were willing to brave the Chevy. The first was my actual girlfriend, a swimsuit model who was in the gift-ed program at our rich kids' prison of a high school. An animist, she put her hands around her eyes and peeked at the Chevy through the garage door window. "It ticks and groans and makes noises even when it isn't running?" she said. "Have you ever wondered why?"

"Yeah," I replied, "because it's fucked up."

"No," she said, "because it's alive."

Girl two wasn't as kind. Blond, hot-tempered, for her one ride did it. She flew out of the Chevy, coughing, waving her arms. She hit me. "You're nuts. That car is suicide."

Well, so what? Because at Beaverton High School in 1966 it was hip to be dead. Boys who slammed their machines into retain-ing walls and were buried for their efforts got big rewards. Classmates held candlelight vigils in front of their homes and many of the best-looking girls openly mourned their ghosts. It had occurred to me, in fact, that I'd be ten times more pop-ular at school if I were six feet under. But the truth was the Chevy was dragging me down. I couldn't figure out why, given that I could plan cars so well, I couldn't build one for shit.

Oh, I'd made improvements. I'd gone to Radke's Auto Supply out in the heart of industrial nowhere in East County. Radke's was a ground zero of desire, a galaxy of chrome and speed. Christmas morning. Except no present was yours unless you had money from all your flag waving, towel snapping, or taco bending to pay for it.

Occasionally, I did. Enough for two chrome reverse rims and a Coveco "racing" steering wheel. But that was about it. My hours after school were spent clawing my way up

Chevy parked like a trophy in front of the service bays—and his review of my efforts—"Christ, Mark"—stung.

The end was near. Shortly thereafter I loaned the Chevy to a friend who had a problem during a drag race with a Corvette. ("Sorry man, but when I hit second gear your hood ripped right off. Lucky it didn't smash through the windshield.") And now

the executive ladder at Taco Time, just to keep gas in the tank. And for what? It was like owning a hot rod built by Dr. Seuss.

Though I was on no one's short list for prom king, I was not a very alienated kid. A photo ID from the time shows me staring out at the camera, long-haired, more pretty than handsome, smug. Still, I was 6'3" and built like a dandelion and I didn't need any smoke-belching, crazy boy's car to advertise the fact that I was—as my girlfriend had remarked—"from Planet X."

I had driven the Chevy to the service station where Bill Winfree worked—his beautiful white '55

*Climb into my Chevy, dump the clutch in first gear, and you got pistons all over three counties.*

my dream machine looked like it had been eaten by a bear and shit off a cliff. My friend Jimmy Huygens attempted my rescue. In his suit of lights, old Levis, and a new white J. C. Penney Towncraft crewneck T-shirt, he came to the garage to get things done. He saw the world in simple terms. Right was right, wrong was wrong. Climb into Jimmy's freshly assembled '32 Ford roadster, dump the clutch in first gear, and you got two lines of scorched rubber a block and a half long.

Climb into my Chevy, dump the clutch in first gear, and you got pistons all over three counties.

I was glad for Huygens's help, grilling as I was oatmeal burgers 30 hours a week to support a car I couldn't drive without a B average I couldn't get because I was grilling oatmeal burgers 30 hours a week. Huygens approached a car as a series of problems that could be solved by logic, work, and money. I approached a car as a series of problems that, pray to Christ, could be solved by jumper cables. Too, there was my pretty swimsuit-model girlfriend (after all, that was what the Chevy was supposed to help me get, wasn't it?). Frankly, it was more fun being entwined together on a sofa in her parents' basement listening to "Monday, Monday" and her dreamy tales of crazy relatives than being crouched down in a grease pit under a filthy ceiling of rusty mufflers and dripping oil pan, and Jimmy Huygens could only do so much.

That the Chevy saw the road again at all was thanks to Jack, the owner of Jack's Shell Station, which sat across the pitch-and-putt golf course behind our house. Jack was a wiry man with a graying crew cut and veins that stood on his forearms. He was direct, rugged. The kind of man who had helped win World War II. I bought two heavy-duty shock absorbers from him and he adjusted my leaking four-barrel carburetor for free.

And thereafter, he spent hours working on the car for almost no money. The Chevy would roll in smoking so bad it was magic that flames weren't shooting out the rear end, and he'd say, "Gimme a half hour," and 15 minutes later it would be back on the road. One afternoon I watched, handing him tools, as he replaced the plugs, belts, and almost every gasket on the engine. This time it took hours. He charged me $8 for labor. When I said something (fearing he meant $80 but had dropped a zero), he said one day I'd learn which end was up and be able to help out somebody myself. I could hardly believe my good fortune. And, in some ways, Jack's death put the end to my hot-rodding career. One morning when the Chevy wouldn't start, I rolled it out of my dad's garage, jump-started it off his Toronado, and wheeled the smoking monstrosity in front of Jack's pumps. I saw a chubby new face through the windows of his office. I got out, went inside. "Where's Jack?"

"He hung himself." The guy wiped his fingers on a red rag. "He got in a fight in a bar. His wife heard him come in late, went out to the garage in the morning, and found him twisting from a rope."

# OREGON IN THE 1960S
# CONFESSIONS OF AN AMERICAN GLUE SNIFFER

## BY MARK STEN

I had a normal introduction to drugs; I began experimenting with alcohol in my early teens. But juice only led to more juice. I entered college in 1965, and the immediate result was a short-lived but drastic rise in my intake of spirits. Fortunately, Reed College was a selective school and had already come to harbor a flourishing drug netherculture. So when the opportunity to turn on presented itself I equivocated for a day or two, then bought a lid and smoked 12 joints. What a charge. The next month was the best of my life, better than getting laid the first time, or even the second. I finished off my freshman year with hair to my shoulders and a D–grade point. I was a dropout. I was hooked.

You might say that marijuana led to use of the harder stuff, if you run by that brand of causality. The Summer of Love is generally remembered for *Sergeant Pepper* and for all those psychedelics, but my crowd numbed its way through sultry June evenings with Freeze, the frosty cocktail glass chiller that came in cans at –200 degrees Fahrenheit. You sprayed it into a bag and let it warm up for a while before you inhaled it, or you died. There were a few frozen lung stories in the paper that summer, even one from eastern Oregon, but we'd lost interest by the time the locals figured it out and cut off our supply. I moved on to other inhalants.

It startled me to freak out on laughing gas. My body suddenly shut down as my consciousness shot up through some interior ceiling to emerge for one of those five-second eternities onto a surreal and achingly unhappy mental plain, a psycho-geo-graphic zone etched in harsh, dry tones by a dying red sun. I'd find myself trapped on a parched and shattered inner mountain range which bespoke a terrible desert deso-lation. Really.

Mescaline, on the other hand, bored me to tears. Acid on training wheels, acid through a muffler, acid in a bra, acid with a hernia, hip capi-talist acid. I mean, gagging down all that cactus certainly can be a chal-lenge, but it's beyond me why other-wise sane people bother with a shod-dy imitation when the real thing lasts longer for the same price. You can see almost as well on mescaline as on LSD, but with acid you get the other 19 senses as well.

Mainlining speed was warm and good, subtly so, but not enough to justify either the crash or all those small broken blood vessels in the brain. And cocaine? Ha. Fine distinc-tions have always eluded me. Help me out here, is there actually a dif-ference between snorting coke and guzzling coffee while you flush twen-ties down the toilet? Not like there's a difference with acid. Or airplane glue.

I met Sidney around Christmastime in 1967. He was an Oakland black who had been in Reed's Upward Bound program the summer before, and he stayed in town afterward rather than return to California, where he was wanted for burglarizing an electronics store. Sidney had become quite a whiz in computer technology, organic chemistry, and so on. He made the evening news while he was still in high school, the day his parents called the bomb squad to come remove a quart of homemade nitroglycerine from the family refrig-erator. The Panthers had high hopes for Sidney.

When I first encountered him I was baffled by his chronic incoher-ence, his vacant and glassy stare, his pronounced lack of interest in . . . anything. I was baffled until the night he whipped out his bag and offered to share.

It wasn't actually airplane glue per se that he was using, but rather the more potent active ingredient toluene, which was widely available for about $3 a gallon. A phenomenal bargain, as drugs go. I was game. Seating ourselves in adjacent toilet stalls, we began passing the bag back and forth, inhaling the heady fumes rising from paper towels soaked in toluene . . . .

What can I say? I guess you deserve some description of the high, but words are at their weakest in this realm of human experience. Glue is one of a class of drugs that act through obliteration: real crush-ers like ether and Freeze and gasoline and various oxygen deprivants, bag drugs whose effects stem from gross and massive disruption of cerebral function, probably from extensive tissue damage to the brain. Toluene is a powerful organic solvent, and I figure intoxication is simply the sensation of neurons dissolving. It's the greatest feeling in the world.

It opened my mind. It expanded my consciousness—or narrowed it to a pinpoint. Conversations became transparent, people stood revealed, their grasping personal motivations shimmering through like dead goldfish at the bottom of a pond. It wasn't exactly awful, just funny. In fact, it was all just one howler after another. An egoless hilarity prevailed.

I even had a religious experience on glue, just sniffing away and these . . . beings . . . started talking to me and . . . . don't get me wrong, I come from a good atheist background . . . but I felt the only polite thing to do was answer . . . .

There, you still don't know how it feels.

**T**hat first night I left the toilet stall three hours later with a new lease on life and a headache. I had found true happiness; I could

YOU SPRAYED IT INTO A BAG AND LET IT WARM UP FOR A WHILE BEFORE YOU INHALED IT, OR YOU DIED.

hardly wait to rush out and buy my own gallon. On my way to the paint store I crossed paths with a friend majoring in biochemistry who reeled in horror at my story. He assured me with all the vehemence he could muster (not a lot, being a science major) that toluene was laughably toxic, it would turn my central nervous system to oatmeal, and my IQ had probably dropped ten points already.

Brain damage. That would take some thought. I had to admit Sidney looked like a wreck, so I resolved to monitor my physiological sensations on my next glue trip, that evening.

It didn't work. I passed right into a coma. I came to at four in the morning on my hands and knees, with no memory of the previous hours. I crawled out of the bathroom and staggered down the hall, rebounding softly off the walls until I reached my room, where I dropped into bed and vibrated off to sleep.

Sensing in toluene a potential for lasting neural disaster, I renounced, though the odor of paint, thinner, and other industrial incenses came to evoke an unbearable longing and nostalgia. In drug raps I never missed a chance to mention that airplane glue was my favorite high. I developed a bag fetish.

I stayed on the wagon for two years. I didn't go hunting it, but when it found me in the fall of 1969 resistance was futile. The student newsrag I worked on used bottles of an unwholesome white substance to paint out typing errors, and when I read Warning: Vapor Harmful, well, I took a tentative whiff, just for old times' sake, and it was all over. I slipped from the office with a bottle up my nose. By the end of the week I had made off with their entire supply. By the end of the week I was also a drooling wreck, so I quit again until the next year, 1970, when I was seized by a compelling urge to get high. It was late in the evening and the paint stores were closed, but what were chem labs for, hmmm?

The windows in the Chemistry Building were usually left open at night. Of this I'd been assured by acquaintances playing pool down in Lower Commons. I prowled the organic labs deciphering labels until I found the stuff and rushed it back to the poolroom, pausing long enough to grab a few plastic bread bags from a passing garbage can. Some fun seekers had already set off a party after forcing entrance to the community's music listening library, which was usually well barricaded by its staff. As the toluene made the rounds, everyone gave up trying to shoot pool and started Borning Out on the vending machines instead. Borning Out originally described some bone-crushing maneuver used by Portland pro wrestler Tough Tony Borne, an eroding middle-aged bruiser who would have been over the hill years before if pro wrestling were sport rather than theater. The term somehow came to be identified with the practice of knocking over cigarette and candy machines, which was equal parts sport, theater, and the Revolution. The ritual ran like this: the protagonist addressed himself to an unguarded machine, tipped it forward until it hung in the balance, yelled *"Tony Borne!!"* and threw it face down on the floor. The hapless mechanism was then lifted back to its upright position, the coins and stray goodies were scooped up, and the process was repeated until no more plunder was forthcoming or until the looters got edgy and bugged out. A generous unit might yield $10 or $12 in, say, six dumps, plus a dozen or more packs of cigarettes. When we ran out of machines we kicked in the pool room door.

Truly a people's spring.

That summer I found myself touring the Seattle area with a traveling sideshow that billed itself as The Only Moving gallery.

The idea was to display humans in various states of freakhood as exhibits, sort of a "Hi there, I'm a work of art" routine. Actually, the idea was that the art world, being in a state of flux and radical innovation and all, was ripe for a picking, and our nouveau bullshit approach smelled like a winner. I was cast as a drag queen cleaning a gun. I decided to overcome stage fright and jazz my act by getting looped on glue.

So around noon, hours before curtain time, I procured a quart of toluene and stayed loaded until sunrise the next day, sticking tight to my bag through an endless churning kaleidoscope of cars, buses, restaurants, stores, street corners, bathrooms, hallways, dressing rooms, art galleries, front lawns, back yards, strange basements, and my sleeping bag, with the gig lost in the middle somewhere. I just lay back and let the promoters shuffle me around walking-wounded style. Once onstage I did get it on for the market, gawking rubes who'd walked off the street and paid their money, and suddenly here's this androgynized trauma in lipstick and a miniskirt waving a rifle and a bag of model airplane cement and raving about man's fatally maladaptive genetic propensity for aggression, and on the more general theme of organic evolution as a necessarily self-abortive process. They probably thought it was just me.

The night rolled on, and one by one the rest of the troupe wandered off and fell out. Finding myself alone with the bag, I grew thoughtful and turned my attention again to the question of brain damage. The problem vexed me: How to stay high without trashing my nervous system? As dawn approached, the glimmer of a solution appeared on the horizon, a long shot, to be sure, a remedy so mechanistic, so materialistic, so

IN DRUG RAPS I NEVER MISSED A CHANCE TO MENTION THAT AIRPLANE GLUE WAS MY FAVORITE HIGH. I DEVELOPED A BAG FETISH.

*Western*, it could only have been inspired by such a brutally technological drug as toluene. I would take the scientist's leap of faith, I would abandon any lingering beliefs in spirit or soul, in essence, or life beyond death; I would declare myself a material event, a bag of parts, a machine.

*My head hurts. My chest hurts. My kidneys hurt. I'm all mess up. I'm gonna croak.*

How could I get off this sinking ship? How to I separate the real me from all this neural equipment I'm yearning to smash up? What was the real me? If my identity lay in matter and not in essence or soul, maybe I could physically extract it from the doomed shell of my body. Maybe I could home in on those memory molecules, RNA or protein chains or whatever, and find the shortcut to immortality of consciousness. My chem-encoded memories could be stashed away in jars until such time as recorporealization techniques are perfected and my mind-identity could be reintroduced into living flesh.

This could be tricky. To avoid the development of an individualized second identity, the memories would have to be injected early, preferably long before birth. Assuming the psychic jolt didn't send the fetus around the bend altogether, there would probably be numerous memories lost due to the undeveloped state of the physical brain. But the information would be replicable, and the memory fixes could be re-administered periodically until the identity took hold (I could use an occasional memory fix myself.)

At first I assumed that my identity would be reincarnated in clones of myself, but then it occurred to me that it would be just as easy to ease someone else's body. I could be my best friend for a lifetime. I could change sexes. Or species! Apes and porpoises and large carnivores are obvious crowd pleasers, but how low could you go? A bird? A tapeworm? A tree? Why stop there? As the techniques of genetic engineering are perfected, as man learns to impose his will upon yielding germ plasm, we shall mold for ourselves whatever bodies may suit our fancy. The faint hearted will quail at the work of the new genetic artisans, driven and possessed like all artists before them, drawing on past forms to create shocking new aesthetic syntheses (who is this bitch, anyway?), breathing fresh life into the primeval archetypes which still haunt the racial subconscious. Werewolves will roam the world then, and trolls, vampires, sabretoothed cat people and cold-eyed lizard men and all the half-human spawn of a planet unhinged by this final union of technology and primitivism, of ecstasy and terror.

I smiled into the bag and reached slowly for my quart of toluene, confident that a galaxy of endless revelation and sensation lay well within my grasp.

# BEST SHORT STORY EVER WRITTEN ABOUT EASTSIDE PORTLAND COPS

# LASER

## By Kent Anderson

*This story, excerpted from Kent Anderson's novel-in-progress,* Night Dogs, *takes place in Southeast Portland in 1975.*

It was a two-story apartment complex in the kind of neighborhood where, when things were slow, Hanson would cruise the streets looking for cars that had been stolen for joyrides, then abandoned when the gas ran out.

A beefy young white guy in jeans, motorcycle boots, and a Harley-Davidson T-shirt opened the door to apartment nine. "Good evening," Hanson said. "What can I do for you?"

"*Good* evening?" he said, looking up at the drizzle hissing past the porch light. He had a gold hoop in one ear and a carefully trimmed Fu Manchu. The urban pirate look. "Tell me about it. It's been over an hour since I called you people."

"What's the problem?" Hanson asked.

"Tell him, Steve," a woman said, stepping into the doorway. "I'm tired of the guy's shit," she said, jabbing her cigarette at the door, then sucking on it as if it were her only source of oxygen.

She was wearing tight shorts and a sleeveless black T-shirt with no bra. In her early 30s, she was five or six years older than Steve, lean, with short black hair. The tattoos started at the hollow of her throat, curling and twining over her collarbones, spilling down the ridged cleavage into the scoop neck of her shirt and out onto her shoulders. Every inch of skin Hansen could see, from the throat down to the edge of her shirt, was covered with tattoos, black and purple, dark green, orange and maroon, the colors of bruised and rotting fruit. Her arms and legs were pale and untouched. "Tell him," she repeated.

"I'm trying," Steve said, looking down at her, stroking his mustache to show he wouldn't be hurried. "There's this *soul* brother who lives upstairs," he said, turning back to Hanson.

"He's been driving us batshit with that pounding," the woman said. "For *days.*"

How many hundreds of hours, Hanson wondered, trying not to look down her shirt, had someone worked on her with a stinging elec-

## HANSON took out his wallet, folded his ID card, and held it up. See, he said, it's me.

tric needle, stitching ink under her skin and beading it with blood.

The TV was on in the room, divers with spotlights kicking down through dark water and silver bubbles.

"Did you talk to him? Ask him to keep the noise down?" Hanson asked Steve.

"Ha," the woman said, exhaling smoke. "You mean like conversation? An exchange of ideas?" She pushed past Steve and looked out at the dark courtyard. "With some stupid nigger in this for-shit neighborhood? Not fuckin—"

"Cool it," Steve said, pushing her back inside. "I'm talking to the man, OK?"

"*Talk* to him then," she said. "I can't sleep with the noise—"

"I'll *handle* it." He slammed the door behind him.

"I'm fuckin' *sick* of it," she shouted through the door.

"Motherfucker," he muttered. "Look, my fiancé has a nervous condition, and that fuckin' *brother* up there has got her on my case, OK?"

"Which apartment?" Hanson asked.

"Right above us, man. Seventeen. Go in the door down there, and take the stairs."

"I'll talk to him."

"I'm not prejudice, either. I'll fuck a man up I don't care what color he is, and I'll tell you one thing right now—"

"Tell him later," the woman yelled from inside.

The door slammed behind Hanson when, out of habit, he stopped to write down the license number of the green Pontiac in the space numbered for their apartment.

He crossed the muddy courtyard and took the interior stairs to the second-floor hallway where it smelled like a week's worth of burned suppers, the doors identical except for the numbers. Down the hall a radio was playing. He imagined a game show where the contestant had to choose which door to answer. If he opened the right door he'd find a pretty girl in a bikini draped across the hood of a new car, but if he opened the wrong door he'd find a pack of hungry Dobermans or a naked man with a shotgun.

*Shotgun Hall.* That would be the name of the game show.

Hanson knocked on the door to number seventeen.

It sounded like someone was moving furniture in the apartment. He knocked again. "Police officer," he said.

The sounds stopped. After the click and snap of hardware and locks, the door cracked open the width of a safety chain. The man who looked at Hanson had an acne-scarred face and was wearing an OD army hat. For an instant Hanson thought he knew him.

"Howdy," Hanson said, "can I talk to you for a second?"

"You got some ID?"

"Well," Hanson said, holding the front of his shirt out, "I've got this badge and uniform. I left my special hat back in the car."

"Anybody can get a police uniform," he said. "You got some kind of ID card? Photo ID?"

Hanson took out his wallet, fold-

**The man who looked at HANSON had an acne-scarred face and was wearing an OD army hat.**

ed his ID card, and held it up. "See," he said, "it's me."

When the man leaned closer, to read the card, Hanson saw a skull on his shirt. "OK," he said. "What's the problem?"

Hanson nodded at the pin on the army hat. "Hundred and First Airborne?" he asked.

"Yeah," the man said, "who were you with?"

"Uh, Fifth Special Forces."

"Uh-huh," he said, "sure you were."

Hanson laughed. "It's gotten to where I feel like a liar when I say that. Hey, I *knew* some guys from the Hundred and First."

"That right? Where?"

"Down at Phu Bai when they were still there. I was up, you know, Cam Lo, Dong Ha, and then kept going. North. An A-camp."

The black man put his face closer, looked up and down the hall, then unhooked the chain. "Come on in," he said. "Can't be too careful, you know what I'm talking about. Everybody's a Vietnam veteran now. Seem like's it's one in every bar. Half of 'em claim they were Green Berets.

Wait," he said, hooking the lock again. "You not CIA, are you?"

"They wouldn't have me."

"Come on in."

As soon as Hanson stepped through the door the man closed it, locked it with a deadbolt, and dropped a two-by-four into a pair of iron brackets attached to the reinforced door frame. "Hanson," he said, reading Hanson's name tag. "I'm Millon."

He was wearing jungle boots, baggy OD fatigue pants, and a T-shirt with the grinning death's head and the words KILL 'EM ALL AND LET GOD SORT 'EM OUT.

He looked, Hanson thought, like someone who's been on 24-hour alert, his camp under siege for a long time.

The only furniture in the apartment was a broken-down sofa and a TV set with a screen full of static, hissing like grease in a skillet. Newspapers and magazines and books were stacked neatly, precisely on both sides of the sofa. Dozens of photos, snapshots, and curling Polaroids, the colors fading, were thumbtacked to the wall above the sofa.

In some, soldiers are saluting with cans of beer in Vietnamese bars, their arms around Vietnamese whores with beehive hairdos. In others the soldiers are shirtless, wearing bush hats and fatigue pants, leaning against the gun tubes of 105 howitzers, grinning as they eat out of C-ration cans, and posing with M-16s on some bleak fire base, the blowing red dust turned metallic orange now and some of the figures fading from the emulsion.

It was hot in the room, and Millon smelled like rotten onions. The two windows had been reinforced with two-by-fours, bars bolted across them. Hanson said, "Glad to meet you," looking for weapons in the folds of Millon's fatigues.

The small dining nook across the room had an arched ceiling. A Silver Star medal on a red, white, and blue ribbon hung from the peak of the arch, centered, as if it could ward off evil. "Silver Star?" Hanson said.

"Uh-huh," Millon said, rubbing his eyes.

"They don't just hand those out," Hanson said.

"What? What's *that* mean?"

"Not many guys *get* Silver Stars."

The ceiling and walls of the nook were papered with aluminum foil, throwing light like an evil force out into the rest of the room. A plywood sleeping pallet was raised above the floor on two-by-fours, and the floor was completely covered with a checkerboard of cardboard-backed, plastic picture frames, dozens of them, face down like tile.

"My stateside bunker," Millon said. "I been working on it. Gotta scrounge some sandbags and stand-off wire."

"Right," Hanson said. He glanced at the locked door, wondering if he were going to have to shoot Millon before it was all over.

"What you want with me?"

"The people downstairs called to complain about the noise," Hanson

**MILLON** turned and looked at him, cradling the heavy beam in his arms as if he were trying to guess its weight.

said. "I guess from when you put all this reinforcing on the doors and windows." The TV hissed, blue static twitching across the screen.

"Shit," he said, smiling, his eyes bloodshot with fatigue. "The tattoo bitch sent you. *She* the *reason* for this." He gestured from the windows to the plywood bed. "I got to get some sleep. I tried sleeping out in my car, but *she's* out there at night, three, four in the morning, with her clothes off. Walkin' those tattoos around. Some nights I'll go to the window, and she's right underneath it, looking up at me. I put that up last week," he said, pointing to a convex truck mirror he'd mounted on the window frame, "so I can look down without, you know, exposing

myself."

Hanson thought about using a packset to call for another car, but knew whatever was going to happen would be over before they could get there, even if they could get through the door.

"I'm just gonna say this," Millon said, "no other way to do it. That tattoo bitch down there? Her old man—*she* put him up to it—shooting beams from a laser up here at me. I know it sounds like I'm, like it's hard to believe, but that's what's goin' on. Nine days now." Suddenly he began scratching his chest, like something had stung him, digging his dirty nails in hard enough, Hanson thought, to draw blood through the T-shirt.

Just as suddenly, he stopped scratching and went on, as if he'd never paused. "Always does it late at night, when all the others are asleep."

"Why would he do that?" Hanson asked.

"She tells him to do it. They hit me in the feet. And here," he bent and patted the backs of his legs, "and in the ass. In the balls," he said, lowering his voice. "That's what she likes. Yeah," he said, his voice lower, "sometimes in the balls. Blue and yellow fire. That's why I built this," he said, walking into the glow from the aluminum foil.

Hanson followed him, scanning the room in overlapping patterns, looking for weapons. The foil reflected the jumping blue TV glow, like an ice cave.

Millon picked up one of the frames from the floor and held it out at arm's length toward Hanson. It was a cheap mirror, and Hanson saw the side of his own young face and the barred door behind him in its rippling silver reflection.

"I get these for $1.89 at the K-Mart," Millon said. "I told 'em it was for a, you know, *art* project. Had to go back to the warehouse to get enough. They reflect some of the laser beams back. Some of them. I thought that might help too," he said, pointing to the TV set. "Leave it on for interference."

He carefully fitted the mirror back in its place. "They don't work too good," he said, adjusting the other mirrors. "Don't work at *all* most of the time. Not heavy enough to stop the beams."

He stepped back to study them, then turned to Hanson.

"I know you think I'm . . . ," he began, almost saying *crazy*. "Lying."

"Where would these people get a laser?" Hanson said. "Why would they go to all this trouble? They're just ordinary assholes."

Millon began scratching his chest again. "What I'm supposed to do? Look at my *place*, man," he said, sweeping his arm across the barren room, the TV screen lighting, then shadowing, his face. "Would I make this up, motherfucker? You think I'd tell you this if it wasn't true? Act a fool for some white fucking cop? I *know* how it sounds."

Hanson watched the muscles working in Millon's neck. A good punch, straight into the throat, would stop almost anybody. But you couldn't be sure with a crazy person.

"I thought you might help me out. That's why I told you the truth. I had some friends over there who were white boys. First time in my life. But the war's over now and everything is back like it always was."

"I'll go talk to them," Hanson said.

"You won't talk shit," Millon said, "white motherfuckers."

Hanson unsnapped his holster. He'd take a lot of heat for killing an unarmed black man, but he wasn't going to fight a psychotic as big as Millon in a locked room. If he got out of this, he decided, he'd carry a little throw-down gun from now on.

"Open the door," Hanson said, "I'll tell him to stop the lasers."

Millon must have heard the snap of Hanson's holster, or understood the look in his eyes. Hanson stood aside as he walked to the door and lifted the timber out.

"You won't tell him shit, will you?" he said, his back to Hanson.

"I give you my word."

Millon turned and looked at him, cradling the heavy beam in his arms as if he were trying to guess its weight.

"Put that down, let me out, and I'll tell him to stop."

"She'll just get another one to do it for her."

Millon threw the timber across the room and began working on the locks. One of the photos closest to Hanson caught his eye. Millon looked young and happy, just like anybody else that age, standing with a couple of white guys, the three of them holding an American flag at shoulder height, smiling over the top of it. A Huey gunship was lifting off a landing pad in the distance just beyond the entrance to the fire base, an archway with a sign that said

**WELCOME TO FIRE BASE DAVY CROCKETT**
*When you're in the right*
*—Don't Never Quit.*

On the way to the stairs, Hanson kept his eye on the door, the clicking locks followed by a *boom* as the beam slammed home.

In the patrol car he began filling out miscellaneous report forms, listing the date and time, the heading Neighborhood Disturbance. Below that, in the lined Summary section, he wrote, "Re: Millon."

He clicked his pen a few times and wrote, "First name refused."

Christ. He could have called for a backup and dragged Millon to University Hospital and filled out all the forms and hoped the intern shrink on duty would admit him. But he'd probably act sane once they got to the hospital, and the shrink, who'd been on duty for 24 hours, half-crazy himself from exhaustion, would decide that Millon posed no danger to himself or others. He hadn't really *done* anything, there weren't any beds available anyway, and Hanson would have to take him back home. Besides, it was much too late in the shift to get involved in all that paperwork.

It was a dark night, no moon or stars, the streetlights all broken. The drizzle hung over everything like a heavy fog and Hanson imagined for a moment that he was drifting through space in the patrol car, alone in the universe. He put the pen in his pocket and looked down the rain-swept, empty street before pulling the mike off the radio.

"Five-sixty," he told the radio, "going to channel three for a record check."

The woman answered the door. Hanson looked down at her and their eyes locked. "Well?" she said, taking a drag off her cigarette, her breasts swelling against the soft black cotton of her T-shirt. The hooded porch light flapped in the wind, squeaking and throwing shadows. Hanson saw hollow eyes and open mouths down beneath the edge of her shirt, then thought it must be shadows.

She took the glowing cigarette from her lips and, her eyes still on Hanson's, blew smoke out the corner of her mouth. She leaned over, her shirt falling away, and said it again, softly, almost a whisper, "Well?"

It wasn't shadows he'd seen. Only the bottom parts of her breasts were tattooed, the tips pure white, like islands in a midnight ocean of undulating dragons.

## "I'm no child molester, man."

Hanson's face was wet from the cold mist, and a drop of water rolled down his neck. She ran a hand up into her short black hair, her breasts shifting, a tuft of hair showing under her arm, and Hanson wondered what her skin tasted like.

"The guy's a little crazy," he said, imagining the taste would be salt and green tequila.

"Tell me something I don't know."

"He hasn't been sleeping much," he said. A hook-billed raven on her shoulder seemed to preen when she flicked ashes off the cigarette. "That might be the problem."

"He keeps his lights on all night," she said.

"He says you all are shooting laser beams at him."

The woman snorted.

"I told him that was hard to believe."

"Now why would you say that?"

Hanson smiled. "Can I talk to your fiancé for a moment?"

"Steve," she called, turning her head. "Steve!" she shouted, looking back over her shoulder, the tendons in her neck cording like snakes down into the T-shirt. "The cop's back."

She took another drag off the cigarette and turned back to Hanson, looking him in the eyes again as smoke bubbled out her nose. "You think you're really something, don't you?" she whispered.

Hanson looked up as Steve came to the door, barefoot.

"So what's his problem?" he said.

The woman's cigarette smoke drifted out into the fresh, damp air and over Hanson's shoulders.

"He's crazy," the woman said.

"Who? The nigger or the cop?"

"The nigger says we're shooting lasers at him."

"Right," Steve said. "Go on inside. It's cold out here. I'll take care of it."

"Don't tell me what to do, motherfucker."

"I'm not, I'm . . . OK, please. How's that?"

"You *better* take care of it," she said, going inside and stretching out on the tape-patched Naugahyde sofa that faced the door.

"Did you tell him to keep it quiet?" Steve asked.

She hung one leg down on the floor and hooked her other foot over the back of the sofa, straining the material of the shorts, hiking them up her long, pale legs to where green-and-gold palm fronds flickered in the hollows of her thighs. She smoked and watched Hanson.

"Look," Hanson told him, "If you *are* shooting laser beams at him, would you promise not to do it anymore."

"What the fuck are you talking about?"

"Lasers," Hanson said. "Stop shooting him with lasers." If he licked her thighs, Hanson thought,

GOOD CITIZENS ARE THE
RICHES OF A CITY

they'd taste like the sting in your nose when someone punches you in the head, the copper taste and black stars.

"Let's close the door," Hanson said, reaching past Steve to pull the door shut. "I ran your name, Steve, and found several outstanding warrants for your arrest. Two counts of possession for sale of a controlled substance . . . ."

"I took care of those," he said.

Hanson smiled. "No you didn't. Then there's one count of furnishing a controlled substance to a minor, and one count of sodomy with a minor."

"What?" he said, his eyes cutting left and right, poised to run.

Hanson stepped on Steve's bare foot with his steel-toed boot, grabbed the collar of his leather jacket, and pulled him close.

"You better not run on me, Steve. I'll shoot you, no problem."

"The possession for sale, yeah, but I'm no child molester, man."

"I believe you, Steve. She probably looked older. But the law's the law." Hanson let go of the jacket. "But, hey, this is your lucky night. I'm willing to forget all about it, if you do me a favor."

"What?"

"Promise me you'll stop shooting lasers. Just say, 'I'll stop shooting lasers.'" Hanson smiled and nodded, as if he were speaking to a child.

"Just say it."

"I'll stop?"

"*Shooting lasers.* I'll stop shooting lasers. All four words. A complete sentence. I'll stop shooting lasers. Now . . . ."

"I'll stop shooting lasers."

"Great. Good job, Steve," Hanson said. "Good night, now," he said, backing down the steps. "But I'll be checking back. I'll have those warrants in case you let me down."

He walked back upstairs, up the urine-soaked stairwell where winos could sleep and junkies could wait for people to come home with their social security checks.

He knocked on the door. "Millon." He knocked again. No light showed under the door, not even the TV. "I told him to stop. You can get some sleep now. Go talk to the VA, to a shrink. Tell him what he wants to hear and get some disability money. OK? Millon?"

Hanson put his ear to the door and heard nothing but the roar of the ocean and his own pulse.

When the barmaid flicked the lights on and off at 2 a.m., Hanson left with Judy Bellah, one of the girls in Records, and went to her apartment. She was small, with short dark hair and pale skin. Her apartment was decorated with bamboo-shaded Japanese lamps, and when they went to bed he turned them off so he could see tattoos coil her breasts, ripple along her ribs, whip her belly, and flare inside her thighs like black lights.

---

## TAXI TO THE LAUNDROMAT

Rows of washers stare, blink
in the flap of a sleeve.
Between cycles your mother watches
*As the World Turns* and sips gin
from a waxed paper cup. Like a miner's
headlamp, her swollen eye leads her
   face,
the bruise spreading into her collar.
You want to collapse in foam
as the ladies watch your pocked face
pale as sheets churning in bleach.
They stick a curl with a painted nail,
fan their taunt into a beat
their platform toes can tap.
*You've got a hole in your pants.*
   Clap, clap.
*You've got uh high waters.*
   Clap, clap.
*You've got a hole in your pants.*
*You've got uh high waters.*
   Clap, clap.
This time you wish yourself
spun dry, clean enough for them
to see through and out front
past the Summer Sale 25¢ sign
to the cab and the next green light.

—JUDITH ROOT

# PEOPLE

PHOTOGRAPHED BY DALE MONTGOMERY
TEXT BY SUSAN STANLEY

Oh, Portland's got 'em, all right, more quirky folk per capita than anywhere this side of Oz. A grandmother who glowers from billboards and the pages of national magazines. A recovering lawyer who gussies up like a fairy princess and ends up jawing, as it were, with Leno. America's First Drag TV Evangelist. An appliance dealer with a crew cut lands on the silver screen. Meanwhile, a tall, quiet man tends his backyard amusement park. We're talking municipal flavor here. We're talking what distinguishes Portland from, say, Topeka, Kansas. Tom with his sensible Gloria. Gert and her billboard-worthy tattoo. Stephanie and her homemade Elvis. Anne and the coffee room at Powell's. Sister Paula . . . Barron . . . Darcelle and Roxie. Would they play as well in Topeka? Doesn't matter. They belong to us.

**STEPHANIE PIERCE AND "ELVIS,"** Performance Artists

After years of holding court across from Dan and Louis' Oyster Bar, she reigns now on the second floor at Southwest Broadway and Ankeny. The proprietor of Where's the Art? gallery and the Church of Elvis is a fortyish erstwhile attorney with AT&T in NYC. When Jay Leno arrived, he didn't seem to get her, if you know what we mean. His loss. As for Elvis, he can be seen at the Saturday Market, singing and strumming his cardboard guitar for spare change. Q: So why did she ditch corporate law? A: Because real princesses don't wear pantyhose.

**GERT BOYLE,** Chairwoman of the Board, Columbia Sportswear

By now, most of us have heard the tale of the plucky teenaged immigrant who helped in papa's glove factory—she who became the plucky widow who, along with her young son, built the world's largest manufacturer of outerwear. Modestly, she admits, 'twas she who designed the company's hugely selling, much-imitated multipocketed fishing vest. The brilliant, hilarious ad campaign cooked up by Portland's Borders Perrin & Norrander is a natural for the grandmother willing to spike her hair and sport a tattoo for her good cause. Suffice it to say that Gert Boyle is a downright laff riot and one of the most unpretentious females on the planet. Long live the Tough Mother.

**TOM & GLORIA PETERSON**, OWNERS, TOM PETERSON'S & GLORIA'S TOO

If ever there was an icon, it's Tom Peterson, looming over the city with his toothy grin and crew cut, the cheery mutant offspring of Big Brother and Alfred E. Newman. In the days of late-nite TV movies, Tom was forever grinning and knocking from the other side of the screen. And lo and behold, there he was playing the police chief in Gus Van Sant's *My Own Private Idaho*. There was that bankruptcy thing, but . . . well, Gloria knew all along he should've stayed away from all that stereo stuff. Suffice it to say he's back.
WAKE UP! WAKE UP!

**BARRON**, P R O P R I E T O R , W O O D S T O C K   M Y S T E R Y   H O L E

The hole was there all the time, he says. It just was full of dirt that had to come out. Don't expect any further explanation of the Woodstock Mystery Hole, no-last-name Barron's backyard amusement park, complete with the Tower of Faith and Gift Shoppe. Play your cards right, know the right people, you might end up on the Church o' Fun mailing list and receive the works: the odd (quite) newsletter and, best of all, an invite to the annual Meteor Shower Party. Don't even think of sending an R.S.V.P., though. It's just not done.

**ANNE HUGHES**, RESTAURATEUR

Remember way back when, that poster with a nude Anne Hughes in an armchair, promoting her art gallery? (It related to a quote from Gertrude Stein, OK?) She's also run a Northwest Portland guest house and monitored an election in Nicaragua, where she palled around with Daniel Ortega. And she started up the coffee room in the Western Hemisphere's largest bookstore. Now there's the Anne Hughes Kitchen Table in Southeast Portland. Oh yeah, another thing. A while back she walked all the way home, alone, from San Francisco. It was just a little something she'd been wanting to do, she says.

**SISTER PAULA NIELSEN**, AMERICA'S FIRST DRAG TV EVANGELIST

Tall and endearingly gauche, given to a rhinestone-smitten suburban matron's taste in clothes, Sister Paula projects a screen presence that is, putting it mildly, riveting. When she flashes onto the screen, even those who've thrown in the spiritual towel can't help lingering, fingers involuntarily frozen over the remote control. Lest you think otherwise, Sister Paula is completely sincere in her convictions, and in her mission. Lean back in that recliner and enjoy the show: nobody has ever said "Jesus!" with the same intonation, or with as many syllables. And who knows? She may win your heart and soul.

# BEST SUBVERSIVE

# *Darcelle*

## BY SUSAN STANLEY

Bobbie Callicoatte, dead.

Carlotta the headwaiter, dead.

Sandi Dee, dead.

Even Myra —"Death Breath"— is gone, snuffed out by The Plague.

T.N. Tina Sandell is sick, but hanging on, hanging on.

Paula "Red Hot Mama" Nielsen pops up on regional cable these days as "Sister Paula, America's First Drag TV Evangelist."

Chef Shirley is head cook down at one of the California universities.

As for Julio, Julio of the Spirits, God only knows where he is. Someone said they saw him a month or two ago.

But Darcelle herself, she's still there, strutting out onstage with the "Rhinestone Cowboy" number, bouncy bare butt-cheeks festooned with lipsticky kiss and all. Roxie is still tap dancing in roller skates, though she doesn't turn the cartwheels since the heart surgery.

I loved these guys. They saved my life, maybe.

The first time I stepped into Darcelle's, that dimly lit, smoky drag bar in Northwest Portland, it was the mid-'70s, and Old Town was still Skid Road.

---

*Who says there are no second acts in American lives? In the early 1960s Walter Cole (right), known then as Walter Cole, first made his mark on Portland when his coffeehouse, the Cafe Espresso, became the mecca for area beatniks, jazz musicians, and high school kids willing to spend $20 for a matchbox full of oregano. Later, Walter Cole became renowned as Darcelle XV, king of Oregon drag queens, pictured here with Roxie. Though he/she is now an Oregon institution, no one has gone against the various local grains so long and so well.*

*Photographed by Dale Montgomery*

Onstage were four or five dancing maidens, two surprisingly beefy but glittering in sequins and satin and a shimmering froth of feathers.

In the persona of Darcelle there was a practiced sense of the ridiculous, mated with style and force of character. Self-parody—and just a touch of the mean. I was stunned by a passing apparition. Surely it wasn't REALLY Gloria Swanson, but... black slingback pumps, shapely calves, black '50s dress with beaded appliqués, black stole, tasteful pearls, black gloves to the elbows, rhinestones, white hat with long, long pheasant feathers extending out on both sides. The hair is just right. Soulful eyes. A mole drawn just so on the chin. Perfect. Except that the neck was off somehow. . . .

A young man done up in elaborate female costume passed on his/her way to the ladies' room, flinging out a compliment as he passed: "HEAVENLY tits, dahling!"

Darcelle's was the sort of place people from the 'burbs could visit for a good, live show. Wednesday through Saturday nights, the club's regular troupe—the "corps de ballet"—performed two shows, the midnight male strip show following on weekends. Tuesday nights were for "Catch a Rising Star," hosted by an absolutely spectacular drag queen

THE HAIR IS JUST RIGHT. SOULFUL EYES. A MOLE DRAWN JUST SO ON THE CHIN. PERFECT. EXCEPT THAT THE NECK WAS OFF SOMEHOW.

called Champagne. (Beneath makeup and wig, a mild fellow who toiled days at the phone company.) Some Tuesdays, the emcee was the tall and imposing Paula Nielsen, resplendent in Sophie Tucker sequins and feathers. Sundays were reserved for charitable events. Mondays, the club was dark.

Each Christmas Eve, the club held a party for employees and friends. For many, I suspect, this was the biggest event of the holidays, perhaps the sole invitation. (I wonder: It's hard enough for some parents to learn their son is gay. To learn he also wants *to dress up like a girl and flounce around in public*, well . . . he's not coming home for Christmas, and that's final!) I have a cloisonné hair clip I got at one of those parties, a gift from a male stripper, and I wear it a lot.

In odd moments of reflection—falling asleep, say, or staring out the window of an airplane—I find myself thumbing through a handful of vintage mental snapshots, strangely sweet pictures always, always lumping my throat.

October 1977. *For my 35th birthday, I perform onstage at Darcelle's as "Bubbles*

Wolkofsky and Her Flying Buttress," warbling "My Heart Belongs to Daddy," backed
by a chorus line of towering men tarted up
as showgirls. A black- and-white 8 x 10 of
that performance is framed and hangs in my
kitchen: newspaper editor, PSU faculty wife,
and mother of two grade-schoolers, struttin'
her stuff in black sequins and feather boa, slit
skirt and ample cleavage, mountain of teased
hair and makeup.

An all-time life highlight: an audience
member, unaware of the gag, calls out to
Darcelle at show's end, "Has Bubbles been
a girl all her life?"

★

Five years later, I was on my own:
no husband, no job. I went to
my friend Darcelle and asked to wait
tables.

Me (sad but brave): I'm broke. Can you
give me a job?

Darcelle (aghast): I'll give you some
money.

Me: No, I want a job.

Darcelle: Oooooooo-kay. . . let's try it for
a while and see how it goes.

It was the best job I'll ever have. I
worked as Bubbles the waitress five
nights a week, clad like the other
waiters in black slacks and vest,
white shirt with black bow tie. My
long hair was swept off to one side
in a ponytail, a "do" my compatriots
assured me was dreadful.

" 'Nother round here? How 'bout
some more nachos? If you have more
than one glass of wine, it's cheaper

to buy a whole bottle." (We were
awarded per-bottle bonuses.)

March 1982. Darcelle and Roxie and
Julio of the Spirits and me and what's-his-
name—that gorgeous guy who "does"
Marilyn Monroe so divinely—we're all sitting around at two-thirty or so, drinking the
two drinks that come free after each night's
work. Marilyn and I have already done our
night crawl, pawing our way on hands and
knees across the gummy floor for coins and
the odd dollar bill dropped by the lousy tip-
pers.

They relax now, these great tall men in
their finery, their rhinestone-festooned satin
gowns held together with safety pins and
last-minute stitches, their massive headdresses
carefully placed on the cooling stools. Darcelle
in particular is looking pretty ragged, heavy
stubble poking through the half-sweated-off
greasepaint. He looks at me thoughtfully, at
the almost-40-year-old divorced daughter of
an Anglican priest.

"Wanna fuck?" he asks kindly as Roxie,
his mate, smiles benignly.

"Yeah. I do," I answer. "But not you.
Thanks, anyway."

They all laugh. And as usual, Darcelle
and Roxie, whose house is near mine, drive
me home, waiting, in loco parentis, until
I'm locked inside before driving off.

I have never felt so safe as I did in the
care of those men.

★

Oh, they were worried about me,
all right. Not only were my
tips pretty crummy (every night, I

spilled at least one drink onto a customer), I *wasn't getting any.* They dragged in their straight brothers and co-workers. They urged me to flirt with cute customers. Michael, the small, compact, beautifully muscled star of the late-night strip show, took me aside one night.

"I do girls, too, you know," he murmured.

Seeing him leave the bar more than once with a tipsily smitten customer, I'd suspected as much.

"So, if you, you know, need a little ..." he trailed off, patting me awkwardly on the shoulder.

"Thanks, sweetie," I said. "That's always a good thing to know."

Later that night, the beautiful red-haired lesbian Bettina shyly approached.

"Here," she said. "Wear this. Your tips'll be better." Thrusting a bundle of slimy black knit fabric into my hands, she fled. I was left holding a V-neck sleeveless leotard and a wraparound skirt that would reveal plenty of leg.

Bettina was right. I dumped the slacks-vest-bow-tie getup and let the bosom show. Now I could answer the nightly customer question: "Are those *real?*"

★

April 1982. *Darcelle's pretty blond daughter is getting married, and all the club's employees are invited to the elegant affair. The proud father of the bride is for-mally resplendent in striped morning coat and dark trousers, white gloves hiding his alter ego's glued-on, Dragonlady-red ceramic talons. A true gentleman: after giving their daughter away, Cole assumes his place in the pew alongside his wife, Jean, while Roxie— Roc today—sits in back with the rest of us.*

*There are probably a couple hundred people at the wedding reception in the Neighbors of Woodcraft Hall. This is a class act, the bride's father splashing out for his beloved daughter. Champagne fountain, orchid trees on each table, a sumptuous buffet, an open bar, a live band.*

*Dressed in their best non-drag duds, employees clot together like shy kids at a junior high dance, unsure of what they're supposed to do on "the outside."*

*Across the room, a lone man in drag approaches, visibly drunk. He wears a baggy housedress of flowered cotton with fake fur flip-flop bedroom slippers, and for a purse carries a pink curler bag. He hasn't shaved, and shoulder-length hair hangs in greasy tresses. He is greeted and embraced warmly: anybody's eccentric aunt at any wedding.*

June 1982. *I defy warnings to stay out of Chef Shirley's face: she's on the rag tonight. The creator of Darcelle's famous Fettuccine Shirley is going through the hormone treatment that precedes sex-change surgery. She cries a lot and suffers from hideous, visible hormonal changes as she chops and dices, chops and dices, looming over the hot stove in the club's basement kitchen.*

*It's hotter than hell down here. Which pos-*

sibly, but not necessarily, explains why this 6'3" person with football-guy shoulders is clad tonight in a pink see-through babydoll nightgown with artfully scattered rosebuds of yellow satin ribbon. With her bony face, her haircut makes her look like Prince Valiant. I'm talking to her for two reasons. One, I like her. Two, she's a fabulous cook and I'm not. I want to see how she does it.

Pauline, her song-and-dance act over, stands here, too. Bawling me out, as usual. Panning bottom-to-top, here's how she looks: 6-inch spike heels and fishnet tights that make the long legs seem even longer. Male giblets tucked away back there somewhere. Naked from the waist up, with just enough hair shaved to make a girly chest. Beard showing through thick makeup. One of those hair-smoothers on the head to make it more wig-receptive, but no wig. She glares at me in my slinky Bettina getup:

"God, Bubbles! Honestly! If you'd just lose some weight and wear some makeup, you could look just as good as me!"

Weeping softly at some unseen sorrow, Chef Shirley stirs on, ignoring us.

★

August 1982. *My biggest problem is Myra—or Death Breath, as everyone calls the twentysomething waiter, even out of drag. Tall, elegant, thin as a swizzle stick,* keeps wondering what I could be doing here, unless I'm a narc?

Finally, one night, I've had it. I grab him by one of his icky trademark butterfly pins and haul him around a corner.

"Look, you little pissant," I snarl, "I've had enough of this shit."

"What? Shit?" he said, batting his infuriatingly long eyelashes at me. Ye gods, he really is scared of me!

"You tell one more person I'm a narc, and *I WILL GET YOU FIRED.*"

**"GOD, BUBBLES! HONESTLY! IF YOU'D JUST LOSE SOME WEIGHT AND WEAR SOME MAKEUP, YOU COULD LOOK JUST AS GOOD AS ME!"**

Myra, whose boy name was Chris, had one great ambition. And that was to be anointed as a member of Darcelle's corps de ballet. He, she, was a "dragette," a queen-in-training. He wanted us to go shoe-shopping, to tell me about his dates, to give me handy makeup and fashion tips. I still have a pair of dangly aurora borealis earrings he gave me.

Chris was staggeringly beautiful as Myra—a fact not lost on his father, who finally came in one night to see his son onstage. With each double scotch rocks served him, his face got stonier. He didn't stick around to talk with Myra/Chris afterward. Just walked out, tripping a little over the threshold.

September 1982. *I'm sitting in the dressing room area, yakking with Roc and Walter as they transform themselves into Roxie and Darcelle. Roc slathers on the greasepaint, his head pink and shiny as a first-grader's new eraser on the first day of school.*

*T.N. Tina Sandell approaches me shyly. Offstage, he's a quiet, dignified man named Jerry—a full-blooded Klamath Indian. Onstage, with shiny black butt-length hair and flawless moves, she's the best lip-syncher of them all, especially performing Tina Turner and Janis Joplin.*

*"I just melted two holes in this with my cigarette," she says, holding up a low-cut blood-red Quiana nylon knit gown. "And I want to wear it for 'Proud Mary' tonight."*

*I tell her to fetch a needle and red thread and a light bulb. There in the middle of the chatter and the smell of greasepaint, 75-watt bulb serving as a darning egg, I carefully repair the holes in the slippery fabric, using sock-mending techniques learned a quarter-century earlier in Miss Chrisman's seventh-grade home ec class at Irving Junior High School in Lincoln, Nebraska.*

December 1994. *I'm back in Darcelle's basement dressing area. My longtime sweetheart and I are flying to Las Vegas tomorrow, to get married there in the Graceland Chapel. What to wear, what to wear? Sequins, obviously. So here I am.*

*I try on this, I try on that. Finally, we settle on two gowns, one of red sequins, the other of bright blue glitter, and add a boa of hot pink feathers. I look like a sackful of kittens on the way to the river. I hie myself to that bra joint out on Northeast 122nd Avenue, where I buy nearly a hundred bucks' worth of corsetry to redistribute the wealth into an hourglass form.*

*I can't foresee that my roll-aboard suitcase will be stolen at the Las Vegas airport, with the expensive corsets, the half-dozen tea cozies made from vintage linens, the new shoes, and a fistful of family pictures—all lost forever, flushed right down the toilet of life.*

I stopped by there the other night toward the end of a show. Darcelle was onstage. Tilting her head with the huge blond wig, grinning and batting the improbable lashes, she was in her usual splendid form. She held the microphone in one bejeweled hand, smoothing the other over a generous, satin-covered flank. She winked outrageously at the cluster of "bachelorettes" celebrating the upcoming marriage of the blonde named Tawnee, and ended up with the customary crack about how *Here at Darcelle XV we learn to laugh at ourselves, so then we can go out and laugh at EVV-REE-BUDDEE ELSE!*

Later we sat together at one of the little tables, Darcelle and Roxie and my husband and me. While we talked, my friend Darcelle and I held hands, his big paw with the rhinestone rings and the long, red-tipped fingers dwarfing my medium-sized hand with the clipped, unpolished nails.

We talked about old friends, about Bobbie and Myra and Pauline and Chef Shirley.

We talked about how when I quit the best job I'll ever have, Carlotta the headwaiter said it was OK, because he was about to fire me anyway.

Mostly, though, we talked about our grandchildren.

Fifth-generation Oregonian Gary Ewing was one of the first light-show gurus in San Francisco's Avalon Ballroom. I'd first heard about him at the home of friends who ran the Psychedelic Supermarket next to Portland's Lair Hill Park during the late '60s and early '70s, when, if you couldn't get to San Francisco, you came here and were given a flower for your hair.

"Ewing makes giant balloons," they said. "You get inside of them with a band and a light show, and it blows your mind!"

Hard for me to "grok" until I experienced a Ewing balloon at the Bullfrog Festival outside Estacada in 1968. My wife Sherry and I and our babies and her kids, Todd and Carii, then nine and seven, came up from Sweet Home in a '52 Morris Minor pickup with a home-made canvas-covered wagon canopy over the bed, and a tent.

Imagine. A heavy translucent vinyl balloon on a grassy field. Inflated, it was 60 feet long and 40 feet wide and 30 feet high in the middle. It took all of Friday night to inflate by generator.

On Saturday morning, Gary directed us in getting gear placed properly outside the balloon, then cut a seven-foot-high slash to the ground, and while air was flowing out pulled the opening wide to allow us to rush in and out with wood and pipe and stands and movie projectors and overhead projectors and sound boards and clear glass spheroid bowls and colored oils and lots of other stuff.

Gary sealed up the seam, and we waited until the balloon was full of air again before lifting one edge a bit and rolling under it. A sort of space-station-type crawl-through plastic airlock was created, and we awaited nightfall.

Maybe 300 people climbed inside that night. The acoustics were amazing. Colored lights were set in motion by putting drops of oil into two or more bowls, placing the bowls inside each other and setting them atop an overhead projector, then rotating or spinning the bowls in rhythm with the band. In that balloon, the lights danced and undulated on the entire surface, all around us, and clear to the ground.

I remember one square spot on that huge surface, like a window, but in reality a projected Three Stooges comedy. Strobe made the entire space alternate between total black and total white; everything existed for an instant, then for an instant

**BEST HIPPIE**

**by Bill Wickland**

did not. The effect was like living in slow motion, and it required an intense freeing of the sensory inhibitors to move, to trust your body more than your eyes. The scariest and most fun exercise was to jump over a friend lying beneath you, or to be that friend lying under someone who is jumping. It was a leap of faith. Todd and Carii had to coax Sherry and me to try it.

The colored lights on the balloon were as impressive from outside. Sherry and I slipped off up the hill after the kids were tucked into their bags in the Morris wagon. Looking down, it appeared as if the Martians had landed.

Later Gary Ewing became locally famous as the mastermind behind the Crystal Ballroom—a huge room in Portland that had a dance floor suspended on springs and ball bearings. The Crystal had stood empty for years after drive-in movies and television took people from dancing, and in the mid-'60s Gary leased it. His rock 'n' roll light shows there became a Northwest legend, a crown jewel of the Oregon freakout experience. Thousands of young Oregonians like myself went from buttoned-down straight to blown-out freak after a single Gary Ewing Crystal Ballroom experience.

This being the 1990s, the Crystal has now been restored as a brewpub and dance hall.

## OREGON IN THE 1960'S

# Meanwhile, in Vietnam

EDITOR'S NOTE: Kit Bowen was born in an Oregon suburban heaven and nearly died in a Southeast Asian hell. You may have read about him in the Vietnam War book *The Boys of Company C*, the tale of Bowen's endlessly shot-up, blown-up, beat-up infantry unit. Bowen was Company C's medic and saw more violence, horror, and death before he was 21 than almost any ten people put together will see in their entire lives.

Kit Bowen and I grew up together. We were alike. Tall, skinny, mouthy upper-middle-class boys with lots of friends and zero worries. Bowen's parents were artsy, cosmopolitan—for example, they got divorced, which was avant-garde for Raleigh Hills in 1965—and Bowen was a great guy. One night we insulted each other into a brawl, and I gave Kit a fight-stopping black eye a second before he would have otherwise bashed my skull into the pavement of my parents' driveway. But Kit didn't get mad, he got even. A week later at the junior prom he slipped my bright-eyed, delicate girlfriend a raspberry syrup–camouflaged vodka Mickey Finn that turned her into a somnolent upchuck machine.

Bowen was casual. He forgot about college, drank some beers one day, and joined the army. He didn't want to kill anyone, so he became a medic. What follows is one of the more pastoral passages from his war diary.     —M.C.

# SERGEANT BROCK

## BY KIT BOWEN

We got into the choppers, excited after months in deep shit and looking forward to a rest out on Highway 13, the main road that extended the length of the country and supplied all the base camps in Vietnam.

I loved flying and helicopters had become my favorite. It's so hot and humid in Vietnam, the chopper rides were like walking into my basement back home and turning on a fan. I would always try to jump on last so I could be closest to the door. I'd hang my legs out the side and rest them on the running guides. It was a cheap thrill to have the air dry my sweat at 80 miles per hour while looking down at a panorama of rice paddies and jungle. Though there was little pretty about Vietnam from above.

Over the years America's firepower had raised havoc with the land. The craters of the moon rising out of endless mire endlessly bombarded. I couldn't understand how people could live in such hell.

Highway 13 was known as

Thunder Road because it exploded a lot, and as soon as we put down, our unit, Charlie Company, was to set up next to the road—our only job was going to be to walk the highway every morning with mine detectors to make sure our tanks could pass safely. Nice duty. Beer drinking and skinny-dipping.

But as the chopper carrying my platoon began to descend, I saw something was wrong. We were not coming down in nice blown-away-see-every-little-thing-for-miles ruined wasteland, we were being dropped into jungle, right back into the bucket of fuck. Suh-prise, suh-prise, suh-prise, as Gomer Pyle would put it.

We landed, to be informed by our lieutenant that we were to ride shot-gun on Colonel George Patton III's tanks, part of a support system nobody at the LZ seemed to know the first thing about.

So we sat around, waiting for the tanks. Twenty of us, right in the middle of nowhere, and I, for one, was real happy to see the iron monsters come rolling up out of the jungle.

They picked us up. I was on the lead tank, sitting outside up front like a hood ornament. If there were any mines in the road I'd certainly be the first to know about it.

No sooner had we got started than I saw movement along the tree line. About 200 yards away there was a pajama-clad gook walking along just like it was Sunday-go-to-meeting.

I hit the tank commander on the back of his helmet and pointed. He nodded, mumbled into his chin mike and, boom, I was whipped sideways as our tank, and the other others behind, did a snap column left—and opened up with everything they had. These people took war seriously. It was everything I could do to hang on without being thrown overboard.

When we rolled up to the tree line we found one dead, one wounded, and another with his rifle raised above his head screaming, "Chieu hois!" which meant open arms or King's X.

My black pal Smitty took a grenade from his belt, pulled the pin, let the hammer fly, said, "I got your chieu hois hanging," and lobbed it into the little man's chest. Smitty, by nature, was not much of a do-gooder.

One of the gunners, Sergeant Brock, jumped off his tank and,

bare-chested, with a .45 in each hand, walked into the jungle. He fired a round from each and the recoils knocked him on his ass.

He lay there in the mud firing from both clips into the sky. If he'd only been shooting into the jungle I am sure we'd've won the war.

# Best Inner Turmoil

WILD LIFE is proud to present the best bad times any Oregonian ever had, as experienced by Oregon ex-golden boy Larry Colton. Colton, who, as a professional baseball pitcher is best 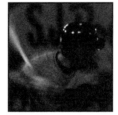 remembered not just for his 122-mile-an-hour fastball, but for his words of wisdom to younger teammates ("Remember, men, it's not whether you win or lose, but how good you look in your uniform"), has adapted the following totems of modern suffering from his classic tale of a golden boy gone haywire, *Goat Brothers*.

Our story begins as Larry has just been dumped by his gorgeous first wife, Denise. He leaves her—and his young daughter, Wendy—in Seattle in the clutches of Denise's handsome model-writer (and soon to be abusive alcoholic) boyfriend.

# CRISIS ONE

by LARRY COLTON

As I pulled back on the highway, I was a lost soul at the crossroads. A few years before, when I graduated from Cal Berkeley, I had it dicked. I had a bonus contract ($8,000) with the Philadelphia Phillies, a Chevy Impala with moon hubcaps, and a gorgeous girlfriend whose mother was a movie star, Hedy Lamarr. This was the way I dreamed it when I was in high school, where I captained the varsity and presided over the senior class.

Now I didn't know where I was going or what I would do when I got there. All I knew was that my pride wouldn't let me stay in Seattle. Nor did I want to go back to California. Too far away from Wendy, too many old friends to face.

I drove south on I-5, stopping in Portland. I had been there several times on road trips while playing in the Pacific Coast League. I liked the idea of being in a town where nobody knew me and I could just disappear into the pine trees, not having to explain what went wrong. Alone to sort through my gloom. I checked into the Heathman Hotel, where I'd stayed on road trips. The bellhop remembered me. From my eighth-floor room, I stared down at the teenagers cruising Broadway below and recalled how, only a month earlier, I had joined my teammates in a water-balloon drop on those cruisers. Seemed like fun at the time.

I was shell-shocked. Within a week my baseball career had ended and my wife had left me. I was camped out in a hotel in a strange town where I had no friends, no family, no job, no clue for the future. I had $800 in traveler's checks, a Buick station wagon I had to sell, an ounce of dope, and two suitcases of clothes, half mod, half country club. Aimlessly I walked the streets until dawn, ignoring the steady drizzle. It was September 15, 1970.

## BEST EX-MUCKRAKER: LOCAL HERO RON BUEL

Just about the time Larry Colton's suffering was beginning to hit its stride, Ron Buel's star shot to the top of the Oregon sky. Ron was Oregon's first power-broker baby boomer, a true revolutionary who did more than anyone else to integrate the post–World War II generation into Portland's economic and social fabric—first by getting his best friend, 31-year-old Neil Goldschmidt, elected mayor of Portland, then by founding *Willamette Week*. Buel embodied what makes journalism great: fighting for good against evil, addressing the towering wrongs, crusading for the poor, and of course, most importantly, really pissing people off.

Short, stocky, and droll, except when he was screaming, Ron Buel made Lou Grant look like Jimmy Olson. He built the first "establishment" voice for the consumer class that rose out of the ashes and haze of Woodstock and Vietnam.

I met Ron while editing the magazine *One Dollar.* The rumor was that *Willamette Week* would eat Portland's "alternative" print media alive. *One Dollar* had good writers, among them Pierre Ouellette, John Shirley, and Mikal Gilmore; and better yet, delicious advertisers—hip stores and boutiques. And I was amazed to hear him say, "I like what you're doing. We won't touch you."

And he didn't. He had bigger fish to fry—namely, the *Oregonian,* then a daily made out of local car crashes, "society news," and wire service clips.

Buel was the best editor the *Oregonian* never had. He scared them into going from bad to mediocre. The guy was fearless. And he wasn't some wimpy long-haired leftist on the outside looking in. He took on city hall after he had *run* city hall. He tackled fat-cat utilities, fat-cat politicians, and fat-cat business. Yes, he had a "progressive wing of the Democratic Party" agenda—but

Buel would expose the wolves who had suckled him if those animals did wrong in the woods.

As a columnist, I milked an effective niche: I was a liar. I "interviewed" then Mayor Frank Ivancie (think of a taller, handsomer, dumber Richard Nixon) and credited him with writing the power riffs to Jimi Hendrix's "Foxy Lady" and "Third Stone from the Sun," as well as lyrics including "Roll over Rover, and let Jimi take over." I also claimed Frank introduced Mick Jagger to Bianca, thus sparing the rock megastar "a life of Preparation H and chance restroom encounters."

Ivancie's lawyers threatened to sue. I asked Buel, "Was that too far out?"

"No," he said. "It wasn't far out enough."

My mandate: Get away with murder. "Kill 'em with kindness," Buel instructed. I claimed that Portland Police Chief Ron Still had written a novel entitled *Cars I Want* which appeared to be only page after page of classified ads for used hot rods, but which had been praised to the sky in the *New York Times.*

More lawyers. A heady time. Finally, I got a call from a writer with the news that I was about to be fired. The writer was so upset he'd developed a stutter. "They think Ba-ba-ba-Buel's gone nu-nu-nuts and that you are proof."

But Buel couldn't have cared less. And I was ecstatic. I had at last achieved the position I had always coveted: teacher's pet.

Sadly, Ron retired to Nike not long after that. The paper had financial problems and he had become a man who was carrying too much baggage. He had taken stand after stand after stand and he had pissed off too many people. I for one was very sorry to see him go.

—M. C.

# BEST PRELUDE TO SUBURBAN APOCALYPSE

## BY PIERRE OUELLETTE

EDITOR'S NOTE: The following is excerpted from Pierre Ouellette's science fiction thriller, *The Deus Machine*.

Here's the setup: In the near future, all hell has broken loose. A secret military cable has created DEUS, a bio-computer complex, outside west Portland. But DEUS has developed a mind of its own and has conjured up a whole new world of monsters and real-estate-devouring horror.

Climb abroad with our hero, unemployed computer expert Michael Riley, as he surveys the scene. Note the quiet relish with which the author sends his very own real-life neighborhood to its doom.

↓

As the helicopter climbs higher and leaves the Oregon Health Sciences Center behind, Michael gets a classic lesson in urban geography. Directly beneath is the topographic spine of the West Hills, which bisects the Portland area into old and new. The old is behind them—the central city, the docks, the ships, the refineries, the smokestacks, the walkup apartments, the residential grid. The new is ahead, where the flat farmland of the Tualatin Valley offers no natural resistance to the relentless push of urban progress, and the suburbs have already covered 15 miles in a mad dash toward the Coast Range on the far side of the valley, absorbing entire communities along the way, turning feed stores into tanning salons, tractor dealers into Honda salesrooms.

But now something is pushing back. Some ten miles distant, a circular area of brilliant green has formed to the southwest. At its center the green sea is nearly solid, except for the thin lines that mark streets and the tiny squares that are parking lots and roofs of buildings and homes. At last report, the Mutant Zone was about 15 feet deep, and had somehow rubberized and collapsed most trees above this height. Farther from the center, the green sea explodes outward in fragments and clumps like a terrestrial version of a globular cluster of stars, so the concentration falls off rapidly toward its circumference. At this height, it appears as though a rowdy growth of moss is rolling over the tidy geometry of the urban landscape.

From a set of remaining landmarks, it is already obvious that the ParaVolve complex is at the center of the malignant growth.

In the chopper, Michael turns his attention to the foreground and the Mutant Zone. Every major road is throttled with cars, which have plunged the street system into terminal gridlock with emergency services paralyzed. Major fires glow like cigarette tips and send fuzzy black pillars of smoke into the overcast sky as office buildings, stores, and apartments burn out of control, with no hope of salvation by the fire department. As they fly over Highway 217, hordes of people march south along its shoulders past the queue of dead cars, past other people lying on the embankments, people too sick or afflicted to walk.

Thirty seconds later, they encounter the outer perimeter of the Mutant Zone and see the bright

green islands of metastasized growth that seem to glow with a vengeful illumination among the houses, apartments, and buildings. The chopper pilot takes them lower, and they spot their first medugator, which is patiently cruising across the parking lot of a supermarket. As they close within 25 feet, the beast acknowledges their presence by rolling its eye pods up to stare at the belly of the chopper.

"From all reports, they don't attack people, but everything else is fair game," comments Dr. Tandy. "I wonder why."

## Best Inner Turmoil

When we left idealistic young pro baseball pitcher Larry Colton at the end of Crisis One, his wife had run off with a blond superstud and left him quasi-penniless. Also, baseball-wise, he had been blown off the mound.

But cast adrift in Portland, Larry found that his bad luck is just beginning . . . .

## CRISIS TWO

by LARRY COLTON

I looked like a musty Buffalo Bill after a hard winter—fringe coat, shaggy hair, droopy mustache. It wasn't bad enough that I was suffering through a marital and career crisis. Now I was convinced I was dying. It started as a painful knot in back of my right shoulder and then just kept spreading . . . from my neck to my armpit and then all the way down my right side. It felt as if I had an elephant and his brother standing on my shoulder. I was up to 15 aspirins a day. I couldn't lift my right arm; the muscles were in atrophy; my appetite was gone.

But I wouldn't go to the doctor.

It was November 1970, two months after my last pitch and Denise's pronouncement that she was ditching me for another man. I had rented a one-bedroom clapboard house on half an acre in Garden Home, a wooded suburb of Portland. It had apple and plum trees and a pumpkin patch in the backyard. Not that I cared. I was in a deep funk, living alone in a strange city, positive I was headed to that great coast league in the sky. Dead at 29.

Every day was the same: I woke up at noon, drove downtown in my '59 Chevy pickup camper, and went for a walk along the Willamette River, then up to picturesque Washington Park overlooking the city. Walking

**IT FELT AS IF I HAD AN ELEPHANT AND HIS BROTHER STANDING ON MY SHOULDER.**

and worrying. Worrying and walking . . . the melancholy lyrics of "It Don't Matter to Me," a sappy song by Bread, echoing through my mind, its words trying to convince me that it was okay if Denise needed some time to be free . . . that it didn't matter to me if she took up with someone who was better than me, because her happiness was all I wanted.

No longer able to lift my arm, I finally went to the doctor. He referred me to a neurologist, although judging from his concern, he might as well have been sending me straight to the mortician. The neurologist, a pompous twit, looked even more concerned. I weighed 165, ten pounds less than my beanpole days in college, 55 less than my chubbo spring training of 1966.

"What do you think it might be?" I asked the neurologist.

"That it could be a tumor on the spine or ALS."

"ALS?"

"Lou Gehrig's disease," he replied.

"What should I do?"

"Go home and put your left hand on one side of the mirror, your right hand on the other, then look yourself square in the eyes and tell yourself there's a 50-50 chance you're dying."

# PECKERNECK COUNTRY

BY WALT CURTIS

Lots of stumps. Brush. And peckerwoods about the size of a logger's middle finger. The thickness of a choker cable, or less. No self-respecting gypo'd try to cut that stuff. He needs something he can sink his crosscut into. A diesel cat pulling three-footers down a muddy logging road, Lyle. Lyle is a dead boyhood friend who used to work on his old man's logging crew. That's when money grows on trees.

How do you skin a cat, whistle punk? First, you pull his foreskin back. Yowlee!

Pecker poles. Yessirree and dipsydoodle, that's where Peckerwood Pete lives and puts his good ear, the cauliflower, stump-blasted one, next to the bone-bleached fire-burned totem to fathom the rhythms the woodpeckers beat. Ratatat-tat! Forest rock-and-roll. Rockin' ruffed grouse thumps on a hollow log drum. Woody Woodpecker and Woody Guthrie are good neighbors. Pete puts his schnozola in the breeze tryin' to catch a whiff of menstruatin' doe.

Hot-blooded old duffer dripping Copenhagen juice on Fritz the frisky chipmunk. Sort of gets on your nerves. When cabin fever sets in. That sound of whanging woodpecker whacking off on a spar pole. The running creek is a watery flute, soothing the jittery noodle. Burnt bacon and blasting caps for breakfast.

Out past Vernonia in November. Where'd you get that gosh-darned name? Vernon's home? A type of begonia? No pretty flower'd grow out here on a stump farm! So long, it's been good ter have known ya. Vera of Vernonia. Veer off, Buster! On your own. The maples are Chinese red and Florentine gold, just like silken patterns on women's dresses. Nighties. Of the '30s. Or saffron leaf falls on Buddhist monks immolating themselves on the bonfires of the season.

I hear a doe rattling the second growth. Let's shoot a sound shot. Even the cottontails are scared shitless. Ever' peckerneck carries two or three thirty-ought-sixes or Savage thirty-thirties in the back window of his beat-up pickup just to let you know who's the boss. He is. He could blow a hole in the gut of a buck at half a mile or blast daylight in a man the size of a galvanized washtub on the rainiest day in wet heaven. Do you remember when Mom used to wash out clothes on a washboard in the backyard, then hang them on the line to dry?

Out past Vernonia where the logging trestles are marvels of the world. The size of an Egyptian pyramid. Spanning the canyon. I lost my head and heart in Mist, Oregon. On the sensuous Nehalem, splattered with bright yellow maple leaves, handprints, like the patterns on a woman's dress. A liquid Jewell. The river is.

I've never been to Buxton. What the fuck's in Buxton? Where all the male deer have a ball. Antlers in the Treetops by Who Goosed a Fourpoint. Drinking Blitz beer and hunting humans.

A general store. A goddamn barking dog. As the white mist rises from dun grass meadows like smoke from past campfires, or smoldering slash burn. You can tell there was once giant lumber out in this country by the monumental stumps, high up above

the ground, with huge notches cut in them yet, platforms for two-fisted men to stand on and earn some blisters. A boy blows on a pennywhistle agitating the fleas in the mutt's ears. He howls some more. Buxton— you've been there!

The ghostly fields of the dear dead past. Why do they call them "pastures"? Because that's where the past manures and inures. The waxing bright almost-full moon is like a magic chicken egg rolled out from some hidden straw nest, in a silvery, weathered, tumbling barn. Where's the mysterious chicken who laid this gigantic egg?

Well, I'll tell ya, greenhorn stranger. The hen is hid up in the rafters because of all the chicken prickers around here. Terrible strange critters.

A-cluckin', they pull feathers off the neck of a chicken. Pluck it, jerk it off, as they plunk it! Drives the bird insane. A-squawkin' and a-runnin'. You're darn lucky to find an egg up in the sky. Cock a doodle do!

You don't say? The hell you say! I didn't know times was so tough.

If you stick out your pecker just to take a pee, the bird's pecker, the beak I mean, might hit you on the neck. Make it go numb clear up to yer elbow. That's another reason they

**I HEAR A DOE RATTLING THE SECOND GROWTH. LET'S SHOOT A SOUND SHOT.**

call it Peckerneck Country. And every cow for miles around is stump-broke.

Loggers are a fiercely horny breed. They bunch up cock-knockin' with peevees that they use to pole logs with in the racing river. If a man falls in, his hard-on is washed away when his tin pants sink him straight to the bottom. I seen a logger leave his cork boots on and prickly red woolen long johns in bed in a whorehouse out by Pittsburg. But kicked the woman out for eatin' soda crackers! What a tinhorn! Even the widowmaker couldn't knock a lick of sense into that knothead.

You better be able to back up what you say, butthole!

If I eat enough beans, I sure enough kin.

"What'd he do? Is that why he's sleepin' in the truck—his old lady kicked him out?" And other wisdom. At the Sunset Inn. On Highway 26, headed back to Portland. It's like Pete smellin' at a wide spot in the middle of the road where a skunk got run over. I love the taste of that old-time religion. "Ain't That a Shame" playing on the jukebox. I walk back to the washroom. The rain falls like tears. Logger graffiti covering the slippery walls. Wanted: two short niggers for mud flaps.

I felt like a logging truck was lifted off my shoulders when I left that redneck tavern, going to hell in a hand basket. The Hamms beer at 40 cents a bottle the bargain. Must've been happy hour.

The "pecker tracks" are everywhere in the wilderness. In the woods, on the ceiling, in your hair, on the walls of my eyes. Sticky stuff! Pecker is a wild animal. Like a cougar or a bobcat. Capable of touching and attacking you anywhere. One of the most dangerous game in the world!

If you can't say nuthin' nice about nobody, don't say nuthin' atall. If you cain't keep it funny and clean, don't mention it in polite company. We'll wash your mouth out with soap. This goes for a town, a country, a locale, a mountain boomer's home, a neck of the woods, a piece of ass, your buddy's girlfriend on the rag, an enemy, a game being hunted, a mother-in-law, another starry cosmos worse than this last.

So long, it's been good to Vernonia. Keep it to yourself. I won't say nuthin' bad about it, if you don't. Pecker Tree Cuntry. Where the pricks live back in the woods. And the deer are smoochin' at ya and winkin' eyes begging you to come and get up on a stump.

The "pecker tracks" are everywhere. Sign of the most dangerous game in the world. Capable of attacking you anywhere. Even when you're driving down the road in your pickup truck.

# Best Inner Turmoil

Can it get any worse for King of Oregon's Ex-Young Larry Colton? Of course it can. It always has, it always will. When we left the newly ex-professional baseball pitcher at the end of Crisis Two, his doctor had just informed him that there was a 50-50 chance he was going to die. Does he? Read on.

# CRISIS THREE

by LARRY COLTON

I was at the hospital five agonizing days for tests, including a myogram, electro-neuroanalysis, and a biopsy. I lay flat in bed, no word from Dr. Pompous as to the results. He never even peeked his head in the door. On the sixth day, he finally showed up. He was wearing his power-of-life-and-death face. I bolted upright—a definite no-no so soon after a myogram—and barfed Jell-O all over the doctor's leg. I was aiming for his crotch.

"The good news is that it's not a tumor or ALS," he said. "The bad news is I don't know what it is. Your tests were all negative. We'll just have to keep monitoring it. You can go on about your life."

My head ached too badly to celebrate.

# EXTRA! EXTRA! AN ENTIRE SECTION DEVOTED TO JOHN SHIRLEY!!

# PUNK

"John Shirley writes ghastly horror novels that scare the living crap out of people. A lot of people are pretty scared by John Shirley. When people actually meet John face-to-face they become even more scared."

—BRUCE STERLING

"God is dead and I want his job."

—JOHN SHIRLEY

Some people throw parties, John Shirley threw nightclubs. On weekends during the punk explosion, Shirley would simply *heist* a whole floor of any empty building he happened to find around Portland. In would come the bands, the beer kegs, the biker security, and the masses.

When the police arrived, bloody bare-chested John would be the last to be seen flying out a fire escape.

Meantime, industrious John was writing novels. He had maybe 30 paperback sci-fi novels published by the time he was 30. Would there, could there have been a *Blade Runner*, an *Escape from New York*, a *Road Warrior*, or a *Neuromancer* without Shirley? No. For Shirley was, in William Gibson's words, "Cyber-punk's Patient Zero, first locus of the virus, certifiably virulent."

Gibson—whose novel *Neuromancer* launched the "cyberpunk" movement in science fiction—gives credit for creation of the cyberpunk sci-fi genre where credit is due. "That Oregon boy remembered today with a lank forelock of dirty blond, around his neck a belt in some long-extinct mode of patent elastication; orange pigskin, fashionably rotted to reveal cruel links of rectilinear chrome spring: Johnny Paranoid, convulsing like a galvanized frog on the plywood stage of some basement coffeehouse in Portland . . .

Discovering Shirley's fiction was like hearing Patti Smith's "Horses" for the first time: the archetypical form passionately reinhabited by a debauched yet strangely virginal practitioner, one whose very ability to do this *at all* was constantly thrown into question by the demands of what was in effect a shamanist act."

I met John when I was fresh out of college and he was maybe 19. I'd just walked into my friend Dennis Kealey's house. A yellow-haired blur came sliding and screaming down Kealey's banister to land with a crash at my feet. Some tall blond kid in full American Indian regalia—feather headdress, war paint, buckskin duds. An out-stretched hand, a firm shake, and a brisk "Hey. I'm John Shirley."

A year later, as editor of *One Dollar*—a Portland monthly magazine—I published his first short story. He brought it in pieces and I assembled it like a jigsaw puzzle.

He used to worry that he was "a poseur." Which made no sense to me—the John Shirley I knew was as nailed down as a jailhouse floor—until I realized, he's right. He among this legion of lost souls was the most found soul of all.

Here is a seminal John Shirley short story John wrote for a Portland underground newspaper in 1976, that wan, blemished year of the United States' bicentennial.

—M.C.

# TRICENTENNIAL

## by JOHN SHIRLEY

### I

"Precisely what do you suggest I do about it?" asked Ollie.

"You're hedging. You know what has to be done. You got to go get one," said his sister Lem coldly.

"Look—we can make one for him out of cardboard—"

"No. He wouldn't fall for it. He has to have the real thing. Cloth. With the official Tricentennial medallion on the stick. He's not *that* far gone. And if we don't do it Pops won't sign the release and he'll die without turning over the stall to us and then we'll be out in the street. And *you* are the oldest, Ollie-boy. So you are elected."

"I don't know if I want to stay in this grimy cubey. I could be in the Angels. I got a Hell's Angels Officer's School commission and I

Army, except they've got the Rape Decree to back up anything they do. But big deal. You get your rocks off but do you get a decent place to sleep?"

"Okay, okay, then. But—I ain't going alone. No way. If we're gonna get it for him, *you're* goin' with me, backup. Because there's no way to go two big ones on 53rd alone without getting it in the back . . . . Look, are you sure we can't get one in Building Three?"

"I'm sure. I've called around. All the dispensaries are out of them except Eleven."

"Maybe we can roll the old man on the 100th floor. He's got one."

"He's got microwave barriers. We'd fry."

Ollie sighed. "Then let's go. And when we bring it back I hope to God the old sonuvabitch is happy with it. Because if he's not, Father or no Father—"

"Okay, don't get toxed. Let's go."

## II

At first, the metal streets seemed almost deserted. The frags and the joy-boy gangs and the hustlers and sliders were there, just out of sight, but Security was keeping them off the street for the Tricentennial Procession. Ollie'd heard the proces-

sion might traverse the 53rd Level, but he'd assumed it would move through some less dilapidated end of the street. Maybe it all looked this way.

Crusted with gray-white scum from exhalations of methane engines and human pores, the kelp-fiber walls of the five stories visible on the 53rd Level bulged slightly outward with the weight of excess population—each stall cubey held at least five people more than regulations.

Ollie cradled the Smith & Wesson .44 he'd received at age 14, on his Weaponing Day. He held it now, five years later, as another man might have clasped a crucifix, and he whispered to it piously, while his eyes swept the rust-pitted streets, sorting through the heaps of litter waiting for the dumper, the piles of garbage, the half-dozen corpses that were as much a part of any street as the fire hydrants. The streetlights extending from the warped and peeling faces of the buildings were all functioning and the vents near the ceiling within the plasteel girder underpinnings of the 54th Level were all inhaling, judging from the thinness of the smogs wreathing the dark doorwells. There were only about 25 homeless or gangbugs on the street and no cars—nearly desolation, compared to

> "YOU DON'T BELIEVE ALL THAT STUFF THEY TELL YOU AT THE ANGELS RECRUITING OFFICE ABOUT THE CYCLE CORPS, DO YOU?"

any other time. Apparently the Procession was near.

Ollie and Lem, crouching just inside the doorway to their home-building, rechecked their weapons and scanned the sidewalk for booby-traps. "I don't see anything we can't handle," Lem said.

"We can't see into the alleys or doorways or that subway entrance. And—" Ollie was interrupted by the blast of a siren. A few ragged silhouettes shuffling the street scurried for doorways at the wailing from the cornice speakers. Others hardly looked up. "Looks like all that's left are dope-heads who don't know from shit. Christ, they're so far gone they don't know the clear-streets when they hear it."

As the siren wound down Lem asked, "How long since you been on the street?"

"This is the first time in three years. Looks pretty much the same. Only more dope-heads."

"Always more dope-heads. They don't get gutted much because they don't have any money."

"Well, let's go. Maybe we can dash the whole two blocks. I mean, since the streets are almost empty—"

"You haven't been on the streets in three years. You don't know—" Lem began.

"You're jimmy for venturing onto the streets when you don't need to. We've got everything we need on our floor, all the dispensaries and spas are there, and it's the same everywhere anyway and since you can't leave the Zone without a permit or unless you go with the troops, why bother?"

"We've got a half hour to get to Building Eleven. Let's do it."

Both of them were dressed in scum-gray clothing, camouflage, their faces smeared with gray ash so their pallor would blend, as much as possible, into the walls.

Lem, tall and thin, the fire in her curly red hair extinguished with ash, stood and checked her brace of throwing knives, then inspected the Uzi she'd got two years before on her Weaponing Day, and the cans of acid bombs affixed to the two khaki belts crisscrossing her chest.

Ollie examined his own equipment, certified that the extra pistol he kept in his shoulder-holster was loaded and ready, the knives on springs lashed to his forearms primed. His .44 loaded and cocked.

Lem behind, walking backward to cover the rear, they set off, looking like some odd two-headed predatory creature. The lineaments of the dour metal streets converged in a mesh of streetlamps, girders, stairways, and furtive figures, made tenuously unreal by the smudged air and dim mucus-yellow lighting. The vista, shackled by metal ceiling and street merged in the distance, had all the elegance of a car crumpled into a cube by a hydraulic-press compactor. Ollie adjusted his infrared visors to see into the darker lairs. A frag, there to the right. The frag was a woman, left breast burned off to make room for a rifle-strap, a patch over her right eye. She waited, leaning back against the wall, her lower half hidden by a multiplex heap of refuse. Ollie hadn't been on the street in years, but the indications were the same: the suspect looked casual, relaxed—and that was bad. If she wasn't planning to attack them, she'd look tensed, in defense. So she was preparing to jump.

She was 20 feet off, on the low right, standing in the well of a barred basement doorway.

They carried $40 for their Old Man's toy. Frags could smell money. Even penniless, they'd be jumped for their clothes, guns, and on general principle.

The frag made as if to tie her bootlace. A signal. "Down!" Ollie cried.

Lem and Ollie went to a crouch as the woman who had seen her accomplice's signal leapt from the doorway immediately to her right, and only her M-16's jamming saved them. Lem stepped in and, with an underhand cut, gutted the frag and withdrew the stiletto before he could reach for another weapon. By this time the other frag was swinging her rifle around to take aim. Ollie had already leveled the .44.

He squeezed the trigger, the gun barked, the jolt from the recoil hurt his wrist. The one-eyed woman caught it in the gut, was thrown back, rebounded from the wall, and pitched forward to fall on her face. Blood marked a Rorschach visage leering in red on the wall behind her.

He heard Lem firing at the other frags attracted by the gunshots. A young man fell, pistol clattering into the gutter. The others found cover.

"C'mon!" They sprinted, running low to the ground, gaining another 40 feet, three-quarters of the first block behind them. Another block-and-a-quarter, Ollie thought. Something lobbed in a wallowing tinny arc struck the sticky metal sidewalk and clattered past Ollie's right leg; he turned and grabbed Lem by the forearm, dragging her into the shelter of a doorway. The grenade exploded on the other side of the wall, fragments of the flimsy wall-fiber flew, laughter erupted from nearby frag-niches to echo from the distant ceiling, laughter as acid-drenched as the shrapnel that took out two dope-heads across the street. The blue smoke cleared.

A bullet struck the wall by Ollie's head, flying splinters stung his scalp. Swallowing fear—it had been three years—he crouched, panning his gunsight back and forth over the gray-black-engraved prospect. Sniper? From where? He looked up—the window, fourth floor. Glint off a barrel. He snatched free an acid cartridge and clipped it hastily on the launch spring welded to the underside of his pistol's barrel.

He cocked, squinted, and fired. The sniper's rifle went off at the same moment, another shot too high. Then the acid-bomb exploded in the sniper's apartment. A scream that began as a rumble, went higher and higher in pitch, finishing as a bubbling whine that merged perfectly with the return-ing off-streets siren, a growing, piercing ululation. The sniper, slap-ping at his boiling skin, threw him-self whimpering out the window and fell, writhing, three stories, striking the ground headfirst. Stripping the corpses of the sniper, joy-boys, and the two dead women, the frags were momentarily distracted. So Ollie and Lem sprinted, zigzagging to make poor targets.

Bolting across the intersection, they drew fire. Four strident *cracks*, four *pings*—four misses. They achieved the opposite corner. Crouched behind a conical heap of excrement and plastic cans, their left side protected by the extruding metal sidewalls of a stairway. "Three-quar-ters of a block left," said Lem.

But frags were closing in from the right, at least a dozen piebald figures creeping hastily from shadow to shadow like scuttling cockroaches.

One of the frags caught another unawares and slipped him a blade. There was a bubbling cough and that was all.

"One less," said Lem. "But they'll cooperate to kill us before they turn on each other again."

A scratchy recorded fanfare announced the Tricentennial Procession. The street was 20 yards from gutter to gutter. The Procession filled the street for half a block: two long, six-wheeled armored red-white-and-blue sedans surrounded by 12 Security Cycles. A recorded voice from the chrome-fanged grill of the front sedan announced over and over:

REJOICE INDEPENDENCE DAY REJOICE INDEPEN-DENCE DAY REJOICE INDE-PENDENCE DAY MAYOR WEL-COMES ALL CITIZENS TO SEYMOR COLISEUM FOR PM PUBLIC EXECUTIONS PARTY REJOICE INDEPENDENCE DAY REJOICE REJOICE.

Dimly, through the green-tinted window of the low, steel-plated limo, Ollie could make out the faces of the High Priest of the International

Church of Sun Moon sitting beside the man he'd appointed as mayor, whose name Ollie could not recall. A few token bullets bounced from the limo's windshield. The silhouettes within waved at the faces crowding the windows. A handful of excrement splattered the roof, cleaned away an instant later by tiny hoses in the windshield frame. One of the Security Cycles shot a microwave shell into the apartment from which the excrement had been thrown; there was a white flash and a scream, and a thin wisp of smoke from the shattered window.

The Security Cycles were three-wheeled motorbikes, propelled, like the limousines, by methane engines fueled by gases extracted from human excrement. Issuing blue flatulence, they rolled slowly abreast of Ollie and Lem. The cops inside, figures of shiny black leather, heads completely encased in black-opaqued helmets, were protected by bells of transparent plasteel from which their various weapons projected cobra snouts. The cop nearest Ollie methodically snuffed dope-heads and careless frags with casual flares of his handlebar-mounted microwave rifle. "Hey," Ollie breathed, "maybe they'll help us. If you call them for help getting to the corner they can't refuse, seeing as we're right in front of them and all. Hell, with the High Priest watching . . . "

"Ollie, don't be an asshole—"

But Ollie was already out in the street, waving his arms, shouting, "We need an escort, just a little farther, we are citizens, we have to go to Building Eleven to buy a—"

He threw himself flat and rolled, wincing as the invisible microwave beam singed his back. The cop fired again but Lem had thrown a smoke-bomb, and Ollie took advantage of the thick yellow billowing to return to cover.

"Wish I could afford one of these microwave rifles," Lem remarked wistfully.

"Hey, Lem, maybe if we keep just back of the procession we can use it for cover and get the rest of the way."

Lem nodded and they were off.

Most of the frags were flattened to avoid the microwave beams; the cops ignored their shielded rear, so Ollie and Lem sprinted along behind, and Building Eleven loomed ahead. Ollie grinned. There! The stairs!

They were scrambling the two flights up the stairs when the doors to Building Eleven swung open and a pack of joy-boys, none of them over 12 years old, stampeded directly into Lem and Ollie's reflexive gunfire. But there were too many of them to spray dead at short range. Five went down, another ten were upon them—naked but for belts bristling with makeshift knives. Their gap-toothed mouths squalling, drooling like demented elves, they chattered and snarled gleefully. Their sallow, grimy faces— seen as blurs personifying aggression, now—were pockmarked, the eyes dope-wild. Swinging the gun-butt in his right hand, the spring-snapped knife in his left, Ollie slashed and battered at the small faces, faces like rotted jack-o'-lanterns, and time slowed: fragments of skull and teeth flew, black-nailed hands clawed at his face, his own blood clouded his visors.

Ollie plowed forward, kicking, elbowing, feeling a twisted shard of metal bite deep into his thigh, another below his left shoulder blade, another in his right pectorals. He was two feet from the door. He left his knife in someone's ribs. He glanced at Lem; three of them were on her back, clinging like chimp-children, clawing relentlessly at her head, gnawing her ears with ragged yellow teeth. He dragged them off her with his left hand, wrenching viciously to keep them off his own back, and brained another who flailed wildly at his own eyes—and then he and Lem were through the door.

It was cool and quiet outside.

A young man, a custodian chewing synthabetal and squinting at them, leaning on his mop, said, "You got some holes in you."

"Where—" Ollie had to catch his breath. He felt weak. Blood soaking his right leg—have to bind that before heading back, he thought, try again, ask: "Where we buy . . . flags?"

"Fifty-fourth level if he's got any left."

### III

Luck was with them. They made it back with only two more wounds. A .22 slug in Lem's right arm, a zip-gun pellet in Ollie's left calf.

Lem slumped outside the door to bind her wounds and rest. Ollie took the flag from her and staggered into their two-room apartment, stepped carefully over children sleeping on the crowded floor, tried not to stagger. He was dizzy, nauseated. The tiny cubicle seemed to constrict and whirl, the stained yellow-white curtains over the alcove where his father lay dying on an army cot became malignant leprous arms reaching for him. He cursed, his right hand gripping the small, rolled-up flag. He felt he could not walk another step.

Ollie sank into a chink of clear floor-space. He glanced wearily at one of the sleeping children. Eight-year-old Sandra. She woke, a pale, hollow-eyed child, nearly bald, a few strands of wispy flaxen hair. "You take this to Pops," he told her. "The flag. Tell him to sign the goddamn release."

Seeing the flag, the little girl's eyes flared. She snatched the bright banner away and ran out into the hall, ignoring Ollie's shouts.

She got three bucks for the flag from a man on the 100th Level.

A penny a year.

# PUNK STORY

## OREGON IN THE 1970S

"These are serious times. We are forced to re-evaluate our tactics. Gone are the days of clandestine meetings in dank cellars . . . . Our ultimate goal: eradication of the enemy (The Hippie)."

—FROM *Search and Destroy* MAGAZINE

Formica, of Formica and the Bitches, née Randee of Randee and the Randees, was restless. It was opening night at Revenge, Portland's premier New Wave dance hall, and she was petulant and impatient to rock. The club, a musty old walkup on the city's lower southwest side, was packed with Oregon's punk elite, dressed in the height of mondo bondo fashion—leather, short hair in every Crayola hue, chains, and tight, tight pants for everyone.

One hundred fifty fans screamed for action.

Formica led the Bitches onstage. Taller than most men, she had salt-white skin, and her lips were so thick that they looked like the wax lips kids used to get in their trick-or-treat bag at Halloween.

"Okay now," she shouted in a cross-cultural stab nonpareil, "we're gonna sing 'Louie, Louie' for the coal miners." The Bitches whacked into it.

Formica howled! Formica strutted! *Louie Louie we gotta go yeah yeah yeah yeah!* The drummer, with her white skin, big black eyes, and shiny mop of straight black hair that glistened under the stage lights, looked like an angelic vampire. She whacked her drumstick with a blurring regularity suggestive of superfast windshield wipers. Chewing openmouthed in time to the music, she adjusted a wad of bubble gum with her tongue and it ballooned forward between her teeth. She was 14. A third Bitch, Andrea, pounded out a throbbing backbeat on guitar. Outfitted in jeweled teardrop glasses, tight black pants, a T-shirt that reads Rock Against Racism, and boots with needle heels, she looked like a glitter Bolshevik from Oz.

On the dance floor everyone pogo-ed. Après the mosh pit, a lost art form. Ideally pogo-ing was accomplished with hands and feet bound. You and your partner jumped up and down and tried to strangle each other in time to the music.

Repertoire exhausted after three songs, Formica and Co. exited the stage and in came the leader of Portland's first all-punk band, King Bee. Known to the phone company as Mark Stanley, to his readers as Mark Sten, and to the rest of the populated universe as Stenula—when the mood struck he wore fangs—Stanley/Sten/Stenula was designed to stop the hearts of every suburban mom and dad who ever had late-night horrors about the whereabouts of tardy teenage daughters.

Oozing into the room in long, narrow sections, big eyes beaming all over the place, hand-rolled cigarette hanging out one corner of his mouth, Stenula looked as if he had been assembled in Dr. Frankenstein's laboratory by Ricky Nelson. He went to Reed College back in the days when you had to have a big brain to get in. From his experience came his scholarly classic, "Confessions of an American Glue Sniffer."

Stenula had helped plan this coming-out party here at the Revenge with John Shirley. Shirley, then 24,

looked like a poster boy for what he so recently was: a member in bad standing of the U.S. Coast Guard. Blond, short-haired, Gatsby handsome. This was years before he was to become the founder, with William Gibson, of cyberpunk fiction, but he had already sold two novels and become the protégé of Harlan Ellison, who rhapsodized that in John he had "finally met an equal."

Shirley had hung out with the Sex Pistols, whose fans he enthused "looked like things found drowned at the beach." The Sex Pistols were tough—they beat each other up onstage and barfed on people at airports—but America destroyed them. They couldn't handle Houston.

Shirley returned to Portland to form Terror Wrist, which was to cap the evening at Revenge.

Singing lead, Shirley appeared onstage wearing a spiked leather dog collar. Stripping off his shirt, he tore at his chest and stomach with his fingernails until his skin flamed with welts. Singing hard, he squeezed his neck until his eyes bugged out and his face turned purple. The pogo-ers loved it,but Shirley and Stenula had made a serious planning error that would doom this event: they hired bikers as security.

The bikers did not get the pogo. But they did get the old ultraviolence, the old twelve-on-one, the old stealing the show by throwing a member of Terror Wrist headfirst down a flight of stairs.

Portland Punk. No product of Woodstock Nation, not about peace and love. Stenula defined it as "reaction against peacock rock, hero guitar, 1970s pretty-boy superstar schlock" music for all the unhappy-faced kids who never "have a nice day." The New Wave Rock 'n' Roll Collective—home of sorts to Formica and the Bitches, Stenula, self-described "urban aborigine" John Shirley, et al.—was located in a great big mansion out in north Portland.

The rooms seemed bigger than they were because there was almost no furniture; just two or three chairs and a portable TV, in front of which sat a chubby little rocker in army fatigues. Her hair was chrome yellow and she was watching *All My Children* with the sound off. She showed me a photo of a youngish blond hippie wearing a T-shirt that read Powered by Blitz. "My old man," she explained.

"Your boyfriend?" I asked.

"Course not," she corrected, "My dad."

Mike King descended the stairs, rubbing sleep out of his eyes. He was a tall, dough-faced 19-year-old with braces. Even among Portland punks, Mike King had gone the extra mile. Descending that staircase, he wore a black kimono and shoul-dered a guitar with "Inept" scrawled across the side. His hair was black above his ears, white down the mid-dle. An orange line ran from each ear to each temple. This was puz-zling until I realized, *Mike dyed his hair with his glasses still on.*

King claimed his locks had been every color of the rainbow except chartreuse, puce, and sea green. Asked why not sea green, he replied, "Because sea green was a fad."

Saturday night at the Revenge—John Shirley's instant nightclub, made out of the third floor of an abandoned building John found downtown. Star billing goes to the Mentors. Years later the Mentors will be primal inspiration for Nirvana and Pearl Jam, but on this night in 1978 they are mostly famous for being so fundamentally charmless that no woman, no matter how desperate, would ever have any-thing to do with them.

They appeared in Arnold Palmer golf shirts and black executioner's hoods. "I can see you're all bored tonight," announced the drummer, "and wondering what I had for dinner."

With that he knifed into his golf shirt, and what was either dinner or chicken entrails spilled out. The Mentors called their music "secretary hump rock," and during their second set a woman dressed neck-to-ankles in skintight leather mounted the stage and beat them all with a whip.

Rozz Rezabek-Wright proved belle of the ball. Until recently he had been just another power-pop Peter Frampton manqué from Salem or Medford or someplace, but as lead singer in Negative Trend, he'd hit it big. His breakthrough came the night he put a garbage can over his head while singing "I Wanna Be Your Dog," and then leapt over a drum set and broke his arm in six places. It got him a spread in *Search and Destroy.*

With Stenula on bass, the Revenge Club rang with a ground-zero-at-Hiroshima sound as Rozz howled through "Human Failure":

*Wish your mama had taken the pill!*
*Your daddy hates you and he always will!*
*Cuz you're a HUMAN FAILURE,*
*HUMAN FAILURE!*

Rozz yanked off his shirt and belted into "Target for Disgust." His chest, like an immense, elongated chicken neck, had been graffiti-ed with nouns like "filth" and "hopeless." Black machinist's tape formed a circular target centered on his belly button.

He writhed around the stage howling "target for disgust"—and then heaved a glass of Coca-Cola in a crew-cut young lady's face. She maced him.

"I'm a target for disgust," he continued to bleat, tears streaming down his face, "a target for disgust!" Frantically, his pals threw water in his face, trying to get the mace out. But Rozz could handle it. In San Francisco an outraged Rozz fanatic had doused him in lighter fluid and tried to set him on fire before the cops dragged the guy away, flaming matches still in hand.

Ross scrambled to the top of a speaker and leapt into the crowd, microphone in hand, never missing a beat. His friends were still heaving water in his face; the stage was soaking wet. A lone biker became the unwilling voice of reason. "Stop it!" he shouted into a mike. "You can't throw water around all this electrical equipment! We're all gonna fry!"

Formica was leaving America. She couldn't take it anymore. All the disco-screamers, fast-food and psychedelic service stations. She and co-Bitch Andrea were headed for greener pastures. England. To hang out with the Clash.

Tonight the New Wave Collective was giving them a send-off. Rozz was there, tied up in a ball. He had his head and shoulders between his legs and was rolling around on the kitchen floor screaming into a microphone. This allowed everybody in the house to hear Rozz's innermost thoughts. Whether they wanted to or not. Rozz screamed stuff into the mike: "You're all insane! I'm a terrible guy! Dis! Gust! Ting!" etc, etc. In a party mood, he filled his cheeks with beer and spit it on anybody dumb enough to bend over and inspect him at his eye level.

Formica was in black. Black leather jacket, black blouse, black skintight pants, and black leather boots. She had refused to give me an interview, having locked herself in a bathroom covered with posters of the Dils, White Boy, Patti Smith, the Screamers, and the Lewd, and yelling, "Go away! You're just an icky capitalist reporter! Here to rip off our culture!"

Meanwhile, another creature sidled up to me. "Rozz used to be a homosexual," he hissed.

"Huh?"

"He used to be a fag," the guy repeated, and produced snapshots to prove it. Staring out from Polaroids was a tall skinny figure in a dress. It might or might not have been Rozz. I didn't know what to say. "Nice legs."

I picked up a copy of *Magazine X* off a table—documentation to make

up for my lost Bitches interview— and Mike King said he'd "kick my ass" if I didn't pay for it. Which could have presented a problem for Mike, for though he was over six feet tall, he had the muscle tone of a cherub.

Then the little drumming Bitch, the milk-skinned she-Dracula with the glistening maroon lips, wanted to know: "What is the Old Fart doing here?"

Gee, and to think, at the time I was only 29.          –M.C.

# Portland Cops:
# AMERICA'S BEST

Say what? How boooj-wa. How can we call WILD LIFE a revolutionary-Marxist-Leninist-People's guide to Oregon and name Portland as having the "Best Cops."

But think about it. Say you are a

heroic black revolutionary Trotskyite crackhead who, in your battle against the oppressor state, is liberating a Beaverton 7-Eleven of $320 cash and five cartons of Marlboros with a nickel-plated 9-millimeter at three-thirty one Saturday morning and bang, you're busted.

Which future do you want:

a) a hamheaded SWAT team "pig" slamming you in the back of a black-and-white, beating your head to bratwurst with a lead-core Kevlar truncheon? or

b) a nice yuppie with a $40 haircut, a badge, and a master's degree in Deviant Psych explaining how, after you do the hard five, you'll be eligible for your GED plus . . .

Yes, Portland cops carry guns. But fear not, Che. Just think of them as social workers who can kill you. Say, for example, you foil your arrest by grabbing the 7-Eleven clerk and holding him hostage. Pull that stunt in New York and the cops'll let you blow the clerk away and then yank your psychotic ass out of there, and 15 minutes later 250 different carp fishermen will be using you for chum on the Hudson. Pull that stunt in L.A. and the LAPD will call in an airstrike and then run over your goo with a tank. But in Portland, likely as not the cop will stretch yellow tape 20 blocks around the place and call in a helicopter with a flannel-shirted shrink hang-

ing out of it imploring through a megaphone, "Che, let's stop all this craziness and talk about your mom."

–M.C.

# Best Inner Turmoil

Careful readers will recall that, at the conclusion of Crisis Three, our narrator, King of the Ex-Young Larry Colton, didn't die of the mysterious disease that had laid him low for months.

Instead, he got married. To beautiful young Kathi. They had a baby, Sarah. Kathi went to nursing school and Larry tried to stay faithful. Will they live in the uninterrupted bliss Larry Colton so richly deserves? Was Albert Einstein dumber than a rock?

# CRISIS FOUR

by LARRY COLTON

It was Kathi's idea to go to Rooster Rock, a nude beach on the Columbia River 15 miles east of Portland. I agreed, not wanting to seem unhip, unliberated. These were the '70s.

We had been married four and a half years, and if there was such a thing as a driver's seat in a relationship, Kathi was now steering the bus.

In the early days of the marriage, when I was still sneaking phone calls to Denise, it was Kathi who was insecure. But somewhere along the way the tide had turned and I was the one feeling threatened. And suspicious. I sensed that as soon as she finished nursing school and could support herself, she'd blow me a kiss and head on down the road, taking Sarah with her.

We spread out our towels and stripped naked. Sarah, who was then three and a half, headed straight for the water. There were about 50 other nude sunbathers spread out along a quarter mile of beach. A small fleet of speedboats was anchored just offshore, the boaters drinking beer and ogling, as were the people with the binoculars on the cliff behind us. It seemed I was center stage in *Oh, Calcutta!*

"You sure you want to be here?" I asked.

"They're the ones with the problem, not me," my wife replied.

I suspected that Kathi, who had always been relatively modest about her body, was trying to make a statement about her new liberated state. She was attending a women's consciousness raising group once a week. She talked about needing her "space." Okay by me. I felt barely able to claim the spot my own body occupied—she was welcome to the rest of the remaining universe. When she stopped shaving her legs, I commented I preferred smooth legs on women, making it clear that I was

simply expressing my personal preference, not issuing an order. I was doing my best to be politically correct, but walking on marital eggshells.

After spreading Coppertone over my body, I pulled out a notebook and began to work on my latest freelance article, a feature chronicling a day in the seamy life of the Portland Greyhound depot. I'd come up with the idea after spending so much time there waiting for Wendy, 10, to get off the bus from Seattle for her bimonthly visits. I was to be paid only $150 for the story. Still, it was crucial money. Child-support money. With Kathi in nursing school, our finances were strained. After three years teaching at Adams High, I was burned out—and because I refused to take classes that had zero relevance to my actual teaching assignment, the school district was threatening to suspend me. The more I fought them, the more nervous Kathi got. "You've got a family to think about," she said. "You can't afford to lose your job."

Another family with a little girl Sarah's age arrived on the beach and set out their towels about 50 feet from us. In time, the little girl wandered over to us and began playing in the sand with Sarah. Soon, her naked father strolled over to make sure she wasn't bothering us. He stood next to our towel and struck up a conversation. Kathi was sitting up, eye to eye, so to speak, with this guy's penis. Here was my wife talking directly to another man's dick. I had not yet evolved to this stage of liberation. Especially considering that this guy was hung like Trigger.

It was the last time we went to Rooster Rock.

## UNDERSTANDING MEDIA

### BEST UNDERGROUND NEWSPAPER:

# P D X S

A newsprint hand grenade. This is the best alternative newspaper since the *Village Voice* actually was the *Village Voice*. Impossible not to read. *PDXS* is alluringly unpredictable and almost never stoops to dogma. Publisher Jim Redden's bright idea was to discard the traditional chassis of an underground newspaper— hack retread left-wing breast-beating—and resort to a much smarter framework: reason.

These guys are eons ahead of me on the evolutionary scale. Stuff I can't begin to comprehend is commonplace to them. For example, why it is important to rag on *Willamette Week*, the way *Willamette Week* rags on the *Oregonian*? *PDXS* keeps calling *Willamette Week* "the once-alternative newspaper" as if *WW* had abandoned a sacred creed. To me *WW* was never an alternative newspaper, it was simply an excellent alternative to the reactionary hayseed lapdog-to-the-establishment early-1970s *Oregonian*.

### BEST PUBLISHER:

# Feral House

O regon hosts wonderful book publishers. Graphic Arts Center Publishing Company publishes beautiful, lavish nature photography books as big as manhole covers, and nicely written too. But for audacity, originality, and relevance, who can compete with Adam Parfrey's nationally renowned Feral House?

Nobody. Check out: *Kooks: A Guide to the Outer Limits of Human Belief*, *Cad: A Handbook for Heels*, and what Feral House describes as "the most gruesome document of all time," *Tortures and Torments of the Christian Martyrs*. Books whose subjects tend to live between the edge of rational society and the edge of irrational society. Pygmy nymphomaniacs, two-headed babies, and folk from the Flat Earth Society (those so-called "live broadcasts" from the Apollo space program did look cheesy—was Neil Armstrong broadcasting from

Tranquility Base, or NBC Burbank?) to the bio of Charles "Smitty" Schmid, the charismatic, homicidal Elvis Presley lookalike who stuck crushed beer cans in the bottoms of his motorcycle boots to make himself taller and who, before Charles Manson, was the true modern American killer-scuzzbag archetype.

This isn't wacky tract publishing. The writing—from two dozen different authors—is sane, smart, compassionate, and often funny, without condescending to the subject matter—people who are dynamically deranged, murderously psychotic, and occasionally probably just plain *right*.

## BEST UNUSUAL PUBLICATION:
# Craphound

A phantasmagoria of clip art and ideas. A lot of cheery bizarre sex stuff. *Craphound's* encyclopedic exposé of local sleazemeister Robert "KOOL* Man" Duprey was the best case of killing a fat ant with a sledgehammer in literary history.

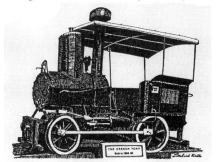

## BEST GROCERY STORE:
# Strohecker's: Supermarket of the Gods

### BY DAVID KELLY

*Oregon is home to the best grocery store in the world. Our leader samples its wares.*

I'm putting together a pretty good picnic lunch for four here, and with a little restraint I think we might keep the whole thing under $2,000. What gives me hope is that today Strohecker's seems to be, uncharacteristically, out of something.

For 94 years, all of them in the same family, Council Crest's neighborhood corner grocery has perched atop the slippery slope of Southwest Patton Road and Old Orchard, halfway up a mountain of million-dollar vintage Portland homes. Even at these fiscal altitudes the natives don't phone in orders for delivery anymore, but they don't expect to hear "no" from the staff, either. So executive chef Gena Eller (a grocery store with an executive chef? She's earned the title, it's that kind of place) is somewhat abashed as she admits that there won't be any more of the medallions of venison in port sauce until tomorrow.

Peasants who live down on the flats of distant Irvington like me can be even pickier for having had to ford the river and claw our way up from Goose Hollow. So the apparent limitlessness of Strohecker's was the first thing I noticed a couple of decades ago when I moved to Portland. Here, thousands of miles from my old Kentucky home, was a butcher who not only understood the difference between a Kentucky country ham and an ordinary Smithfield, but could produce one.

And not only that, my jones for Crosse & Blackwell vichyssoise wouldn't have to go unsatisfied, nor would my nostalgic craving, awakened by the sere and blowing leaves of a fine fall day, for a certain San Gimignano white Chianti that was a private Brown-Princeton game tailgate tradition between me and a certain girl many long-lost bright college years ago.

But obscure Italian whites are as nothing to Strohecker's. The wine collection, expanded in the 1960s by Wayne, father of the present owner John Strohecker, is housed in a veritable Aladdin's cave of which the modest supermarket appearance of the store above gives no hint.

When she was about to be 73, my beautiful and sophisticated mom advanced me enough of my inheri-tance to get me into the big, leaky fixer-upper I and my numerous children still inhabit. A special birthday present was clearly in order. Mom loved good claret. By sheer luck Baron Philippe de Rothschild, proprietor of Chateau Mouton, had just published a witty and wicked memoir in which, between description of his love affairs, he told how he persuaded famous painters to do his labels.

Powell's had the book. But how to get the wine here in far-off Oregon? I mentioned my problem to Mr. Strohecker (père), who asked if I could excuse him for a few minutes. When he returned it was with an armload of the Mouton Rothschild artist's labels, including a Dali, a Warhol, and the 1973, by Picasso.

Lots of moms with kids do their daily shopping at Strohecker's, pushing carts and forking over cash or plastic as they leave just like this was Safeway. The store ceased to carry accounts in 1988, just after it replaced its old wooden building, which looked like a ranger station, with the current brick anonymity. There's nothing particularly danger-ous aboveground here, if I can just steer around the smoked pheasant and the fresh beluga and, over in deli desserts, the chocolate mousse and the die-for-'em fresh fruit tarts. Today there's Vivaldi on decent speakers and an exhibit of Doug Byers's soothing black-and-white photos of beautiful women and industrial kitchens.

Still, we have been slightly tense. No medallions of venison is a big relief because we would have been tempted to partner them with the '70 Chateau Petrus, a real budget buster at $1,200.

We tell chef Eller and wine consultant Brett Huebner that we will be opting instead for the wine-poached salmon and a bottle of the '89 Joseph Drouhin Montrachet, a mere $325.

Having been restrained about the entrée maybe we can turn up the volume a little on the overture to our off-the-shelf Strohecker's picnic with—yes!—a pound of the beluga on crostini toast points and a champagne that's worthy of it, an '88 Rose Crystal (Roederer, $210).

Variety is the very soul of a picnic, so let's add some duck pâté, some English Stilton, a Ledel de Claron triple-creme, and assorted French olives with more crostini.

Next, vitamins: fruit salad, Caesar salad, iced gazpacho—focaccia on the side, and a second Montrachet, this time a '93 Dominique Lafon ($300).

As we push our cart over to the line of moms pointed back toward a parking lot full of their BMWs and Mercedes wagons, we try to remember a grocery in our collective Manhattan or Los Angeles pasts that

can equal Strohecker's. And we can't. If the Big One hits and Council Crest slides into the gully, you can look for me poking around the rubble of Strohecker's for those medallions of venison and that Chateau Petrus.

Meanwhile, I suppose I could add things up on the way to the register and see whether we are going to come out under $2,000. But what fun would that be?

# Best Inner Turmoil

We didn't have the money to pay for Larry's heartfelt, beautifully written story of the breakup of his second marriage. But suffice it to say that it was all you would have hoped for and more.

We find our narrator now at a breathtakingly low point. No longer a professional baseball player, no longer a teacher, Larry is trying to make it as a freelance writer. Tune in now as the suffering gets even worse.

# CRISIS FIVE
by LARRY COLTON

Women and money, man, they were driving me nuts. It was a cold, drizzly morning in January 1979. I was 37, supposedly prime time for a man to hit financial and emotional maturity. Instead, I had two ex-wives, two ex-careers, two exdogs, and a beat-to-shit 13-year-old Chevy Nova with a broken transmission. It had only one gear that worked... reverse. On the bright side, I'd just completed a gig as a department store Santa. Six Santas sharing the same beard—it was like breathing goat barf. But the check was in the mail.

I was rushing my daughter Sarah to get ready for school. She was in the first grade, and as she did every Tuesday night, she had spent the night with me. I was still living in the unfinished attic of friends who had offered me a place to crash after Kathi and I split. I had two guest mattresses, one for Sarah and another for Wendy, 13, when she came down from Seattle.

Usually, the friends with whom I was staying let me borrow one of their cars to take Sarah to school, but on this day they were gone . . . and we'd already missed the bus.

"I can't be late," Sarah instructed. Sternly.

I tossed her peanut butter and jelly sandwich into her Princess Leia lunch box and we walked outside to where the Nova had been parked for two months, inert, hopeless, gathering mildew.

**I tossed her peanut butter and jelly sandwich into her Princess Leia lunch box and we walked outside to where the Nova had been parked for two months, inert, hopeless, gathering mildew.**

Maybe it fixed itself, I hoped.

I turned the ignition. It coughed and wheezed, belching carbon. But it started. I brushed the dust off Sarah's seat, then backed down the driveway and out onto the street. There was no use shifting. I just kept going in reverse. . .down the block, left at the corner, then seven miles backward through the morning traffic of Portland. I stayed on the side streets, sneaking across busy intersections, waiting for cars to clear the way. My neck began to get stiff. Drivers stared in disbelief. The drizzle had turned to a downpour and the rain stuck to the Nova's rear window. I poked my head out the driver's-side window, squinting through the deluge. On the radio, KGW's Skywatch announced that the morning commute was going smoothly. Easy for them to say.

A block from Sarah's school, a siren startled me. A cop signaled me to the curb. He said he'd been following me for three blocks. I could only take his word for it—I'd been focused on what was behind me. (Or was it what was in front of me?) I pleaded my case. "I'm dropping off my daughter, then driving straight backward to Aamco."

# Best Inner Turmoil

Larry Colton had what this country is supposed to be all about—athletic ability, brains, personality, and drive. A great athlete—and while he probably wouldn't have put Rhett Butler out of a job, he was a ladies' man too. Still, there was a problem. No money. Here he was 40 years old, twice divorced, the father of two daughters, living alone in one of those flaky-paint neighborhoods where America hadn't quite kept its promise. Making money writing freelance, Colton had discovered, was about as easy as truck farming the moon ...

# CRISIS SIX

by LARRY COLTON

It was a Friday night. Julie, my live-in girlfriend, called home to tell me that she was going to meet a couple of her lawyer colleagues for a drink after work and would be home by 7:30. I told her I'd have dinner ready. Cooking was one way for me to compensate when my cash wasn't flowing. (By all rights I should have been a gourmet chef.)

Julie and I had been living together, off and on, for two years. She had stuck with me through my lowest days of despair—after my DWI, giving me a shoulder to cry on, buying the groceries, encouraging me artistically, loaning me her Honda. (My Nova was dead. Not even a reverse gear.)

My friends told me I was an idiot if I didn't marry her. She was bright, beautiful, and bounteous. But I had met her on the rebound from my second failed marriage, and was dubious about the marital institution, some days even bitter: both ex-wives had been the one to pull the plug; both had blamed me for the demise; both had gotten custody; both had moved on to the greener pastures of disastrous relationships. Another problem was that I didn't trust myself to be faithful. Or her, for that matter. Another was I didn't want to get married when I was still a financial Hindenburg. Another was a fear of failure ... three strikes and you're out.

Julie was 33 and hinting that she wanted children. But I had had my quota, which did not seem fair to her. So why was I living with her? Because I loved her.

At 7:30 I peeked out the window, thinking I heard Julie pull in the driveway. False alarm. Eight o'clock rolled around, then 8:30. And still no Julie. I checked the casserole. It was getting crispy around the edges. I took it out of the oven and fixed myself another gin and tonic. Why hadn't she at least called?

Another 30 minutes crawled by. I wasn't worried that she'd been in an accident—no, I was worried that she was still at work, naked, with one of the senior partners. Or, hey, maybe just one of the interns. Forget that she was a moral Mother Teresa. Trust wasn't my main virtue. At least not with women. Not with myself. By 9:30 I was fuming, ready to head downtown to one of the Friday night meat markets. I'd show her. Only I had no car, no bus money, no cash for cocktails.

It was 10:30 when Julie walked sheepishly through the door, reeking of guilt and piña coladas. I was waiting in the dining room with a casserole.

"Here's your dinner!" I raged, reaching out to dump it over her head.

She threw up an arm in self-defense, sending chicken, rice, and peas flying. I picked up a handful off the rug, and even though the arm wasn't what it once was, started firing. With casserole peppering the room like bird shot, she ran for the door. I grabbed her by the arm and pulled her back, then put myself in front of the door, arms folded, Bull Connor blocking the way. When she tried to pass, I herded her back toward the dining room, using my size as a weapon.

Then I whirled and stomped out the door and into the night. By the time I reached the end of the drive-way I realized I had no place to go and no way to get there.

## BEST HEROIN DEALER:

# Henry Jerrel Johnson

*The thing about Henry was that Henry was a very nice guy.*

Henry Jerrel Johnson, also known as Superman or Superfly, "the hottest pimp in P.O." and the largest volume dealer of heroin in Oregon history. For five years during the 1970s, he was the Horatio Alger of the Oregon underworld: car theft, check kiting, pimping, and executive-level dope pushing.

I went to visit Henry at the State Penitentiary in Salem. Super pimp, Superman, Superfly, whomever. I was not looking at any errant Isaac Hayes or black Pretty Boy Floyd. Of medium height and build, Johnson looked normal.

Henry owned a home in Aloha. Probably the only black man living within five miles of the place. He'd painted his home purple. In two tones. He had a diamond ring with a $16,000 three-carat center stone. "It has 240 diamonds in it, the smallest 10 points."

He owned a Rolls-Royce complete

with bar, telephone, and "the steering wheel on the wrong side!" Race cars with "Henry Johnson" painted on the sides, an airplane, a Ferrari, several Lincolns, a pit bull, and a motorized skateboard.

How? Henry dealt heroin and grossed over $32,000 a week for over two years. To grease the wheels with his squirrelly clientele, he offered perks. Like: he let them "geeze for free" on Sunday.

❖

A good life, certainly, but a great one? "One time," Henry told me, "a guy went to the playground where my stepson was at and put a knife to his throat and started demanding money and dope. My wife didn't have any dope, but she gave him $150."

"Did you call the cops?" I asked.

Henry laughed. "How'm I gonna do that? Call up and say, 'Chief Baker, this is Henry, so and so just attacked my son and stole my dope money. Go catch him.' No, I didn't call no cops. I just put up a $1,000 reward and a piece of dope.

"Later some guys catch the guy down by the Old Town Pump Dance Hall in Portland. They work him over with tire irons, and I drive by and they ask me: 'Do you want us to beat him within one inch of his life or two?' And I say, 'One.'"

❖

Henry Jerrel Johnson was born February 5, 1950, in Portland, the third child in a family of nine held together by a mother he remembered "doing housework for rich whites and in rest homes."

By the time he entered Jefferson High School, home of "the slick blacks. . .them that would later be great pimps and players," Henry was in trouble.

"I became one of the most notorious car thieves in P.O." With his accumulated loot Johnson bought a Cadillac convertible and decided to try his hand at pimping. Sadly, Johnson's first punch took him to the cleaners after he couldn't resist sampling the merchandise. "Bev. I met her downtown in front of the Rip Tides, where all the whores were working at the time. The first thing I did was forget all the rules. The number one rule is never let your little head rule your big head."

To make a short story shorter, Johnson took Bev straight to the Thunderbird Motel, played with her parts, and fell asleep, and Bev made off with his watch, ring, wallet, and trousers. Henry ended up having to hot-wire his hot pink Cadillac in a pair of bib overalls lent him by the motel's gracious manager.

His third whore, Yvonne, would later become his wife. They got married a year after doing business together. One night Yvonne told him she wanted to earn some extra money. Though he thought it was a rotten idea, he gave his consent. "If a whore wants to whore, she's going to whore no matter what, and I didn't want anyone pimping my wife besides me."

It didn't work out. "Her tricks would come by the house at night, and I would hide in another room until they were finished. Sometimes I would listen through the door and peep through the keyhole and get plenty mad and jealous seeing another man be with my wife for $20 or $30."

Henry decided once again to diversify his portfolio by getting into "the Summer 'Ho Market."

"They're young bitches that turn out in flocks during the summer 'cause they're out of school or tired of hanging around the house. They parade up and down Williams Avenue bullshitting and making business bad for the real whores— because it gives the trick a chance to pick up something young and tender and dumb.

"These women haven't been turned out right by no pimp. . .they haven't had no one tell them how to hold their legs when they making a trick, so that he won't jiggle all of their insides loose and give 'em female trouble. They don't know how to take a finger douche or check a man for VD; all they know how to do is parade up and down the street and wave at cars."

Johnson organized a squad of choice Summer 'Hos but eventually gave up in disgust. "No matter how hard I tried, I never made more than $250 a night with all eight of them."

Thanks to his heroin business, Henry was able to rescue dozens of young women from a life of prostitution. It was a young capitalist's dream. Everything was taken care of for him. He had a main woman who cut the dope and packaged it. He had a guy to deliver the dope to each of his 12 salesladies for $25 a drop. And all Henry had to do was keep those gals in cars, clothes, apartments, and spending money.

"You show 'em you care. You show 'em the advantage of selling dope. You tell 'em: 'Don't take no knowledge to lay on your back for $20. You have female trouble before you're 25. You want to better yourself. '"

Finally, however, Henry decided to quit dealing dope, but his white partner, James McFarlene, whom he had grown up with and who was "like a blood brother," started "bugging me about buying some dope just one more time. I said no. But he kept on asking me, said he was in a jam.

"Well, he was in a jam all right. He'd been busted by the cops. They told him it was either his ass or mine."

It was Henry's.           –M.C.

# MAJOR MOUTHPIECES

Didn't do it, and need an attorney? Usually, when you have a generalized legal problem in Oregon, you can just call Chuck Paulson or Frank Pozzi, hand them a couple grand, and forget about it. But sometimes you get into a deep and particular world of hurt and need a specialist. So now it's time for a WILD LIFE bonus. Something you can cut out and put in your wallet. To wit, a list of top catastrophe attorneys found locally. Without ceremony, this is it:

## High Crime

If you're accused of bank robbery, dope dealing, treason, theft of state secrets, etc., and actually *did* do it, call Des Connell. This guy looks like an eagle who played linebacker for the Rams. Connell blew the whistle on the vice in the vice squad a few years back, and could probably spring Pontius Pilate from the hubs of hell.

## Murder

You just blew the top of your brother-in-law's skull off with a .44 Ruger, don't want to go to jail very long, but would like to write a novel about it. Call Phil Margolin.

## Personal Injury

A blotto Ashley Mercedes Squigmount III just splashed you and your Toyota all over a concrete retaining wall with his Sherman tank of a Caddy. What's left of you better get on the horn to Elden Rosenthal. Elden's a quiet, idealistic guy whose hobby is remembering the 1960s, but in court he extracts zillions from the errant and irresponsible.

## Medical Malpractice

Moon-eyed over his comely scrub nurse, love-addled Dr. Owen B. Carthcart (USMC Ret.) gets confused during your "tush tuck" and accidentally sews your ass on backward. Call Scary Larry Wobbrock, past president of the Oregon Trial Lawyers Association. Scary is King of All Justice, a savvy combination of Perry Mason, Mother Teresa, and a well-bred Doberman pinscher.

## You Against the System

The Air National Guard makes a "mistake" during combat exercises and napalms you, your house, your whole town. Call Larry Sokol, Oregon's best-known environmental attorney. He has fought tooth and nail on behalf of squirrels, birds, trees, rabbits, insects, the whole pastoral shot.

## You Against the System: The Sequel

You're an unwilling ratepayer to a monster private utility that's robbing you blind. Call Jay Waldron. He was the one who blew the financial doors off the Bonneville Power Administration on behalf of public-utility power uses, a move that saved Oregon consumers $50 million a year.                    —M.C.

---

# Best Inner Turmoil

When we left ex-jock, ex-husband of Hedy Lamarr's daughter Denise, and ex-golden boy (now pushing 40) Larry Colton, he had just walked out of his own life. He and his second wife Kathi—no, excuse me, not Kathi, she was out of the picture two crises ago—he and his girlfriend Julie had just had a falling out and Larry, penniless and without prospects, found himself back on the street.

Once again, financial constraints nix publishing the blow-by-blow account of how he pulled himself out of the gutter, but Larry did agree to sell us key sentences that will give you the gist—

That said, let's get on with Crisis Seven.

# CRISIS SEVEN

BY LARRY COLTON

The last question on the Portland School District's job application form asked: Why are you applying for the position of substitute teacher? Hmmmmm. Because it has been my lifelong ambition. Because I love school lunches . . . .

I needed the $57 a day.

The first call came on a Monday morning at six o'clock. Could I teach an eighth-grade class for the whole week? It was supposed to be the toughest middle school in the district. Let's see. Five times 57. I was out the door and on a bus in ten minutes.

Thirty-five students were waiting at the door. Two boys raced to a record player at the back of the room and cranked up Ted Nugent full volume. "Our regular teacher lets us do it," they explained. A boy in the back row was choking himself to get high; the boy next to him pulled out a tin of Copenhagen and put a pinch between his teeth and gum, then spit on the back of the AC/DC sweatshirt of the girl in front of him. She didn't notice—she was way too busy ratting the hair of the girl next to her.

I told them to take out their math books. Zero for thirty-five. Nary a one budged. Okay, I never liked math much myself. How about writing a descriptive paragraph about your family. One paper was turned in:

*My mom has brown hair and likes to sit. My step Dad has black hair, green eyes and*

*likes to drink. I might sneak into his room at night and shoot him with his .357. Don't ask me how old my real dad is because I only see him once a year. He has trouble with his back and doesn't pay child support.*

Then there was a boy who called himself Captain Fantastic. He was a cross between the Fonz and General Haig. He wore full army dress, including combat boots, and his favorite sport was smashing inanimate objects with his head.

I opened the top desk drawer. There was an envelope marked "Jimmy's Ritalin." Jimmy was already at Club Speedo, sitting at his desk, mainlining Milk Duds. During the writing assignment the boy next to him started pounding on his desk and kicking his chair. I asked him to stop. He picked up all his papers and books and flung them in the air. "Fuck you!" he said. I moved toward him. "Don't touch me, motherfucker, or I'll sue your ass!" When he threw his chair across the room, narrowly missing my head, I . . .

## Oregon's Elvis,
# COURTNEY LOVE

"Courtney is the definition of a star."　　　　—DAVID GEFFEN

"In the sad, fun, true tradition of Janis, Jim and Jimi, Courtney Love has proven herself a worthy one-woman sack of hell."
　　　　—CHUCK DEAN, *ROLLING STONE*

"Her early life took her all over the globe, [to] New Zealand [and] Japan, where as a 14-year-old she worked as a stripper; Ireland, where she hung around Trinity College; Liverpool, where she infiltrated the rock scene; Taiwan, where she stripped again; Hollywood, where she stumbled in her first attempts at screen stardom; New York, where she hung out in clubs and continued to rock; Minneapolis, where she rocked some more; Alaska, where she again stripped; and Spain, where she appeared in Alex Cox's unwatchable film, *Straight to Hell*, after having already had a bit part in his acclaimed *Sid and Nancy*. If any place could be called home base, it was Portland, Oregon. '*My Own Private Idaho* is the story of my early adolescence,' she says with perverse pride."
　　　　—KEVIN SESSUMS, *VANITY FAIR*

"Look at the record: lost a husband, gained a Michael Stipe; threatened to sue her shrink for getting her hooked on drugs...saw her estranged father *Hard-Copy* out on her, kicked around (figuratively) with some Tibetan Monks and had her site unplugged by America Online! Look how she rattled Madonna at the MTV Video Music Awards. Poor Madonna was left shaking in her hair extensions, but that's rock & roll: fright and intimidation, aiming for the mightiest and leaving a photographable blood trail."　　　　—CHUCK DEAN

"I've got the same taste as fags. I like to suck. I go for the rough-trade boys. I'm a total drag-queen fag."
　　　　—COURTNEY LOVE

"When she was in second grade in Eugene, Oregon, she was having a lot of nightmares. I had no idea what to do. I took her to a psychiatrist just to try to find some way to bring her some solace. The psychiatrist said she needed to join Girl Scouts."
　　　　—LINDA CARROLL, COURTNEY'S MOTHER

# SMALL TOWN GIRL MAKES LOUD

by MELISSA ROSSI

Portland International Airport didn't seem so terribly international when teenage Courtney Menely blew back into town from England, mentally reviewing her exploits and sexual scores the entire trip. Now a bona fide New Waver, with a British accent and a fondness for tea, she couldn't wait to hit Metro and La Patisserie to brag. Ha. She'd shown them. She'd cut a few more notches on her belt, and they were Big Name notches. She had proved that she could weasel into any scene, and her exploits abroad confirmed what the headstrong hell-raiser and cops already knew: she was unstoppable. The Unsinkable Courtney. With her new artillery of star-quality names that she had personally partied with, she blasted her way into the swelling music scene—at the time richer, more diverse, and far more festive than Seattle's would ever be.

Portland, as Kurt Cobain later said, was the birthplace of grunge: Courtney's kind of place, where hundreds of Courtney stories—of rip-offs, break-ins, and fires—first snaked through the gossip lines. Those who hadn't heard of her before couldn't help but notice the pushy, obnoxious noisemaker and get out of her way.

Fueled by raging insecurity that translated into relentless drive, Courtney made her mouth her most powerful weapon. Like a chain saw, it ripped through anything in its way. A plump pair of lips, often smeared in reds, served as the entry-way to the sneering slash, a gaping gash from which shot nonstop ban-tering, a verbal cyclone brilliant and comic, self-pitying and cruel, in tones sultry or shrill, a dizzying whirlwind of ideas, gossip, and con-fessions punctuated by the rapid-fire names of musicians, authors, and titles of heady books.

The mouth flapped day and night, wrapped around receivers in hours-long tele-thons to the far corners of the world. One minute she cooed or confessed, the next hissed and issued death threats or passionate declara-tions of love. Her relentless yam-mering mouth would not shut up until it got what it wanted.

But Courtney was more than a mouth. Within seconds of seeing her, the eyes took over.

Those piercing eyes that sized up in an instant, that gushed tears on command, that blazed a scorching brand on those who had wronged her, eyes that had an almost psychic ability to fall upon the rising stars. For years, these eyes were the only semblance of beauty anywhere on the blubbery dynamo that once was Courtney, and she knew how to work them for maximum effect.

Her nose, until resculpted, was a blight on her already coarse-featured face, a nose that appeared to have been broken, or bludgeoned, and then given a twist. This nose could sniff out a trend faster than the hottest *Newsweek* reporter, and track down a love object like a blood-hound.

There were the pale legs, originally flabby and hidden under frumpy old-lady dresses and dust jackets. But even then they were long, allowing her to tower, offering the confident superiority that comes simply from being tall.

Then there were the hands, with fingers thick and coarse, that seemed better suited to a steelworker than a wannabe tiara-wearing star. These rough grimy hands, long before they picked up a guitar, had learned how to seduce and caress, and pummel anyone who got in the way.

Her hands, like her feet and nose, seem to have come from her father. All it seems Courtney inherited from her reserved mother, besides intelligence, was an ability to flip off societal norms, and the lineage to a trust fund that she'd rip through every month.

And it's the pieces of Courtney Love's body, seen in their original state, that give a clue to the heart of the girl that stepped back into Portland. Put mildly, she was not the classic American beauty, this tall dumpling-bodied sack of a yapper who even then, before it was fashionable, was prone to dress in ripped vintage clothes.

But Courtney had perfected the skills required by less-than-pretty girls to get along in the world. Because if you're less than lovely, if you're only "pretty on the inside"—the name of her debut album—there are but two choices: sit back and take whoever comes along, or aim high and devise a bag of attention-getting tricks. Courtney opted for the latter, becoming a self-educated expert on sex, seduction, and manipulation. Even back before she was a star, even before she had showbiz looks, there was simply no ignoring Courtney.

In 1982, when Courtney returned, the town was filled with writers, actors, artists, singers, dancers, and poets. But the most prestigious of all the creative arts was music. Half the town was in a band. The guy at the grocery store, the guy at the espresso machine, the guy who worked by day as a mechanic were all by night cranking away on the stage of Luis's La Bamba, the Long

Goodbye, the Earth, or one of the dozens of clubs that popped up every few months, often disappearing in weeks.

In fact, before long, she knew all the hot bands. And vice versa. She was a groupie, rumored to blow anyone vaguely connected to a band, just for the chance to talk to the singer.

She befriended Greg Sage, a tall, albino, alienlike recluse whose song "Over the Edge" would a decade later show up first on a TK Records single, then on a Hole EP. There was Billy Rancher, the recent winner of a David Bowie lookalike contest. He'd started a group called Billy Rancher and the Unreal Gods, who were luring major-label scouts to town. There were punk bands like Napalm Beach, Poison Idea, and John Shirley's Sado-Nation—and searing rock bands àla the Confidentials.

But of all the hot bands in town, Courtney's favorite was Theater of Sheep. The lead singer was Rozz Rezabek-Wright. Tall, pale, anorexic-thin, and punklike, Rozz looked like a cartoonish take on a baby bird mixed with a British rock star.

It was the latter quality that Courtney saw when Theater of Sheep played the Metropolis, a beat-up number nicknamed the Met. One side of the club was the all-ages part, where the kids danced up on a runway, looking into a mirror. In the bar, a wall away, chickenhawks and trolls gazed at that night's dancing pickings from the other side. The mirror was two-way.

The club was managed by a young visionary named Dean Matthieson. Short, sharp, sparrowlike, and gay, Matthieson was the Andy Warhol of Portland, and always had a coterie of young boys following him around. He saw the potential in Courtney and hired her as the club's DJ.

Not long into her stint, the dive packed out when Theater of Sheep took to the miniature stage, followed by a flock of teenage girls.

Lead singer Rozz was as mutable as the syntho-glamrock music the band played; reminiscent of David Bowie and Boy George, a ham who seemed like he had spotlights following him even when they were turned off. He reeked of that show-biz quality that groupies can sniff out, many rows back, years before talent scouts do. So dreamy was the set that from that point on, Rozz would cause a mob scene of kids just by walking down the street.

His potential didn't go unnoticed by Courtney, who'd watched him from the DJ stand, cross-armed and smoking.

After the gig, she pushed her way across the room, and into his life. "Who do you think you are? David Bowie? With your mock rock-star poses? You'll never make it wearing those atrocious green-checkered pants!"

"And who do you think you are with that fake British accent?" he asked.

She threw her drink at him. He spit on her.

He was scared. She was in love.

❤

Two days later, Rozz received a letter requesting a secret midnight meeting on the fire escape of a downtown cafe, Metro on Broadway. The note was unsigned. Inside was a rose. And a small packet of blue and white pills.

When he showed up, there she was: that fake British loon. He almost bolted, but there was something that compelled him to stay. A feeling of danger. A feeling of traversing the edge. In seduction mode and black dress, Courtney looked rather alluring. And she'd done her research well. She understood that drugs and drunkenness were her friends, that with their help, she could lower his defenses and seep in.

The drugs were a key to Rozz's heart. He loved pills, barbiturates and tranquilizers especially, the sort that made his muscles relax and made him laugh a lot; he'd developed a taste for them at the age of 15, when a beam fell on his back and a doctor prescribed extra-strength painkillers.

The pills she'd enclosed in the letter, the ones they went to her apartment to take that night, were Tuinals—a pharmaceutical that was half Seconal, a barbiturate, and half truth serum—and yes, there is such a thing, which may have been the attraction for Courtney, who by then was known as a chronic teller of tall tales.

The bedroom she led him to was a wreck. Clothes, papers, magazines, records, books, tapes everywhere. Somewhere beneath the stuff was a mattress.

She lit candles and burned incense, which swirled through the room, competing with the scent of Oscar de la Renta that she'd sprayed on a bit too heavily. Billie Holiday played from a scratchy record. They drank tea and orange brandy. She brought out pictures from Liverpool, told him about her dad. They talked through the night about music, love, and the celebrity Rozz would someday be. She could see it, she could feel where he could go, if he just changed his wardrobe and got rid of his keyboardist, a pearl-wearing swankster.

Courtney gave him stage jackets (supposedly swiped from Echo and the Bunnymen's lead singer, Ian McCullough) and suggested that perhaps *she* could play in the band.

He was amazed by her command of the language, her brilliance, her tales. She was amazed that in Portland, she'd found exactly what she sought: a rising star. He just didn't know how to market himself.

The next time they met it was at his place, where he showed her his library—a collection of 37 books. All of them *Valley of the Dolls*.

The third time they went out, this time to a movie, Courtney proposed. The only snag was that Rozz was already engaged.

"Marion" was the perfect suburban rich-kid brat. Fine-featured, well-heeled, pretty, stable family, parents still together. Everything Courtney wasn't. Everything that Courtney considered her mother to be, the mother that Courtney described as "a majestic-titted blond debutante without a drop of poetry in her soul." And it became Courtney's purpose in life to shove Marion out of the way. Her first step was to announce all over town, in the clubs and through the cafes, that she was going out with Rozz. It was a bit of a stretch—their meetings had been platonic, Rozz unwilling to succumb to her advances despite his relaxed

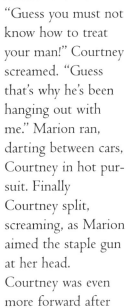

state.

But there was something about that big doughy sack of intensity. Rozz saw the braininess, the style, the humor, the charisma, the way Courtney could ionize a room. Nobody else saw what he called her "biblical eyes." They saw only the fat chick with the funny nose, who towered over her peers.

One night while Marion helped Rozz staple up posters for an upcoming show, they ran into Courtney on Northwest 21st.

"Guess you must not know how to treat your man!" Courtney screamed. "Guess that's why he's been hanging out with me." Marion ran, darting between cars, Courtney in hot pursuit. Finally Courtney split, screaming, as Marion aimed the staple gun at her head.

Courtney was even more forward after that, simply dropping by with pills and coos. Rozz had plenty of fans, but Courtney made him feel like a star, continually etched the chance of international fame in his head. They'd stay in bed for days, just writing through the night or singing songs from *Valley of the Dolls*. Singing was the way to her heart, no matter her mood: sing to her. Like a mother to a child.

He'd awake from a nap to find books filled with scrawled lyrics and ideas for movies, and Courtney would be working the phone.

Despite her eyes, her coaxing, and her pills, she still couldn't convince him to dump Marion. Or, for that matter, to actually have sex with her. But she was pulling him in, as she spun her narcotic web. He was growing more and more fond of her, and found himself affecting her fake British accent, asking from the bed, "Oh Courtney, love, might I have a spot more tea?" She soon announced her new name: Courtney Love.

❤

She was rapidly making enemies. One Portlander despised her so much he set a house she lived in on fire.

Courtney's living arrangements told a tale. She'd move, owing several months' rent and sky-high phone bills. She was known for stealing clothes, boyfriends, and drugs, and for her calling-card scams. On one occasion, while housesitting and in need of cash, she simply relieved the apartment of all its valuables—and sold them to a downtown antique store.

On nights when she wasn't working and wasn't able to secure a bedside appointment with Rozz, she often stood outside Satyricon, a new club. It was a dark cave, with black lights and graffiti-ed walls splashed with neon murals, where Napalm Beach and the Wipers often played. She was too young to get inside, so she hung outside smoking cigarettes, waiting for the sweaty masses to emerge during breaks.

It was there one night that she was kidnapped. A group of skinhead girls, sick of Courtney's chronic mouthiness, grabbed her and drove for six hours to Bellingham, Washington, near the Canadian border, where they dumped her onto the highway, naked. She was livid, humiliated, and vowed revenge. After that, her absorbed anger was a barrier, projecting, "Do not fuck with me!"

❤

Rozz. For seven months, it had been on again, off again. Her trump card had yet to be played. Finally, she had an installment from her trust fund. And she showed up at a Theatre of Sheep show with champagne, more pills, and tickets to San Francisco. They flew there that night, spending two days in one of the four-star hotels, singing in bed, writing, laughing, popping pills.

They consummated their relationship at last. It was actually quite cruel: Rozz refused to look at her face, and made her write poetry while they got it on.

She was wild in bed, her hands instruments of seduction, her spirit willing, the pills making it all a subconscious dream. He might not look at her, but Courtney had him.

❤

The next night in Portland, Theater of Sheep played Starry Night—an old church converted to a balconied all-ages club. The show was packed, and in the middle of the show Rozz looked up to see a fury in white, literally splitting the crowd. It was Courtney. In a wedding dress. She shoved fans out of the way and stormed up to the stage. Once there she glared up at him, and tossed a bottle of peach brandy and Tuinals at his feet—a reminder of the day before. So much for discretion.

❤

# E p i l o g u e

Courtney was so obsessed with Rozz and his band that he suggested she start up her own. She bought a Casio keyboard and drew up a list of all the feistiest women in town. Soon the word was out: Courtney was bragging that she was going to form a girl group and be a rock star. Laughter echoed through the bars.

**BEST HOT MEAT:**

# House o' Beef

BY SUSAN STANLEY

It's the end of a bad week and I don't want Thai, I don't want Vietnamese, and I certainly don't want some dork announcing he's going to be my server tonight. What I want is *real food*, and I want it to announce its arrival in my mouth, *pow!*

Despite our Latte Consciousness, despite knowing it's considered kind of rude to eat anything that once had a face or a mother, sometimes there arises the craven desire to eat meat. Red meat! Greasy red meat! Where you have to wash your face afterward. When that shameful urge pins my nobler nature to the mat, I start whining to be taken to Buster's Texas-Style Ribs.

There are ribs and there are ribs, and God only knows Portland has a bunch of justly esteemed rib joints. Ah, but Buster's has it all. You don't stay in business 17 years, and open two other locations, unless you've got something going for you.

Here's how it is at Buster's: You go through a cafeteria line to get your food. Like barbecued brisket, chicken, ribs (beef or pork), ham, turkey, pork loin or link sausage. The three-meat dinner is $10.95; two-meat dinner, $8.95; one-meat dinners are also available. That's with garlic bread and two side orders: BBQ or pinto beans, coleslaw, potato salad, fries, or green salad. There are BBQ sandwiches, chili, and really good pecan pie. You can even "Texas-s!ze" your meal for another three bucks.

What *really* cheers me up on a Friday night at Buster's is the ambiance. We're talking flashing blue neon cacti and neon Lone Star beer signs. Wall-mounted stag heads, complete with antlers. Rattlesnake skins and longhorn bull horns and dumb pictures of John Wayne and Indians and a gas fireplace. There's a framed poster of all kinds of cowboy boots. Bathrooms are labeled Necessary Room for Gentlemen and Necessary Room for Ladies. The music piped in the other night included Loretta Lynn's "Coal Miner's Daughter" leading into (what else?) "Chattanooga Shoeshine Boy"—followed by Patsy Cline warbling "I Fall to Pieces."

And the ribs, one must emphasize, are absolutely delicious, especially with the hot sauce. You just have to hotfoot it to the Necessary Room afterward and wash your hands before you re-enter what passes for Real Life in these parts.

BUSTER'S SMOKEHOUSE
TEXAS-STYLE BAR-B-CUE
*17883 S.E. McLoughlin Boulevard, Milwaukie (503) 652-1067; 1355 N.E. Burnside, Gresham (503) 667-4811;*

*11419 S.W. Pacific Highway, Tigard (503) 452-8384.*

## BEST SHOPPING:
# HANGIN' WITH THE HOMIES AT GOODWILL

BY SUSAN STANLEY

I have a Nordstrom card. Oh yeah, I have 'em all—Meier & Frank, Sears, Ward's, J. C. Penneys. Back in the golden age of dimestores, I even had a card from J. J. Newberry's. But what I'd *really* like is a card for the Goodwill As-Is store.

My very favorite place to shop—if that's what it should be called—is that football-field-size store, over on Southeast McLoughlin Boulevard where the Mill End store used to be. Officially the Goodwill Outlet Store, this is where you can drop off the old crud you don't want any more, then fill the car back up with the stuff other people have foolishly discarded. It's where you go to find those '70s orange fondue pots (missing their lethal prongs for spearing your oil-soaked tidbits). It's where you go to find loved-to-shreds homemade rag dolls. It's where you go to find books on macramé, and earth-tone yarn embroideries of owls, mushrooms, and butterflies. And it's where you go to find *me*, most Saturday afternoons.

Last Saturday noonish, there must have been 200 customers, each hell-bent on finding a specific Holy Grail. Me, I look out for hand-embroidered pillowcases, derelict patchwork quilts, and other needle-work. (I turn them into tea cozies for friends and family, or ship 'em off to my childhood pal Sandi to peddle in her Scottsdale antique store.) I keep an eye out for clothing ($1.19 a pound) with interesting old buttons (mother-of-pearl, bone, and Bakelite) and for furniture (I insist upon owning an expensive station wagon so I can haul around $10 chests of drawers and other bulky finds).

Last Saturday, I got a pair of red-wood chaises for the deck, needing paint but including usable cushions,

## GOTTA BE AN EASTSIDE CHICK

Hi, my name is Donna. My two friends and I are looking for a man that is physically incapac-itated and in a wheelchair, but not sexually incapacitated. We're looking for somebody to nurture and take care of, and we kind of just want to be the wind beneath his wings and help him become functional in a society that looks down on those that are physically chal-lenged. It would also be an added bonus if this man was well-endowed.

—PERSONALS AD IN *PDXS*

for $10 each. Also a handmade wooden train set for two bits. I've gotten tons of cotton duds (good for quilts) with great buttons. A few weeks back, I got a down and feather comforter for two bucks. (OK, it did cost $15 to have it cleaned.)

I've scored other good stuff. An old LP called *Richard Chamberlain Sings.* (A perfect match for my Tony Perkins LP, bought decades ago at a Nebraska yard sale.) A portable crib for $15; a blue Hall teapot, missing its lid, for a dime. Good stuff, right up there with the velvet painting of the nekkid Burt Reynolds, found languishing in a Dumpster five years ago.

But it's not just the meat, it's the motion. The air is richly textured with the jabber of different lan-guages. Russian immigrants, delight-ed to find such usable, cheap castoffs, keep an eye on daughters with gauzy, fluffy hairbows, and on sons with odd homemade haircuts. Hispanic mamas pile rusty grocery carts high with dresses and T-shirts, with sheets and towels and mattress pads, chiding their frisky offspring: "Maria! *Ven aquí!*"

An elaborate code of courtesy seems transmitted by osmosis. West Hills matrons, their manicured hands protected by vinyl gloves—swiped from their doctor husbands' exam rooms, I wonder?—smile politely as they daintily plunder alongside swarthy, muscular migrant workers. Teenagers punked out with purple mohawks and dumb puce-dyed white-kid dreadlocks offer up to young mothers barely used "one-sies" and pajamas for the toddlers fidgeting in grocery carts.

There's plenty to take home, and plenty to leave for fellow pilgrims. One must have standards. I don't, for example, take home really skanky Barbie dolls, or anything with obvious bloodstains. Ditto My Little Pony toys or used underwear or 8-tracks of *A Jim Nabors Christmas*. A once-worn, swiftly discarded bridesmaid's dress, now that's another story, if the billowing yards of fabric are reusable for a quilt, or a pillow.

Nurturing my inner bag lady, I can mutter audibly to myself or to inanimate objects without feeling odd. ("Hmmm . . . you still have some good wear left in you. And I *love* your buttons. Want to come home with me?") The only person I'm likely to run into is a well-known writer I know, digging for books to keep, or to resell to Powell's.

I'm not sure what my personal Holy Grail is. But when I find it, it's probably going to be in the bins of the Goodwill As-Is, slightly tarnished, thoroughly hidden, and costing only $1.19 a pound.

GOODWILL OUTLET STORE,
*8300 S.E. McLoughlin Boulevard,
Portland.*

## THE BEST OF THE BEST

Oregon hosts the track & field center of the universe, Eugene; the best suburb in the United States, Lake Oswego; America's most celebrated ad agency, Weiden & Kennedy; the best humiliated U. S. Senator, Bob Packwood; the most prominent exemplar of *haute* white trash, Tonya Harding; the best ski lodge in the world, Timberline; America's first mall, Lloyd Center; the best grocery store anywhere, Strohecker's; the most elite slacker college, Reed; the top omnivorous/ enlightened megacorporation, Nike (if the Nike Swoosh does not pass the hammer and sickle, the swastika –and perhaps even the cross– as the most ubiquitous icon of the 20th century by the year 2000, then Phil Knight's promotion department has only themselves to blame); the best unsolved killings of all time, the Peyton-Allen murders; and the world's fastest, hippest, smartest computer–an Intel behemoth out in Beaverton which is able to make a trillion computations per second. So there.

## THE BEST OF THE BAD

Oregon also has produced the best of the bad. For example, the anti-Elvis, Courtney Love. And we're home to some of the very best bad guys. And what list of H-O gauge modern anti-heroes could be without DB Cooper, Bart Simpson, and Gary Gilmore? Oregon has produced two of the  best bad beers in the world–Blitz (for labor) and Henry Weinhard's Private Reserve (for management) and the world's best bad football coaches–ranging from Rich Brooks to June Jones (even John Robinson spent time coaching in Oregon). We've got best bad college football team in the U.S., Oregon State. And tell me the Portland Trailblazers–who make the playoffs every year only to be eliminated every year –are not the best bad professional basketball team anywhere.

–M.C.

# THE BEST PANCAKES

## BY BILL WICKLAND

I was feeling low on a recent wet, dark spring morning, the fifth in a row, when my old buddy Gary Ewing called to say, "Let's go to Hildegarde's for pancakes!"

Hildegarde's, where's that?

Halfway from Portland to Seaside on State Highway 26, aka Sunset Highway. The inn sits at the junction to Vernonia and Timber, logging towns in wild country just 40 miles from the city. To say "rustic" out here means at least one rusted-out Dodge Power wagon or loggers' crummy in each side yard.

Ewing is flapjack-finicky. "These are great—the fluffiest I've ever eaten," he said. "They must be three-quarters of an inch thick!"

I had to wonder about Gary's praise, for in 25 years I'd never seen him produce a normal pancake. His were filled with raisins and wheat germ and blueberries and whatever else he had around the kitchen, big and heavy, filling, but not my idea of breakfast, or even food. Even today I make excuses when invited to breakfast with Gary and Karen and their eight-year-old, five-foot-three-inch son Aaron. Gary stands

six-six. These people require nourishment, not necessarily cuisine.

The most wonderful meal Gary ever prepared was in the old Victorian where we lived in '71 or '72, one morning when we had no money, no pancake batter, no bread. Just eggs and bananas, a little milk, and some curry. Gary said, "I know! I'll do a banana omelet."

Save me, thought I, but now I serve it as brunch for friends, with strawberries and orange sections on the side. Exquisite; if you do it right, the banana slices are still a bit cool in the middle.

Anyway, Hildegarde's. I'd always wondered about that place on the way to the beach. You'd expect a huge, buxom Nordic blonde bellowing fjord songs, but you get Richard McMullin, a slight, quiet, tough-looking guy around 50 who looks like he'd be more at home setting chokers than making pancakes.

Gary had told me that Richard was sort of standoffish, but Ewing still has (now gray) hair to his waist and even today just the sight of him can make people stand back. Turns out Richard is friendly; he just doesn't overdo it. And he doesn't alter the items. You get what it says on the menu.

Like biscuits and gravy, or ham scram, or even crab scram with toast. At lunch you can get a half-pound logger burger, or a buffalo burger, or a meatball sandwich, or a cold ham and cheese. All regular dinners are $5.99, and the specials, surf and turf or steak and oysters, go for $10.95.

Gary called for two cakes plus the sausage omelet supreme. I ordered one hotcake on one plate, and bacon and eggs on another plate, then wandered into the bar (tavern) in the next room. A country classic. The bar itself is half a log; the bar stools are four-foot logs carved out and padded for your rump. The walls are covered with beer distributor promotional signs. The linoleum floor is worn away behind each bar stool, and in the center, from dancing. The jukebox is an old Motorola.

A sign behind the bar advertises: A Pair to Draw to—Chicken Thighs, Large and Meaty.

The restaurant side is, like the bar, essential old log country Oregon, like a functioning museum. Knotty pine walls, wood tables, oak chairs with the backs and legs painted white. There is an old but not distinctive glass case, an old but not distinctive glass-front cooler, and the same goes for the Pepsi cooler. The coffeemaker sits on a tilt.

A big table held five large people who looked like family. Two guys our age came in for coffee and pastry, golfers stopping on the way to coastal links.

Our meals came. Bacon, eggs, toast (properly, i.e., lavishly buttered), and little oblong hash browns.

The bacon was perfect, and the pancake was as light as it was sweet. Fine with Gary. He likes things sweet, to make up for the sugar he misses since he gave up drinking to keep from losing Karen. As for the potato bricks—"These are tastier than they look."

A friendly-looking couple came in to ask if they could get lunch yet. It was 11:15 a.m.

"Not 'til 11:30," Richard replied.

"Then we'll just sit right here and stare at you," the man retorted.

Regulars.

I took my third cup of coffee to the deck outside while Gary scarfed the hash-brown patties.

Beside the restaurant is a stocked

> This is a city of troll-like creatures, scraggly web-footed homeless, lonely-end-of-the-road desperados, and middle-class white kids seeking a safe refuge to explore the dark side of the subconscious.
>
> —MONK MAGAZINE

quarter-acre trout pond (no license, no limit). You land the fish on a fly rod with a bobber for 30 cents an inch. Two guys were landscaping around the pond. John, in his 20s, took a break and came up on the deck for a smoke.

"I can trim around all the trees on the place in one-fourth the time it takes that lunk," he nodded toward the guy in the distance with the power mower, "to do the lawn. You want to have the lawn mowed before you do the Weed Eater, so you know how short to cut around the trees."

Gary came out with a cup and sat down.

John gazed at the parking lot and spotted a vehicle there. "That Suburban looks familiar; I think I sold it to him. I used to work at Bruce Chevrolet in town."

Then a new Audi pulled up at the bait shack next to the pond and a nicely dressed couple got out and looked around, as if not certain the attraction was open yet.

Taking a big, put-upon breath, John allowed as how "it looks like I'll have to set these people up. Startin' to get a lot of 'em on weekends." This was Thursday. "July, August, the place will be jumpin'."

John made for the shack without a glance at the customer, who was headed for the door of Hildegarde's. Ewing had spotted a zoo-type pellet dispenser with a sign saying SEE THE FISH JUMP! 50¢ and made for that.

Richard came out of the restaurant with the customer and yelled, "John, the gear is in here!"

Fiddling around at the shack, John replied, "Well, I was lookin' for the bait."

Ewing threw handfuls of pellets about 20 feet from shore, and the water roiled with eight- to ten-inch trout.

But John knew what he was doing, once he got around to doing it. He baited hooks with worms for the couple and cast for them about 80 feet out into the pond. They'd have a great time playing their catch to the shore.

Nowhere on the menu does it say that Richard will cook and serve that fish for you. This morning I called to ask about that. At first he told me to call back in an hour. When I did, he said, "I'm busy as hell. Try me this afternoon." When asked how long he'd be there, he told me, "All day and all night." I reached him again at two. He kept me on hold for 15 minutes, then got a little break and was able to explain that they don't fry the trout, but will package them in ice.

HILDEGARDE'S COUNTRY INN, *Highway 26, Timber and Vernonia Junction, (503) 357-1633. Mountain air, mountain people, mountain food. Fair prices.*

## BEST DRY-OUT CLINIC:
# (THE LATE, GREAT) RALEIGH HILLS HOSPITAL

I don't know about you, but before my liver gets so big I have to pull it around behind me in a cart, I intend to dry out. And when I do I'd kill to enroll in the granddaddy of all dry-out clinics, the Raleigh Hills Hospital.

According to local legend, here's how it worked: What you got to do was throw a party for yourself. They were said to have a plush bar with every kind of liquor in it. On the first day, you had an absolute blast—you got totally shit-faced on what you wanted. On the second day, you started all over; however, as soon as you got a good load on, the bartender slipped you an Antabuse Mickey.

Classic mid-1960s behavior mod. Suddenly you were vomiting, writhing in death agony. I liked that. A lot. It appealed to a 12-year-old's understanding of the Catholicism I was being force-fed at the time. Be bad! Get punished!

But it worked, and it still can.

–M.C.

## OREGON IN THE 1980S

## BEST DEAD PERFECT MASTER:
# THE BHAGWAN

Summer 1983. Rancho Rajneesh, aka the Big Muddy Ranch, Wasco County, aka the middle of nowhere. The Twinkies had their hands full. Not only was Larry Colton's TV crew spread all over the place, filming a soap opera about this, America's biggest commune and wealthiest religious cult, but Rajneesh Chandra Mohan, aka Bhagwan Shree Rajneesh, aka God, was breaking a year-and-a-half-long vow of silence to announce the up-and-coming end of the world.

"There will be wars which are

### COLD HARD FACT:
The migration along the Oregon Trail was the largest voluntary migration in human history: over 300,000 men, women, and children made the trek.

bound to end in nuclear explosion…
Tokyo, New York, San Francisco,
Los Angeles, Bombay, etc—all these
cities are going to disappear and the
holocaust is going to be global, so
no escape will be possible."

Now, just an hour after dawn, the
Twinkies—the official hostesses at
the ranch (very good-looking young
women dressed in the height of
post-apocalypse fashion—purple leg
warmers, pumpkin-colored sweaters,
burnt-sienna blouses)—fielded press
queries regarding rumors that the
Bhagwan was planning a mass suicide
here at the ranch that would make
Jonestown look like a Girl Scout picnic, that the Rajneeshees were building missile silos on the ranch to
accommodate their own H-bomb-
tipped ICBMs, and, perhaps most
frightening of all, that Ken Kesey
had threatened to "throw the
Bhagwan all the way back to the
Ohio River," on the grounds that
"there's only room for one guru in
this state, not two."

You remember the Bhagwan and
Co. Those thousands of purple people who were constructing a utopian
society out there in the middle of
the Oregon desert 200 miles from
Portland, a "religious" community
complete with an airport, a gambling
casino, a disco, and enough bars and
gourmet restaurants to start a new
Sausalito.

The Rajneeshees had poured

$100 million into the ranch and
were spending an additional $25
million a year on a spread that had
been, until a couple of years before,
little more than a repository for an
occasional cow pie.

Thousands of Rajneeshees were
"worshiping" here every day.
"Worship" was Rajneeshee for
"work." Twelve hours a day, seven
days a week. Using technology that
allowed them to plant an acre an
hour, 6,000 acres were under cultiva-
tion. 15,000 shade trees had been
planted, and Rajneeshee engineers
had constructed a 90-foot-high
earthen dam to create a reservoir
containing 360 million gallons of
water.

These weren't just a bunch of hippies in Birkenstocks or the kind of
wobble-noggined zombies you find
wearing galoshes and togas and
hawking chrysanthemums at airports.
The ranch was 126 square miles—
two and a half times the area of San
Francisco—and hosted Air Rajneesh,
the Rajneeshee airline, whose flagship was a Convair turboprop for-
merly owned by Howard Hughes, as
well as more Rolls-Royces per capita
than Beverly Hills or Kuwait.

The Bhagwan had come to Oregon
to make his nut. And, in the process,
to become the Jesus Christ of the
21st century. Meanwhile, though, the
natives were getting . . . restless.

–M.C.

# Best Inner Turmoil

The end is near. When we left Larry at the conclusion of Crisis Seven, a crazy kid was attacking him. Suffice it to say, Larry mopped the floor with the boy and then left substitute teaching.

Did we mention that Larry Colton quit drinking? Colton was perhaps the world's only imbibing alcoholic who drank less than the amount recommended by the American Heart Association to maintain a healthy heart. He'd go days, weeks, months without even thinking about booze, and resort to it only when there was no other convenient way to get himself in trouble. He'd wait, say, until that perfect night when he could align a fifth of tequila, a borrowed automobile, and a highway patrolman . . . .

# CRISIS EIGHT

by LARRY COLTON

It was 1984. In a city of beautiful homes, verdant gardens, and scenic vistas of Mount Hood, I was living in a dingy upstairs flat near downtown. Actually, the flat belonged to Sherry, whom I'd moved in with on Christmas Eve after I ran out of heating oil in my rented two-bedroom, flaky-paint clapboard house. I'd showed up at her front door with my typewriter and my four-foot Christmas tree, its lights and ornaments already strung. Sherry, 29, was from New Orleans and had a degree in journalism from the University of Missouri, long legs, big dimples, curly dark hair, electric-blue eyes, and a golden retriever named Wally. She was working for a suburban weekly and I had just spent six months on a locally produced version of my "Pillars of Portland" newspaper serial. My dream was to revolutionize prime-time TV through creation of a nationwide interlocking network of "franchised regional soap operas." The project was written up on the front pages of *USA Today* and the *Wall Street Journal.*

# Larry Exploits Bhagwan to Get Rich

Four hundred thousand dollars from Showtime. Four hundred thousand American dollars. Wasn't that what Portland CBS station manager Steve Currie said he planned to sting the cable company for the rights to "Pillars of Portland"? That would mean, Larry calculated, $80,000 for himself. Eight Gs. That was more money than he'd ever made pitching for the Phillies. Inordinately more than he'd ever made freelancing for *Sports Illustrated.* A score like that would mean nice Christmas presents for his daughters—like maybe a couple of college educations.

Production had commenced and Larry was on his way to the Bhagwan's Big Muddy Ranch to shoot key scenes. Out of Portland, the highway rose to the green fire-shrouded base of Mount Hood, and then eased back down into the desert and prairie lands of central Oregon. A huge blue sky, a herd of cattle, then vast yellow plains of wheat and an abandoned station wagon, red with rust, and the slumped carcass of an uninhabited farm building.

Finally, Antelope, population 95. A minor collection of white houses that appeared slightly shrunken and distorted by time, half lost in the shade of broad-leafed trees. But there were big new pieces of construction equipment here and there, and people all dressed in orange, purple, and red. "Maroonies."

On toward the Rancho Rajneesh. Yellow hills rose up around us. The land became radical, rocky. High up on a mesa, a man in red stood with a walkie-talkie.

In the distance a car approached, feathering up dust. A Rolls-Royce with a silver Lincoln Continental behind. "Here comes the main guy," Larry said, scratching his beard, "the

Bhagwan Shree Rajneesh. Or just plain God to his friends. Every day he drives 40 miles to Madras, turns around, and drives back. Never stops or anything." The Bhagwan passed, behind the wheel of the Rolls, a pretty young woman at his side. Gray hair to his shoulders, a round brown face, large hooded eyes, a guru's guru.

Just past the entrance to the ranch was a convoy of huge dump trucks, then the Bhagwan's huge manmade lake, then his airport. From out of the desert appeared row after row of houses and tents. So here he was. If Larry played his cards right, the eighty grand would soon be piling up money-market rates.

Before letting him on the ranch itself—where he would be met by the beautiful nubile "Twinkies"— Larry was stopped. His car and body were searched for guns and bombs.

"We've got an hour to do the crucial love scene, huh?" said Paul Nixon, the Paul Newman lookalike star of *Pillars of Portland.* "Then don't worry. I can do 60 takes. My first wife used to call me the Minuteman."

Larry, his breath flagging steam in the early morning air, said, "Was that before or after she threw you out?"

"Hey look," Nixon said, "she was gorgeous. I figured her for a dream.

We were married in Nevada. I knew she drank, but after four days in Reno she still wanted to party. The crazy bitch was downing a quart of vodka a day."

Nixon stepped down from one of *Pillars of Portland's* 40 Winnebagos and surveyed Rancho Rajneesh. Matters have been complicated this morning because the Bhagwan has just announced the end of the world—and the Twinkies, scheduled to help with the *P of P* shooting, are busy instead handling a press eager to hear about the impending obliteration of New York, Moscow, Beijing, and L.A.

Nixon sipped coffee. "When I was in Vietnam, I was a door gunner in a helicopter. One of those guys with a life expectancy of about 30 seconds." Sound men and cameramen were moving camera equipment between the two Winnebagos. "Never got a scratch. Three years in the Marines, machine-gunning VC, and not even a Band-Aid. Then I come to Portland, enroll in a karate class, and they put me up against this 95-pound nine-year-old homosexual. On the level. He was already a black belt, the instructor's favorite. He got his kicks watching the little fruitcake beat me half to death. They'd pair us in no-contact and the kid would kick me right in the nug-

> "Your ath, marine! Fight me! Fight me in the street!"

gies. I'd keel over, my knees hugging my chest, and say, 'Hey, little pal, what's coming down? And he'd say, 'Your ath, marine! Fight me! Fight me in the street!' "

Nixon looked over the script. He was playing a successful lumber broker there on the ranch to sell the Rajneeshees either cocaine or plywood—take your pick.

Evelyn Hamilton, a local heiress who had paid for the show's startup costs, stepped down from one of the Winnebagos. She was thin, tall, and pale, and had the stern spacy look most recently in vogue during the Salem witch trials. Like heiresses everywhere, Ms. Hamilton tended to exist above the fray, and since TV production is entirely fray, she seemed a little out of place.

When it was time to shoot, Paul Nixon was standing out alongside the road with about 300 Maroonies watching the Bhagwan drive by in his Rolls, when the Bhagwan's eyes fixed on Nixon's own Paul Newman-like baby blues. Nixon was mesmerized. There was a camera pointed toward his face and the director, Tom Chamberlain, was behind him pounding on his back, hissing, "Act! Act! Act!" But Nixon had been struck dumb, faced with the sight of …God..                    —M. C.

## Best Inner Turmoil

*Pillars of Portland* gathered great local momentum. The *Oregonian* ran a story in its Sunday magazine titled "Is Pillars Too Big for Portland?" Suddenly Larry was the belle of the ball at Rotary and Kiwanis Club luncheons, his tales of major league baseball and incipient showbiz success a popular double bill in a town that was basically bored to death with itself. At the luncheons, Larry was almost certain that he alone was there for the food.

We join him now, however, right after the *Pillars of Portland* television premiere.

# CRISIS NINE

by LARRY COLTON

There was one big problem, though. The show that aired on the Portland CBS affiliate was an Atrocious Bomb. My two partners on the project, the director and the producer, split from Oregon in the middle of the night, leaving me to deal with the unpaid bills. I had talked Rick Wise, an ex-teammate with the Phillies who once pitched a no-hitter *and* hit two home runs in the same major league game, into loaning $5,000 to the partnership He had his lawyer sue, tacking on another ten grand in punitive damages.

"You're welcome to my Nova," I said.

# BEST DEAD PERFECT MASTER:
# THE BHAGWAN
## (CONT.):
### Meanwhile, back at Rancho Rajneesh

Winter 1984. A Bell helicopter hovered against the brown desert hills–darting this way and that–then suddenly bolted across the sky, its rotors beating thwapthwapth-wapthwap over the cold blue. The muzzle of a submachine gun sticking out one side, it swept above the thousand of purple-garbed people gathered along Nirvana Way.

Then, below, a big station wagon appeared. Inside, two men in purple. Mounted on a gun rack, an M-16.

The purple people, the Bhagwan "sannyasins"–young women, old men, young men, old women, kids–began going bananas. For at the end of Nirvana Way was another car. A Rolls-Royce. Inside sat the Bhagwan Shree Rajneesh. He was at the wheel. Dark skin. Big almond eyes. A gray waterfall beard and matching gray robe. One glance and you knew: Perfect Master. Straight from central casting.

His Majesty drove slowly. A man in purple walked behind, cradling an

Uzi. His eyes flicked this way and that, his trigger finger tapping at the stock.

People were now beating on guitars and warbling what sounded like the "Hava Nagilah" sung by the Lovin' Spoonful, drunk.

*Oh, Bhagwan, my sweetest, sweetest love! The love that you give me, I'll give it back to you!*

Sannyasins jumped up and down as if on pogo sticks, laughing and crying, tears zigzagging down their cheeks.

But all was not well here in the Promised Land.

The Bhagwan had plunked down $2.5 million for the Big Muddy Ranch but relations with the locals stunk from the beginning.

Oregon has a reputation for being a very moderate state, but what that really means is that it's the kind of place where liberals hate blacks and bikers vote Republican. And Wasco County is a desert rangeland where the cowboys and Indians are still shooting at each other and where people are inclined to regard folks like John Denver and Willie Nelson as degenerate hippies.

Weird tales circulated: hundreds of Rajneeshees experienced nervous breakdowns after being forced to meditate on the question "Who am I?" An Albany housewife gathered over 5,000 signatures on behalf of an "Alien cult" bill that would have forced the governor to expel the Rajneeshees, because "the Rajneeshees are going to kill all the people who are Christian."

A former Sannyasin claimed that at the ranch the names of new arrivals who had been medically approved for promiscuous sex were posted on a bulletin board outside the main dining hall. A "press release" purportedly from the Oregon State Department of Fish and Wildlife was circulated at the commune announcing "there will be an open season on the Rajneesh, known locally as the Red Rats or Red Vermin.

"These Red Rats may be a little rough to dress out and if gut shot, probably not worth the effort.

"IT WILL BE LAWFUL TO:

• Hunt in a party of over 700.

• Use more than 50 attack dogs in one group.

• Use double 00 buckshot (they are thick-skinned).

•…Possess a road-killed Red Rat.

It is OK to hit one, but don't pick the bastard up."

And after a man who had stayed at the commune was arrested for setting off two bombs in the Portland Rajneesh Hotel—blowing up one side of the building—commune members began arming themselves. With Uzis, CAR-15s, and Galil assault rifles. There were rumors the Bhagwan planned to buy tanks and helicopter gunships. It was awful. You know the rest.                                    –M.C.

# Best Inner Turmoil

When we left Larry and his latest love, Sherry, Sherry had lost her job as a newspaper reporter and the couple was drowning in debt . . . .

# CRISIS TEN

by LARRY COLTON

From my upstairs bedroom I could hear weird noises coming from my daughter Wendy's room downstairs. Shrill and irritating. I hesitated to investigate, but it was definitely intruding on my Saturday-morning sleep.

It was 1985. I had pulled it together. Sort of. Two weeks before, Wendy had moved down from Seattle to live with me and my girl-friend Sherry. I had a regular, responsible nine-to-five gig. My offi-

cial job title was marketing projects director for Nike International, cor-porate doubletalk for "we don't know what to do with this guy now that we've hired him." I spent my days churning out in-house fluff about Air Jordan and all the latest scoops in footwear fashion, and bringing home a steady if unspectac-ular $2,000 monthly paycheck, decent health bennies, and lots of great sneakers to replay my K-Mart Specials.

We'd moved into a comfortable four-bedroom rented house in a nice neighborhood, and I bought a ten-year-old Datsun with four forward gears.

The noise from Wendy's room grew shriller and more irritating. I figured it was probably her newest heavy metal album. She and her cohort in metal mania, Jennifer, a curly-haired blonde with poured-on black jeans and a seductress smile, had been front-row center the night before at the long-awaited Metallica concert, part of the band's Kill 'Em All tour. Metallica was taxing my fundamental belief in the First Amendment in a way I'm sure Elvis never did to my mom.

Wendy's fascination with heavy metal puzzled me—I thought her disposition more suited to the Bee Gees and was clinging to the hope that metal mania, like her weight problem, would soon be a thing of the past. But reality was not my parental long suit. For 14 years I had been a Disneyland Dad to her, making sure her weekend visits were special times—but now she was living under my roof. I was asking her to clean her room and do the dishes. Real Dad demands. I could see changes. She was enrolled at Portland Community College; she had a part-time job in a day care center; she was taking an aerobics class; her eating habits were improving. I wasn't ready to declare myself Father of the Year, but I was pleased.

When the noise downstairs persisted, I went to explore. As I descended the stairs, I heard voices and laughter. Male voices. Wendy heard me coming and was waiting at the bottom of the stairs, her $3,000 orthodontia smile (which took me six years to pay for) lighting the hallway.

"Guess who's here!" She was beaming.

Judging from her excitement, I was ready to guess Tom Cruise or Rob Lowe. Foolish me.

"It's the drummer and lead singer for Metallica!" she exuded. "They're here . . . in our house! Can you believe it?"

"They spent the night?"

"You don't understand, Dad," she continued, "They are the *greatest* band in the world."

Foolish me, here I'd been thinking it was Iron Maiden. Still, if they were so great, why didn't they have a swanky room at the Marriott? I was afraid to ask for details. A voice inside advised me to boot these scumbag pseudo-musicians out of my house, and how dare they take advantage of my vulnerable daughter. But wait. How were these guys any different than I had been as a clean-cut baseball player breezing in and out of towns and leaving behind a trail of one-night stands? Was Wendy going to be emotionally scarred from this?

I hoped not. I doubted it. I headed to the kitchen for a bowl of Grape-Nuts. As I sat at the nook crunching away, I looked up to see one of the Masters of Rock wander in to check out the offerings in my fridge. Wendy introduced us. His name was Lars Ulrich. What was I supposed to say to a Rock Legend? Ask what I might expect on his next album? Or show him my baseball card to prove that I was somebody too? I just waved a friendly greeting. Being the Good Father. I was in the bathroom when Lars and his Metallica cohort left, so I missed my chance to wish them luck on the rest of their Kill 'Em All tour.

## BEST SKI LODGE/SUMMER SKIING IN THE WORLD:

# TIMBERLINE

The main door weighs pounds. The central fireplace is three stories high and contains 450 tons of rock. The six wooden columns in the main lodge are each 32 feet high and cut with a broad ax from logs that, when floated down the Columbia, were six feet wide. Huge ponderosa pine struts are  secured by wrought iron strapping a quarter-inch thick. There are hand-carved banisters, hand-hooked rugs, hand-loomed drapes, and hand-appliquéd bedspreads. Walls are paneled in thick-cut cedar and hung with nearly 200 original artworks. With guests including presidents and movie stars (Alan Ladd and Sidney Poitier refought part of the Korean War down the road in *All the Young Men*; Jack Nicholson skulked about the grounds before going berserk for *The Shining*), Timberline Lodge is the product of a mid-1930s WPA project run brilliantly amok. Originally funded for about $800,000, it couldn't be replicated today for $40 million.

Timberline Lodge is a massive granite castle perched below Mount Hood's Palmer Snowfield. It's 75 yards from the lodge to the lift, which takes you up to 7,016 feet, to 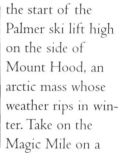 the start of the Palmer ski lift high on the side of Mount Hood, an arctic mass whose weather rips in winter. Take on the Magic Mile on a bad day in December and the wind can whip the spit right out of your mouth. But its summer microclimate must have been designed by Ullr, the beneficent fake god of ski.

The Palmer snowfield is as ancient as the Apostles. Two-thousand-year-old snow packs its gullies in some spots up to 60 feet deep. This frozen mass re-refrigerates on top, even in the middle of August. The heavy moisture of Northwest snow—what makes it inferior to the wonderfully "light" Colorado and Utah snow in the winter—makes it perfect in the summer. The snow glaciates: its crystals are bigger and they stand up, forming something like a huge field of ball bearings. Perfect corn snow, like the stuff they scoop in sno-cones. A very "forgiving and elastic" surface. English translation: you can raise hell on skis or snowboard and still not get hurt.

Afterward, hang out by or in the Timberline Lodge swimming pool, and contemplate the classical lines of Mount Hood's south face looming enormously overhead. From here, floating flat on your back in the jade green 85-degree water, the view is extraordinary.

Room rates are little more than you'd expect to pay at an airport Sheraton. —M. C.

TIMBERLINE LODGE 58 miles from Portland; 6 miles off of *Highway 26 at Government Camp (it's impossible to get lost);(800) 547-1406.*

## BEST NATURAL WONDER:

# THE COLUMBIA GORGE

It is an hour after dawn, the sky a soft baby-blanket blue. Glistening gray, the Columbia River carves a wide path bordered by green grasslands along its shores below. The grassy plain quickly gives way to lush scrub and young trees, second-growth Douglas fir, alder, and cottonwoods grown up after lightning fires and blowdowns.

From high vantage points atop dramatic cliffs you can see for miles and across to the massive gray cliffs on the Oregon side, not far from Multnomah Falls, in an area once alive with fishwheels that scooped thousands of pounds of salmon from the river each day.

The Columbia River Gorge is one of the most astonishingly handsome sights in North America, the result of massive geologic upheavals that began almost 50 million years ago when the western edge of North America rose out of shallow seas. Additional layers of rock were formed by lava that spilled like water from volcanoes in what is now Idaho. Flash forward to six or seven million years ago, when the Columbia flowed several miles south of the present-day Gorge, its course continually altered as uplifting and folding of the earth formed the Tualatin, Portland, Hood River, and Mosier Basins.

Then more great lava eruptions. Today old craters and cindercones can be seen up and down the Columbia, dwarfed by mountains created during the last great volcanic age—Mount Hood, Mount Adams, and Mount St. Helens—part of a chain of active volcanoes, each a little more than a half-million

years old.

Compared to the surrounding land, The Gorge itself is almost brand-new, created during the Ice Age. About 15,000 years ago a vast finger of ice came down the Purcell Trench in northern Idaho and moved up the canyon of the Clark Fork River. It formed an immense 2,000-foot-high ice dam that created what geologists refer to as Lake Missoula, a 500-cubic-mile body of water approximately 4,000 feet above sea level that extended for hundreds of miles up valleys in western Montana.

The ice melted. The dam collapsed. An estimated 380 cubic *miles* of water in a wave over 1,000 feet high (a tidal wave, by comparison, rarely reaches heights of more than 50 feet) came crashing west, obliterating everything in its path, hurtling along with the force of thousands of hydrogen bombs, ten times the force of all the rivers in the world. The water covered 1,300 square miles in Oregon's Umatilla Basin and flooded 3,000 square miles in what is now the Willamette Valley in Oregon.

In less than two weeks, and possibly in as little as 40 hours, the entire Columbia Gorge was created, killing hundreds, perhaps thousands, of indigenous people by the force of the water.

Thousands of years ago, migratory hunters crossed an ice bridge from Siberia to North America following the retreating ice in search of mastodon and giant bison. They came to the Gorge. Their only weapons were spears and darts whipped from slings.

Cool, huh?                    —M. C.

---

**COLD HARD FACT:**

There is more hydro-electricity generated in the Columbia Gorge than anywhere else in the U.S.A.

## BEST WIND SURFING:

# Hood River

They're out there by the dozens, by the score, *schools* of them—sails blown taut, boards knifing and bouncing over the whitecaps, whipping across the Columbia River, zigzagging against the high stone bluffs of the Gorge that loom against the dark, sea blue sky on the Washington side.

Wind surfers.

It is sunny, windy, and chilly. A guy with a buccaneer's hair, mustache, and beard slogs out of the water. His baggy "dry suit" makes him look like a deflated astronaut. Windsurf boards rest next to the shore, fins exposed—great, white, flattened, riveted, pinstriped fiberglass sharks. The parking lot behind is bumper-to-bumper. Cars from everywhere. Oregon, Washington, California, Texas. Beat-up pickups, Brady Bunch–style station wagons, and tons of big four-wheel-drive rigs from British Columbia.

A decade ago Hood River was a ho-hum scenic whistlestop tourist town. At the center of the Columbia Gorge, it catered to sightseers, hikers, and nature freaks. But during the 1980s, the popularity of wind surfing grew at a hurricane pace. And this stretch of the Columbia provided one of the best combinations of consistent wind and open water anywhere. Now Hood River is considered by many to be the best wind-surfing spot in the world.

–M.C.

# THE BEST BAR EAST OF BONNEVILLE DAM

### By John Tilman

The Pendleton Round-up bills itself as world famous. As the second oldest and second best-known American rodeo, it sort of is. But world-class riding and roping alone don't drive droves of tourists down I-84 each September. Nor do they hit the trail just for the parades, street carnival, horse races, Western pageantry, or cowboy and Indian dancing. Many come mainly for the weeklong party.

The epicenter of that party is the Let 'Er Buck Room, a temporary saloon located under the south grandstand of the rodeo grounds. On Friday and Saturday of round-up, it gets so crowded and steamy that Let 'Er Buck resembles the Black Hole of Calcutta with a liquor license.

It can become so closely packed that the overimbibed can pass out without falling. Burly, courteous, mustached bouncers stand at the ready to hustle outside as many hyperventilating claustrophobes as belligerent drunks. But the amateur bartenders are friendly and, considering the crammed-as-a-Tokyo-subway-full-of-booze-crazy-tourists conditions, remarkably efficient. What the drinks lack in variety, they more than make up for in stiffness.

The Let 'Er Buck Room has its own rituals. One is for boyfriends—or complete strangers—to hoist girlfriends—or new acquaintances—on their shoulders. The bartenders ring a bell. The young woman is then obligated to disrobe to the waist and swing her bra, if she is wearing one, over her head as many times as good taste allows, and fling it to the huddled masses, who are obliged to hang it over the bar. Over a decade ago, the Oregon Liquor Control Commission, or perhaps the fire marshal, ruled the bartenders could no longer encourage such behavior. It made no difference. And when the Roundup directors put up posters informing the drinking public that it had to keep its clothes on, the signs promptly became collector's items.

Perhaps because Pendleton's rodeo includes no profession-al cowgirl events—no barrel racing, no breakaway calf roping or goat-tying—women at the Let 'Er Buck Room have established a competition of their own: cowboy gluteus-grab. More experienced contestants opt for biting off the labels from the back pockets of men's Wranglers. Ladies often depart with stacks of a dozen or more.

A new, fire-breathing local OLCC was shocked to learn what was going on under the south grandstand in her bailiwick. She decreed that the legal capacity of the Let 'Er Buck Room must no longer be exceeded. So now people have to stand in line, usually in the hot sun or in the rain, so that, once inside, they stay even longer and get even drunker.

They start herding revelers out of the Let 'Er Buck at six. The party then adjourns to the Rainbow Court and Main. Later, it continues at the Happy Canyon Dance Hall and Casino at the Convention Center.

BEST HOTEL EAST OF PORTLAND

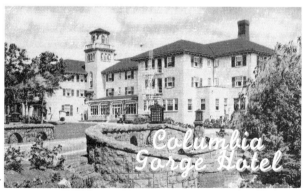

BEST FIRST CHAPTER OF A NOVEL ABOUT OREGON THAT'S NOT
EVEN FINISHED YET BY A TOTALLY UNKNOWN WRITER

# Whipsnake

## by Zorn Matson

### Chapter One

Cindy smiled: inwardly she squirmed. Only 50 more "Camel bucks" to go, and I can buy my own racing-crew windbreaker and never be chilly again.

She idolized the rough 'n' tumble stock-car drivers and was a little bit in awe of the brassy women they were drawn to; but if she had to, she could learn to like the taste of Copenhagen chaw draining down her throat if it meant Roy "The Whipsnake" Millard would kiss her like that again . . . .

❐

"Ya know, Whip, I think that Cindy chick thought you was gonna give that jacket to her instead of Verleen like you did."

Whip rocked back from trying to tune in the police band, sucked the last out of the pint of Jack, and hucked the bottle in an easy arc past the driver's nose. He watched the forces of gravity, wind, and luck direct the flight of the lazily rotating missile to its point of impact, the subsequently imploding windshield of the approaching Mazda pickup.

Through the back window of Gib's cheesy '70 Roadrunner, he watched the small truck veer, over-correct, and flip. Gib hadn't elaborated on the "Fuh?!" that escaped his gap-toothed maw as the bottle skimmed past his face, but Whip knew that Gib was weak and would have plenty to say to survive a police questioning.

Whip felt satisfaction in not having to think through the obvious series of events that this would dictate. His dad would be proud of his hastily developing plan, as it honored one of his favorite old saws: "Turn yer setbacks into opportunities, boy! Otherwise you'll jes' fail the Lord and die mopin'!"

He'd make good use of Gib first, before he killed him.

❐

"Oh fine, Whip! Jesus tell you to do that?"

Whip turned to Gib, who was just finishing a clumsily executed panic stop, and spat through the enveloping cloud of burned rubber and churning dust. "Shit, Gib. We gotta get back there and help those assholes. They might not be dead!"

"So help me, Whip, if I lose my license over this it is the last time I drive you anywhere! I swear to God, you're more trouble than a whole nest of hornets, man!"

Gib laboriously cranked the triple-chromed, welded chain-link steering wheel and punched the gas, which lurched the car into a shuddering bat-turn, pointing it in the direction of the destroyed pickup.

Gib slowed as they approached the over-turned wreck, which had come to rest in the brush-choked gully over the verge of the old highway. At least there wasn't any traffic out here. Other than the logging trucks, everybody used the four-lane between Portland and the coast.

"Gib, I think we better drive to where we can pull off and hide this piece of shit out of sight of any nosy fuckin' loggers, know what I mean?"

"This is *not* a piece-of-shit car, Whip, and we wouldn't have to be hiding anything except that bottle you flung like a dumb maniac if you

weren't such a ..."

Gib feared Roy's smile more than any facial contortion he could imagine; it heralded such unexpected mayhem. He broke off midsentence in the hope that somehow, if he drove away, the smile would remain, frozen, hovering above the crumbling tarmac in his rearview as he pulled away from the pickup and drove toward the first available turnoff. Gib felt like a possum in the lights of an oblivious semi. He sat as still as death, waiting for the unimaginable ...When he glanced over, the moment had passed and Whip seemed lost in thought, as if he had no memory, as if every subsequent second were unconnected, spinning away from a newly desperate promise of happiness...

❏

The hike back to the truck was time enough for Whip to explore a fitting conclusion to his task if he could play it right, and left him feeling that if there were a better solution, it would unfold as God's plan; in no way would he interfere if a better opportunity presented itself. This he had learned. This he could trust, as far as it went.

There wasn't any movement or

> ## Shit, Gib. We gotta get back there and help those assholes. They might not be dead!

sound coming from the truck. Whip wondered why anyone would put a fancy roll bar behind the cab in the truck bed if it wasn't tall enough to save their sorry ass.

"Jesus, Whip, I think her arm's broken...no shit man...these people are fucked up!"

"Shut up, Gib."

"Her head's kinda cut off, Whip."

"Shut up, Gib."

"They're fuckin' dead or somethin'..." Gib's voice trailed off.

Whip slowly climbed the steep incline to the road, and stood with his arms folded, turning his head slowly back and forth, in disbelief or surveying the stump-ridden hills, and said, "Gib, you can keep a secret, can'tcha?"

## I'm gonna take care of this whole problem for you, Gib. Don't you worry...

□

Cindy went straight home after the race, to her cheery little house and poured herself a glass of wine. She was having trouble forgiving Roy for going back on what was an offer made in front of friends and so held the added embarrassment of, well, not wearing the promised windbreaker.

She clapped her hand over her mouth reflexively to stifle the giggle she startled herself with.

Wind-breaker! That describes Whip perfectly. He had, it was known, a problem with holding his own, so to speak. Cindy felt instantly better, and downed her wine in a gulp and poured herself a 'fresher.

Limp-snake, more like, I'll bet. This burst her painful amusement into a howl of glee, followed by a further heroic quaff.

He was cute though, in a scarytingly kinda way. She couldn't believe all that her friends said about Whip, somehow. She didn't think they would probably feel that way if they could see him the way she knew he was inside. It gave her a warm frantic surge, and she hugged her knees tight. Soon they would be together, and he would be so happy that he would become the man she was convinced he could be.

□

Whip reached through the shattered windshield and was trying to undo the safety belt that was embedded halfway through the neck of the girl in the passenger seat. It was weird how some of these safety devices seemed dead set on trapping, mangling, and delivering a departing insult to those who blindly or innocently relied on them for protection.

"She's gonna look like Satan's own Pez dispenser, if we can get her out, Gib."

"Uh...why would we want to get her out, Whip?"

"Why, I imagine she's still warm and probably wouldn't say no, Gib."

"You want to make love to a dead girl, Whip?"

"Well, I doubt it's going to be as romantic as all that, but I am going to at least have a look at her. Gimme your knife so I can cut this safety belt off her."

"You got a knife, Whip. What's wrong with yours?"

"It's back in my jacket, asshole. Gimme your fuckin' knife."

Against every keening note of caution swirling in his head, Gib reluctantly handed Whip his sheath knife and wondered if this was how it felt to voluntarily rest your head on an executioner's block. It was dreamy, and oddly releasing. Then it was all too late.

Gib tried to look through the passenger window but it was shattered in place. The overturned truck was tipped back, resting on the tailgate and the crushed roof of the cab at the height of the chrome roll bar. The hood latch was popped and the hood was hanging, bent nearly in two in front of the vaporized windshield. In order to see anything in the cab, you had to crawl behind it

and fold it back toward the front of the truck, which made it hard to do anything else.

"Hold this hood out of my way so I can move, man."

"I think you ought to get out of there and we should get as far away as possible, Whip. I don't want to have anything more to do with this shit. It's probably murder, and I was driving the goddamn car!"

"You won't have to worry about nothin', Gib."

"What's that supposed to mean?"

"I'm gonna take care of this whole problem for you, Gib. Don't you worry. There's nothin to tie you to this wreck except maybe some lip prints on a pulverized bottle of J.D., but I think I pretty much sucked those off before I tossed it, so if you wanna think it over maybe you wouldn't mind holding this hood off my ass while you're at it, OK, Bro?"

Gib pulled the hood away and Whip sat on his haunches and looked at the upside down girl in the passenger seat. He looked at the driver, whose face was a terrain of blood and pebbled windshield and then it occurred to him that the girl had hardly bled at all, even with a seat belt through her neck. There was a green nylon duffel bag hang-

> "It's probably murder, and I was driving the goddamn car!"

ing from the gear shift knob, caught partially under the dash. Whip worked the zipper open, which loosed a teddy bear and sprung a G-string, a towel, some more worn-looking lingerie, and a two-foot cardboard mailing tube, the ends taped up with blue duct tape. He cut into one end of the tube and was rewarded with a puff of white powder, slowly curling in the dead air of the cab. He said, "Well fuck me runnin', ain't that the most…"

"What's wrong, Whip?" said Gib, immediately regretting such a dumb-ass question. "I…I mean, what now?"

"Lemme outta here, man." Gib held the hood up and watched the tips of Whip's boots plow two long furrows as he backed out from under the engine compartment.

"What's that thing?" asked Gib quietly.

Whip cocked his head and chuckled. "Well, Gib, I think it's safe to say that it's a huge stick of very expensive dynamite, but what kind of dynamite it is, I don't rightly know. My guess is it's either South American or Chinese dynamite, but somebody is gonna get awful sore when they find out it isn't their dynamite anymore." Whip held up the tube and lightly slapped it into his palm, which brought forth a dusty white plume that sifted down to the ground at their feet. "The

Lord giveth, my man, and the Lord taketh away. Wipe your paw prints off the car, Gib. I wanna go some-place less quiet and get a beer. Think this through."

For as long as he could remember, Gib had been dumbfounded by Whip's uncanny ability to cheat the golden rule. It seemed that the more he did unto others and the more suffering he caused, the less he was made to pay. Increasingly Whip seemed to profit by his casual cruel-ties and calculated brutality as if, in some twisted way, God had loosed him on the universe to confound any sense of balance or justice: Whip was severely charmed. It led Gib to a grudging belief that Chaos was the order of things, and that hanging with Whip was suspending him in the eye of the tornado; by associa-tion came protection from the rag-ing shit-storm that emanated from, raged spinning within a hair's breath, but never touched his friend. Gib loved Whip. He always had.

# Burp Gun Party

BEST BASH

A Memoir by David Kelly

**In which Our Leader, moments prior to suffering the stroke that would almost kill him, ate, drank, shot, and was merry at the best party Oregon ever throws.**

If you live in Oregon and can perform El Presidente in six seconds or less, you have probably already been invited to the Last Buffalo Shoot. If you don't understand what I just said, don't worry about it, but this is not a party you want to crash.

If and when the invite arrives, as it did to Bennett and me, be ready to present yourself, driver's license, current registration, and insurance certificate in hand, to a guardian of the northern reaches of the Umatilla plateau at 7 a.m. on a July Sunday morning.

Lo, the hapless and bleary city guys pulled over on the deserted main street of Oracle, Oregon . . . .

Officer Jung Il McIntyre stares through the window of Bennett's Vanagon at the AK-47 and AR-15 lying on a pile of banana clips on the back seat. In New Jersey, he would be crouched in a flash, gun drawn, behind the door of his squad car screaming for backup. But here on the plateau, where they grow enough soft white wheat to keep all Seoul in ramen noodles, a few assault weapons more or less won't get you any special treatment. "Do you realize, sir, that if someone had been coming when you failed to stop back there, you could have been killed or injured?"

Bennett mutters something ashamed and compliant, in the hopes that Officer Jung Il won't run his plates. Bennett's insurance has expired.

But Jung Il, Korean by birth, Scotch Presbyterian by upbringing, calls Bennett's plates to a dispatcher who never sleeps, then slaps a zebra-stripe sticker on the plate signifying that this vehicle may no longer be legally driven.

I stand guard over the guns 'n' ammo while Bennett hikes down to a phone booth in front of the Silo Cafe, where live-wire Baptists are open before church, just as if this was pheasant season. The question has turned from whether we can get a coffee and a slab of marionberry pie to whether we can get to the shoot by eight, when the flag will fly, or at all. A 4-Runner whips by, disturbing a lone tumbleweed in the middle of Main Street. Its bumper reads My Wife Yes, My Dog Maybe, My Gun Never: Support Your Local Police.

We have been busted on the way to a cop convention. Many of the Buff shooters are sheriff's deputies and police auxiliaries. Event founder Merritt Bowman, whose hundred of acres of wheat stretch out all around Oracle and who has made another million in emu sperm, is himself some kind of honorary deputy chief of police. Rangemaster Clint Smith, whose orders we will all be under, is America's leading police weapons and tactics consultant.

Merritt's impulse in founding the Last Buffalo Shoot was, in addition to the presence of a 1,000-yard-long abandoned feedlot on his property, the original 1992 assault rifle ban signed by the traitorous George Bush, that Eastern liberal posing as a Texan. More recently Bush, out of action and polishing his image for posterity, quit the NRA in supposed shock over hearing the ATF described as "jackbooted thugs"—a phrase he had been hearing without noticeable upset, from Representative John Dingle, among others, for decades.

The Last Buffalo Shooters have no respect for Bush nor for the agents in whose name he professes to speak. All local cops hate the Feds. The Feds act superior and get paid more. The Feds are incompetent, as proven by:

☞ The Miami Shootout in which one hood wasted five FBI agents trying to make a felony stop.

☞ The Ruby Ridge Shootout in 1992, in which the FBI, attempting to apprehend suspected firearms violator Randy Weaver, shot and killed Weaver's 14-year-old son and Weaver's wife, nailing her with a babe in her arms.

☞ Waco.

And the Feds are perfidious. Especially when an election is coming. Nobody is sure what Congress will get up to in the wake of the Oklahoma Camo-moron atrocity, but nobody is gladdened at the thought of greater federal police powers and all feel it is a good time to hone critical skills in a way that is fun for the whole family.

Thank God, we have a friend in town. Bennett succeeds in awakening Merritt's cousin Helga, a blonde as ample as her Wagnerian name. She's an aspiring actress, a creamy-breasted extra on *China Beach* and *Murphy Brown*. To urban Jewish sophisticate Bennett, it is a source of grief that Helga digs only cowboys and cops. Bennett tried the matter strenuously last night in Pendleton at the Rainbow Bar, but his Woody Allen charm was lost in a room full of Marlboro Men.

Now Helga is getting up far earlier than she had planned on a Sunday to drive us to the Last Buffalo, where Bennett's surprising aptitude with an AK-47 won't do him any good either, because everybody else is a cop.

We get our coffee and pie. "Eat Marion Berry now," observes Bennett, "and you won't have to blow him later."

We transfer assault rifles and .45s in speed holsters, plus ammo, to Helga's Civic and lock the Vanagon on our clothes and camping gear. Neither Bennett nor I, a fat duck hunter, has a combat shotgun, so we will compete in only two-thirds of the shoot. The assault rifles are borrowed. Bennett is not an Armed Citizen. I own, besides hunting arms and the pair of .45s, an extensively gunsmithed and very accurate World War II Garand M1, but it is not banned, and the spirit of the day seems to demand outlawed rifles.

Arriving at the shoot, it is clear that the spirit of the day demands other things we don't have. The ex-feedlot is in a swale surrounded by golden wheat fields and even now it is collecting heat like a reflector oven. Having promised each other not to wear any camo, Bennett and I are inappropriately dressed as the Corsican Brothers in corduroys, bird-shooter vests, and felt hats. Uniform of the day turns out to be running shorts and Nikes.

**Having promised each other not to wear any camo, Bennett and I are inappropriately dressed as the Corsican Brothers in corduroys, bird-shooter vests, and felt hats.**

Subtract the weapons and the Kill a Commie for Mommy T-shirts, and the Buffalo Shoot looks like a local Saturday motocross or radio-controlled airplane meet. Awnings are rolled out from pickup campers; lawn furniture and Coleman coolers have been deployed. Wives are touching base and keeping kids in yelling range. Husbands are pulling tabs and telling lies. A tall tan mom in halter and cutoffs has her baby in a Snugli carrier on one side, Dirty Harry's six-inch Smith & Wesson in a shoulder holster on the other. And officials!—a committee with a card table, clipboards, and pin-on numbers—essentials weekend America can't function without.

A veteran of hundreds of hours on location, Helga tips back the seat in her economobile and goes to sleep. Wistful Bennett watches her spectacular bosom rise and fall like a Pacific swell, but finally grows bored, and with nothing to sit on or shade under, we turn ourselves in to be registered, checked to make sure we have earmuffs and safety glasses, and warned to keep our weapons clear at all times off the line.

We also arrange to sight in our loaner rifles at the 25-yard line. I'm surprised and delighted to discover that the 1968 Tet Offensive vintage AR-15 shoots the discount store ammo I've brought like God's own woodchuck gun. Five shots go into a group the size of my thumbnail, and I warm to the piece. Hey, this is a part of our heritage, we lost a war with this rifle! Bennett's AK, a choice made-in-Budapest version of the most ubiquitous weapon in human history, is not quite as precise but accurate enough to win with and, I remind him, way more reliable in the jungle.

There's a long expensive burst of machine gun fire and a cheer goes up as a 50-gallon oil drum topples off cinderblocks six football fields away up the valley. More living history: Merritt Bowman has fired the opening shots of this year's Buffalo Shoot from his beautifully restored Bren gun, the mainstay light machine gun of the British army in World War II. The curved magazine sticks up from the top, giving it the quaint period look of something that went ashore with Monty and Lord Lovat. "Piper, Blue Bonnet!"

Besides a humiliatingly detailed FBI background check, it costs Merritt $500 a year for the Class III Dealer/Collector license required to obtain such an object, then the price of a Ford for the object itself. And he has others.

Here in the Land of Opportunity, the rich are different than you and me. Better armed. Television regularly shows us sad, out-of-shape middle-aged militia folk drilling with their

$125 Chinese rifles. But you'll channel surf in vain for a glimpse of the Arizona tool-and-die mogul who has two, count 'em, *two* T37 jet trainers in his private hangar, fitted with hard points for attachment of drop tanks, forward-looking infrared sensors and, come to the point, machine gun pods. Not that he does anything with his ordnance but caress it.

**M**erritt Bowman welcomes the applauding throng, reminding them that machine guns are the safest weapons, only two homicides having been committed on full-auto since they were made illegal to sell over the counter in the 1930s.

Then he introduces Clint Smith, the perfect light infantryman.

Kissing 50, Smith is as aerobically fit as a 20-year-old, a young Gary Cooper in running shorts. As a 19-year-old Marine in Vietnam, his job was to give advanced weapons training to elite ranger and paratroop units, and the legend is that he taught by example. He's been teaching ever since, as chief instructor at Gunsite training center, the old Harvard of American gun schools; as tech rep for Heckler and Koch, showing America's special weapons cops how to get the most from their MP5 submachine guns; and as a founder of Thunder Ranch, the new Harvard of American gun schools now that Gunsite has been bought

by a pharmacist. Smith's back is straight, his jaw firm, his eyes China blue. He is serious and positive.

So we become serious and positive.

As a fat slob on the verge of his first stroke I figure I may as well go first, run the "Rifle Ten" before it gets any hotter.

**I**n the Rifle Ten your five-foot-eight, 260-pound correspondent embarks on the nightmare of an armed 200-yard dash with incidental calisthenics. The venue is the 1,000-yard concrete feed trough that runs nearly the length of this valley. It's a monument to the grain grower's eternal dream of eliminating the middleman. Much of the trough has been bulldozed down to a concrete stripe, a lost sidewalk, but enough of the sides are still standing so that you can almost see the ghostly hundreds, nay thousands, of cattle, beefalo, buffalo, llamas, or emus with their noses or beaks in Bowman provender as the trucks roll slowly by, pouring in more grain. Eventually Merritt realized that the real money belonged to whoever controlled the breeding stock, and he sold off all but a few animals and got into the sperm business.

For a few glorious seasons the feedlot crumbled and weeded into the best pheasant cover in the county, attracting friends of friends of friends from as far away as Martha's

Vineyard. Keeping on Merritt's guest list became a major social priority. Then some convolution of cop-rancher logic made Merritt decide to install a pistol range here, and the local department helped pay for it, giving the cops hegemony. Keep out. Leash all dogs. No hunting.

I stand above a mat on the 250-yard line with Clint Smith, attentive as I thumb ten cartridges into the AR's magazine.

"Lock and load." I pull the charging handle to chamber a round, place the weapon on safe while I strain to see a vaguely human silhouette target in tan and brown camo against the tan and brown earthen berm that is our backstop a mere two and a half football fields away.

I can barely make it out. My real target, which I can't see at all, is a much smaller lethal zone in the center of the humanoid form's chest. Smith curls his thumb around the button of the stopwatch attached to his clipboard, punches it. "Go."

My first task: to do a controlled fall forward onto the mat, acquire the target in the sights of the AR, and place two rounds upon it. Nothing to it, except I forget the safety and nearly dislocate my finger trying to pull a locked trigger. A deep breath. It is absolutely necessary to be calm.

Two shots off. I struggle to rise, but Smith's hand on my shoulder holds me in place: "Lock that piece!" The humiliated fat guy safes his weapon, wallows up, and goes into a trudging jog toward the second mat at 200 yards.

By the time I do the second controlled fall forward I am wheezing emphysemically and the front sight of the AR describes great shaky arcs across the brown smudge of the target. Breath control!

*Wheeze, pop. Wheeze, pop.*

All the great infantrymen were ectomorphs. Clint floats effortlessly at my elbow. At 150 yards I have reconciled myself to life without oxygen and my glasses are swimming with sweat. But the mandated position at this mat is seated, a great favorite with us blobs. I cross my legs and jam my elbows into my thighs. I treat my lungs to six screaming deep ones before forcing them to be still for the two shots into the center-of-mass of this imaginary guy who would have splashed my skull into the sky as I got up off that first mat back there if this were real life.

The fantasy is over. Pride is gone. I am walking, and not fast, toward 100 yards, propelled forward mainly by the derisive stares of the crowd pressing against my shoulder blades.

At 100 yards I must kneel, which means drop my right knee to the ground and jam my elbow down upon my left. This position, useful for seeing charging lions over the tall grass, is horribly unsteady, and to render it viable I sit back on the inside of my right ankle. Painful, but it does allow me to get off two quick ones.

With only 50 more yards to shuffle, a shred of pride returns and my shuffle is brisk. Offhand, which means standing up on your hind legs and shooting like a man, is the least steady position for most, but not Fatty. My left palm cups the AR's magazine and my left elbow rests comfortably on my ample gut. I can almost see the last two rounds strike, just a bit high and left.

Clint Smith's thumb records a time no more than about twice average, and he sings "Cease fire! Clear your weapon! Lock it open!" He is kindly behaving as if my performance were nothing untoward. With even greater kindness he volunteers to run up and retrieve my target while I amble back from station to station, policing up my brass, and with the ultimate kindness that guarantees someday I'll be his customer at Thunder Ranch, if I can just get over this pesky paralysis, he makes a loud cheerful announcement, waving my target at the cloudless sky: "Shooter number one has all shots in the ten ring!"

My God. I'm not dead after all. I would have killed the bastard with my first round.

Bob Roy and his wife Ethyl invite me to bring my warm Coke under the canopy of their pickup, whose bumper reads Save A Logger, Eat Fried Owl. Bob Roy is huge, a millworker and deputy from a depressed lumber town. We agree that Jeez it's hot. I don't mention to him that I am author of a book titled *Secrets of the Old Growth Forest*. I have just performed creditably in a way he can easily beat, and that makes us buddies.

Bennett, normally shaped, halves my score and waves the AK at Helga in glee. "Well, Bennett, where did you learn to do that? The Golan Heights?" she croons.

Bob Roy shoots a Garand like the one I left at home, but it must have a dirty gas port. It fails to cycle at every station, so he has to operate it by hand and finishes way back. The Rifle Ten winner is a middle-aged building inspector from Portland. His wife, a dumpling in matching camo, also places high.

But not to worry, there are plenty of events to come—including El Presidente—and as Merritt Bowman likes to say, "No one gets out alive."

It's not just the heat, I've got a fever. Instead of seeing three simulated bad guys on the pistol course, I see six, and kill them all. Another blow for firearms safety.

Helga doesn't hang around to see the Corsican Brothers take on the cops with pistols. She heads back to Merritt's house to help set up the catered barbecue.

Being broiled by sun outside and mystery bacilli inside, I don't derive maximum enjoyment from the carnival fun: steel plates that go *gong*, helium balloons that wave around and go *puff* from a spoonful of chalk powder inside when burst.

Everybody helps leave the valley cleaner than we found it. Bennett and I hitch a ride with Bob Roy and Ethyl, during which we learn that these tree huggers and nature nazis are all watermelons—green on the outside, pink on the inside. I happen to know that the hills around Bob's town have been shorn of every scrap of commercial timber as if by a gigantic lawn mower. My silent wish for him: a small electronics firm and a cleaner rifle.

Back in Oracle, Bennett risks arrest by moving his Vanagon the few blocks to the Bowman compound. The prospect of riding to Portland with Helga has him chipper even before a shower, cooler clothes, and the sight of icy capacious tubs of beer on Merritt's deck.

The Bowman house wisely turns blank walls to the glare and wind of the Umatilla Plateau and curves Roman style around an atriumlike lawnlet. Helga floats above the bar like a blond cloud, handing out drinks. A cowboy father and son are serving the cops and their families beef seared beyond the possibility of salmonella, superb barbequed beans, fruit Jell-O, cubes of spice cake with white icing, slices of Neapolitan ice cream. When the going gets tough, the tough want baby food.

After dinner Merritt Bowman conducts a graceful awards ceremony. Seems Merritt himself won every event, but failed to register and has been disqualified. So the second-place winners get the prizes, starting with the grand prize of a Dillon reloading press—the best—to the Portland building inspector. Ammo, shooting glasses, pistol cases, and other mementos go to eight more winners, and then my name is called. I am "ninth."

Merritt is down to a stack of baseball caps. Mine says Miami Vice. Bennett is called. He is also "ninth" and his cap says Magnum Force. The next "ninth" is Bob Roy, and his cap says Sea of Love, which gets a shriek from Ethyl.

We'll be back next year to take our revenge.

# THE CONTRIBUTORS:
# A FAN'S NOTES

## No tendril-armed back-biting garret dwellers here: a living obituary of 26 WILD LIFE contributors...

### WILLIAM ABERNATHY

A former editor for *The Rocket* and an expert on guns, hops, rock, and malcontents, William Abernathy is, at 32, barely old enough to be ex-young, and he stoops to critiquing beer.

### KENT ANDERSON

Kent Anderson is a celebrated novelist and author of *Sympathy for the Devil* (a Vietnam War novel that makes *The Naked and the Dead* seem like a Girl Scout picnic) and *Night Dogs* (an epic account of Portland cops living in a world they never made). A former Green Beret and Portland policeman, he is also editor of the best annual literary anthology in the Northwest, *Cold Drill*.

### WILLIAM BOLY

A National Magazine Award winner and author of *Fire Mountain*, Bill Boly possesses humankind's most evolved sense of vertebrate reality. There are few logical quandaries he cannot solve. When he was senior editor at *Oregon* magazine, I'd go into his office baffled. Boly's pen would go to paper. Minutes later, I'd leave his desk marveling, "So that's how you make a perpetual motion machine."

### GIDEON BOSKER

Strange food, psychomachia, architecture, 22nd-century pharmaceuticals—you name it. ER physician, screenwriter, lyricist, author or co-author of 1600 books, Gideon Bosker has got a grip on everything. Take parties: Once Gideon discovered that Portland's city government was buying all new phones and throwing out the old ones. Gideon had a mountain of phones—all still attached to their squawking bureaucrat answering machines—dumped off at a gallery downtown. Then he hired the world's only speed-metal string quartet, scored enough wine to fill a swimming pool, and...you should have been there.

### MARTY CHRISTENSEN

All literature created in Oregon has its origins in my ex-cousin Marty. We receive his vital primal vibe through the fillings in our teeth. He is author of many volumes of poetry, including *Dying in the Provinces* and *My Flashlight Was Attacked by Bats*.

### LARRY COLTON

King of Oregon's Ex-Young. Never too far from trouble, and the soul of charm. Imagine Huck Finn at 50. A former professional baseball pitcher, Larry Colton is a contributor to *Sports Illustrated* and the *New York Times*, and author of the wonderful best-selling memoir *Goat Brothers*. "Larry is the only man in America," according to his friend John Strawn, "to have written more books than he's read."

### WALT CURTIS

Curtis is the Unofficial Poet Laureate of Oregon and a speaker so electrifying that he makes Adolf Hitler look like a wall-flower. So why isn't Walt famous? Is there no God? Distinguished scholar, hero of the masses, sex pervert—Walt has done it all: he's the subject of Bill Plympton's brilliant docudrama: *Walt Curtis, Peckerneck Poet*, and author of the book behind Gus Van Sant's first movie, *Mala Noche*.

## KATHERINE DUNN

Portland poet Marty Christensen has declared, "Western civilization has, unfortu-nately, produced only two great minds: those of Captain Beefheart and Katherine Dunn." And I agree. Katherine Dunn's jour-nalism has appeared in *Esquire*, *The New Republic*, *PDXS*, and *Willamette Week*. She is best known for her genius novel, *Geek Love*, but if you'd like to read an equally awe-some—though very different—work of hers, try *Truck*. Written when Ms. Dunn was only 24, this is an explosive and surreal tale of young love gone way, way wrong—when I finished *Truck* I felt like I had just escaped a flash fire in an opium den.

## MIKAL GILMORE

I published Mikal Gilmore's first work in *One Dollar* magazine when I was 25. My life has been nothing but an epilogue ever since.

## D. K. HOLM

Oregon's best troublemaker. Proof that the pen is mightier than the sword and even the Glock. Few deranged murder-mad, 9-mil-limeter-packing crackheads have caused wider consternation than critic Holm. A zen master at pissing people off, Holm is co-mastermind of Oregon's *PDXS*, pound for pound the best alternative weekly in the country (the *Village Voice* and the *LA Weekly* have a lot more pounds. So what?).

## KAREN KARBO

Karen Karbo is author of two novels, *The Diamond Lane* and *Trespassers Welcome Here*, each

of which was named a *New York Times* Notable Book of the Year. But she is best known for her funny and smart nonfiction. Her article in *Outside* magazine on the root, toot, loot, and shoot full-metal-jacket crowd, "Welcome to Gun Camp," was a classic meditation on the armed citizenry. Her work has also appeared in *Esquire*, *Vogue*, and *The New Republic*.

## DAVID KELLY

For years I have gone to the University of David Kelly. He has explained the universe of Oregon politics, the universe of the for-est, and the universe of all the fucked-up gizmos inside the hinge assembly of the front seat of my old Porsche. Kelly is the former managing editor of *Oregon* magazine and author of the prize-winning book, *Secrets of the Old Growth Forest*. Way back when, Kelly was a river guide, a building contractor, and also taught acid-altered English at Northwestern University. He is currently writing a book, *Gun Nuts*, from which we've adapted two tales, "Urban Duck Death" and "Burp Gun Party."

## JAMES KIEHLE

WILD LIFE designer James Andrews Kiehle —a.k.a. Jake Modern and Uncle Arfo— has been an art director for *Rolling Stone* and *Playboy*, as well as the late great *Oregon* maga-zine. When I met him, I was amazed. He was discriminating—"I like some of the *Mona Lisa*, but not all of the *Mona Lisa*."—he was hip, and for the first time I met some-body who was a writer, artist, and musician all in one. We founded *One Dollar* magazine on the back of Bill Hobgood's Visa card, and after four months I learned to spell my job title: Editor. But it was Kiehle's vision that kept us afloat. He took photos, designed everything, and was so hot at movie reviews that it's a mystery why it's not Siskel and Ebert and Uncle Arfo. This book is as much Kiehle's as anyone's.

## LITCHARD KIEHLE

Before his death in 1993, Kiehle drew many illustrations and paintings of the Oregon Country. He honed his art during a tenure with Walt Disney, as well as art schools in Chicago and Paris.

## ZORN MATSON

I've known bartender/inventor Zorn Matson for years. It's been nice to have a friend who was just a normal non-writing human being. Sadly, that proved not to be the case. Zorn Matson has all the while been quietly creating an existential master-work: *Whipsnake*. Sex, violence, and world-class potty jokes. We are proud to publish the first chapter here.

## ANCIL NANCE

Way up there. See that tiny dot in the sky that— Jeez Louise!—is getting bigger and bigger as it plummets to earth? Or WHAM! Hear that guy on the spacy-looking motor-cycle blow by you on the blindest curve in Christendom? Or, my-oh-my, read about the guy who practically single-handedly saved the otherwise disastrous American Yangtze River Expedition by guiding their rafts through man-killing rapids even though he'd hardly even held an oar before? That was Ancil Nance, the former president of North Paranoid Climbing School, the second greatest photographer in the universe, and the savviest daredevil in the United States.

## DAVID NOONAN

David Noonan is a prototypical Oregonian. A harmonica player and connoisseur of obscure, cheap beer, healthier than he is buff, Noonan talks a lot but listens more, loves quality but hates glitz, and wore flan-nel when it was associated with logging, not grunge. Too bad he's from New Jersey. The author of the novel *Memoirs of a Caddy* (which contains, among other wonderful bits, the best pot-smoking scene of all time)

and the nonfiction book *Neuro*, Noonan is a frequent contributor to *Esquire* and *Sports Illustrated*. He visits Oregon when he can.

## PIERRE OUELLETTE

Pierre Ouellette was an original member of Paul Revere and the Raiders ("they kicked me out because I couldn't learn their dance steps") and a founding partner of KVO, one of the hottest and most powerful high-tech ad agencies on the West Coast. But Ouellette is the anti-fat cat. As the author of two classic near-future science fiction novels, *The Third Pandemic* and *The Deus Machine*, Pierre speaks softly and carries a Fender ax. He was wearing worn-out flannel and holey Levis when Kurt Cobain was still falling out of his cradle, and has been play-ing guitar in bar bands since he was 13.

## JIM REDDEN

Jim Redden, assisted by henchman D. K. Holm's crafty poison penmanship, publishes the best alternative newspaper in America, *PDXS*. Redden's trick was to replace hack left-wing ideology with thinking. He was also the first journalist to delve deep into the radical skinhead and militia movements.

## JUDITH ROOT

The daughter of a former Rose Festival princess, Judith Root is author of *Weaving the Sheets*, the wiliest collection of dark poetry ever.

## MELISSA ROSSI

Lost in a flu fog, I met Melissa Rossi when we were assigned by *Rolling Stone* to cover Bruce Springsteen's wedding in Lake Oswego. One of my mother's friends lived next door to the bride's parents' house— where the ceremony took place—and the idea was that we'd climb up on my mom's friend's roof and spy. I was so sick I don't remember how it turned out. Rossi has also written a book about Jim Rose, a guy who washes down his light-bulb hors d'oeuvres with gasoline martinis. Her book was printed in big, fat, bold letters, so that the entire story was one continuous 83,445-word headline . . . .

## JOHN SHIRLEY
Primal sci-fi visionary and early punk mastermind, John Shirley invented the cyberpunk genre of hip, near-future science fiction later popularized by William Gibson. Want proof? See "Tricentennial."

## SUSAN STANLEY
At a time when hip nonfiction was mostly about exclamation points and bad behavior, Susan Stanley's stories in *Willamette Week* were . . . not. Stanley has been a groundbreaking lifestyle editor at the late and occasionally great *Oregon Journal*, a seamstress in a fake-fur carseat factory, a subpoena server, and a rugmaking instructor. Her nonfiction book *Maternity Ward* is a selection of the Literary Guild, and her work has appeared in publications ranging from the *Washington Post* to *Redbook*. Writing about motorcycle gangs is an old cliché of New Journalism, and I wouldn't have asked Susan Stanley to get within ten miles of a biker were her husband not a biker himself.

## MARK STEN
We thought we were heroes. Sten knew we were boobs. Before Johnny Rotten could spell punk guitarist, Mark Sten was one. A wry prince of post-disco Portland music, gentlemanly anarchist Sten was the first to make a career out of getting attacked by his fans.

## JOHN STRAWN
John Strawn's *Driving the Green* is *the* golf book of our time. When John Updike read at the PGA's 100th anniversary ceremony, he read, not from his own observations about golf, but from Strawn's. John (Strawn, not Updike) taught history at Reed and spent a decade as a building contractor before becoming a member of a golf course architectural firm. He lives in Portland and on airplanes.

## JOHN TILMAN
Rhodes scholar John Tilman is writing a novel that will change the world.

## BILL WICKLAND
Suave and debonair Bill Wickland is Oregon's primordial hippie even though he is a tall, dark, handsome guy who favors golf sweaters and sport jackets. Inside Wickland's vast cranial vault, gourmet psychedelic phantasmagoria has run rampant for 30 years. This guy is out there. He is also the state's top expert on its own best nooks and crannies, and a great writer besides.

# ILLUSTRATION CREDITS

## JAKE MODERN
Pages: 3, 5, 6, 8, 20, 23, 24, 25, 28, 33, 34, 36, 38, 42, 44, 45, 46, 47, 50, 51, 53, 55, 58, 62, 76, 77, 79, 91, 101, 108, 111, 113, 115, 128, 129, 130, 179, 188, 195, 207, 211, 213, 218, 231, 244

## ANCIL NANCE
Pages: 1, 9, 11, 14, 16, 17, 37, 47, 65, 69, 107, 173, 182, 205, 234, 236, 256

## LITCHARD KIEHLE
Pages: 26, 81, 90, 153, 199, 209, 221

## DALE MONTGOMERY
Pages: 83, 163, 169

## COVER:
Photographs by Ancil Nance
Design by James Kiehle
Model: Iris Cole-Hayworth

# *Dear Ms. Information*

Dear Ms. Information:

Please sell me another bar of soap. This book was hyped as written by the best ex-young writers in Oregon. So what about Susan Orlean, the incomparable Richard Meltzer, Todd Grimson (!), Rene Denfeld, Robin Cody, Sheldon "The Al Soltzenetzin of Neakani Bay" Baker, and the 12, 876 highly successful science fiction novelists in Eugene? Not to mention my bosom buddy Barry Lopez.

> THE COMMANDER
> The Farm
> *Springfield*

MS INFORMATION REPLIES: Didn't you read the cover of the book? We said half the best ex-young writers in Oregon. The other half is for next year.